Uganda

Growing Out of Poverty

The World Bank
Washington, D.C.

World Bank Country Studies are among the many reports originally prepared for internal use as part of the continuing analysis by the Bank of the economic and related conditions of its developing member countries and of its dialogues with the governments. Some of the reports are published in this series with the least possible delay for the use of governments and the academic, business and financial, and development communities. The typescript of this paper therefore has not been prepared in accordance with the procedures appropriate to formal printed texts, and the World Bank accepts no responsibility for errors.

The World Bank does not guarantee the accuracy of the data included in this publication and accepts no responsibility whatsoever for any consequence of their use. Any maps that accompany the text have been prepared solely for the convenience of readers; the designations and presentation of material in them do not imply the expression of any opinion whatsoever on the part of the World Bank, its affiliates, or its Board or member countries concerning the legal status of any country, territory, city, or area or of the authorities thereof or concerning the delimitation of its boundaries or its national affiliation.

The material in this publication is copyrighted. Requests for permission to reproduce portions of it should be sent to the Office of the Publisher at the address shown in the copyright notice above. The World Bank encourages dissemination of its work and will normally give permission promptly and, when the reproduction is for noncommercial purposes, without asking a fee. Permission to copy portions for classroom use is granted through the Copyright Clearance Center, 27 Congress Street, Salem, Massachusetts 01970, U.S.A.

The complete backlist of publications from the World Bank is shown in the annual *Index of Publications,* which contains an alphabetical title list (with full ordering information) and indexes of subjects, authors, and countries and regions. The latest edition is available free of charge from the Distribution Unit, Office of the Publisher, The World Bank, 1818 H Street, N.W., Washington, D.C. 20433, U.S.A., or from Publications, The World Bank, 66, avenue d'Iéna, 75116 Paris, France.

ISSN: 0253-2123

Library of Congress Cataloging-in-Publication Data

Uganda : growing out of poverty.
       p.   cm.
       p.   cm.
   growing out of poverty. (A World Bank country study)
   "This report has been prepared by a team led by Kapil Kapoor"—CIP
pref.
   Includes bibliographical references.
   ISBN 0-8213-2460-8
   1. Uganda—Economic conditions—1979–   2. Uganda—Economic policy.
I. Kapoor, Kapil, Ph. D.   II. International Bank for Reconstruction
and Development.   III. Series.
HC870.U438   1993
338.96761—dc20   93-17518
                                                       CIP

GOVERNMENT FISCAL YEAR
July 1 - June 30

CURRENCY EQUIVALENTS
Currency Unit: Ugandan shilling (U Sh)

Official Rate: US$1.00 = U Sh 1214 (December 1992)
Foreign Exchange Bureau Rate: US$1.00 = U Sh 1248 (December 1992)

ACRONYMS AND ABBREVIATIONS

ACFODE	Action for Development
ACS	Aid Coordination Secretariat
DA	district administrator
DANIDA	Danish International Development Agency
DCAT	District Community Action Trust
DENIVA	Development Network of Indigenous Voluntary Associations
DHS	Demographic and Health Survey
FHH	female-headed households
HBS	Household Budget Survey
MAAIF	Ministry of Agriculture, Animal Industry and Fisheries
MHH	male-headed households
MLG	Ministry of Local Government
MLSW	Ministry of Labor and Social Welfare
NGO	non-governmental organization
NIC	newly industrialized country
NRM	National Resistance Movement
NUDIPU	National Union of Disabled People of Uganda
OGL	Open General License
PAPSCA	Program to Alleviate Poverty and the Social Cost of Adjustment
RC	Resistance Council
SIP	Special Import Program
SSA	Sub-Saharan Africa
SWAA	Society for Women and AIDS in Africa
TOT	terms of trade
UCBHCA	Uganda Community-Based Health Care Association
UCOBAC	Uganda Community-Based Association for Child Welfare
UDC	Uganda Dairy Corporation
UNEPI	Expanded Program on Immunization
UNICEF	United Nations International Children's Emergency Fund
URA	Uganda Revenue Authority
WHO	World Health Organization
WID	Women in Development

Contents

Preface ix

Executive Summary xi

Part I: A Profile of Poverty 1

Chapter 1: A Profile of Poverty 3
    Background 3
    Defining Poverty 4
    Poverty Indicators and the Regional Variation in Poverty 8
    Intrahousehold Inequality 10
    Nutritional Indicators 10
    Social Indicators 11
    The Voice of the People 14

Chapter 2: The Poor and the Vulnerable 17
    Who are the Poor and Vulnerable? 17

Chapter 3: The Gender Dimension 25
    Profile of Women's Roles and Constraints 26
    Gender Issues for Poverty Reduction and Economic Growth 28
    The Value of Women in Ugandan Society 29
    Unequal Before the Law? 31
    The Diversity of Households in Uganda 32
    The Gender Division of Labor 33
    Intersectoral Linkages 35
    Conclusion 39

Chapter 4: Impact of Adjustment on the Poor 41
    General 41
    The Ugandan Experience 42
    Rural and Urban GDP Per Capita 43
    Changes in Domestic Terms of Trade (TOT) 45
    Macroeconomic Policy and Its Implications 46
    Implications for Household Welfare 49
    What Has Been Happening to the Incomes of the Poor? 50
    Distortions in Product and Factor Markets 51
    Inflation and Its Impact on the Poor 53
    The Provision of Social Services 55
    Conclusion 55

Part II: A Strategy for Reducing Poverty 57

Chapter 5: Accelerating Economic Growth 59
   Introduction 59
   Prerequisites for Accelerated Economic Growth 60
   How Did Uganda Fare? 63
   The Link Between Growth and Poverty Reduction in Uganda 64
   Structure of Production 66
   Sources of Future Growth 67
   Agriculture 67
   Industry 71
   Savings, Investment, and the Balance of Payments 73
  Annex to Chapter 5: Agricultural Growth Prospects 81
   Traditional Export Crops 81
   Matoke (Banana) 83
   Cereals 83
   Roots and Tubers 84
   Pulses 85
   Oilseeds 85
   Industrial Crops 86
   Horticultural Crops 86
   Livestock and Dairy 87

Chapter 6: Labor Market Policies for Poverty Reduction 89
   The Distribution of Labor Force 89
   Features of the Labor Market 94
   Which Employment Categories are Poor? 98
   The Objective of Employment and Labor Market Policies 99
  Annex to Chapter 6: Urban Employment 103
   A Further Disaggregation 103
   Growth in Public Sector Employment 105

Chapter 7: Providing Key Services and Safety Nets 107
   Introduction 107
   Government Expenditure on the Social Sectors 108
   Incidence of Government Expenditures 109
   Education 110
   Health 111
   Family Planning and Environment 113
   Development of the Rural Areas 113
   The Provision of Safety Nets 114
   Keeping Afloat 115
   Is There Anybody to Help? 117
   Safety Nets for the Future 119

Chapter 8: Institutional Framework Delivering Essential Services 123
      Background 123
      Governmental Institutions 123
      Self-Help Groups 125
      Non-Governmental Organizations 126
      Coordination between Government and NGOs 127
      Creating a Framework for Collaboration 129
      Decentralization 135
      The District Community Action Trust (DCAT) 135
      Conclusion 136

Chapter 9: A Strategy for Reducing Poverty 137
      A. Policies for Accelerating Growth 137
        Policies for Accelerating Agricultural Growth 138
        Policies for Accelerating Industrial Growth 139
        Employment and Labor Market Policies 140
        Policies for Gender-Responsive Growth 141
      B. Policies for the Delivery of Social Services 142
        The Public Expenditure Agenda 142
        Institutional Issues and the Provision of Safety Nets 143

Selected Bibliography 145

Annex I   Statistical Appendix 151
Annex II   Poverty: A Child's View 189
Annex III   Adjustments to the HBS Data 199

Text Tables

Table 1.1   Selected Characteristics of Ugandan Households 5
Table 1.2   Poverty Indicators for Uganda 6
Table 1.3   Expenditure on Different Food Items 8
Table 1.4   Uganda Social Indicators 13
Table 4.1   Growth and Sectoral Distribution of GDP 43
Table 4.2   Foreign Trade Taxes, Trade Deficit and Exchange Rates 47
Table 4.3   Index of Real Farmgate Prices 49
Table 4.4   Real Wages of Agricultural Workers 51
Table 4.5   Fiscal and Monetary Performance 52
Table 5.1   Annual Rates of Inflation 61
Table 5.2   Domestic Investment and Savings 61
Table 5.3   School Enrollment 62
Table 5.4   Average Annual GDP Growth Rates 63
Table 5.5   Average Annual Sectoral Growth Rates 64
Table 5.6   Years Required to Double GDP 65
Table 5.7   Distribution of GDP 66
Table 5.8   Present vs Potential Crop Yields 70
Table 5.9   Key Macroeconomic Indicators 74
Table 5.10   GDP By Sector in Constant Prices 76

Table 5.11   GDP By Sector in Constant Prices (Annual Growth Rates)   77
Table 5.12   GDP By Expenditure at Constant Prices   78
Table 5.13   Balance of Payments   79
Table 6.1   Distribution of Population by Primary Activity   90
Table 6.2   Estimated Mid-Year Distribution of Labor Force, 1992   91
Table 6.3   Some Facts About Urban and Public Sector Employment   92
Table 6.4   Percent of Male and Female in the Work Force   93
Table 6.5   Relative Earnings of Labor in Different Activities   97
Table 7.1   Sectoral Expenditure Performance of the Central Government   108
Table 7.2   Poverty Focus of Government Current Expenditures   109

Text Boxes

Box 1.1   Poverty Indicators   7
Box 2.1   Orphans on Their Own   18
Box 2.2   A Woman Who was an Orphan   19
Box 2.3   I Used to Crawl   20
Box 2.4   Meet the Core Poor   21
Box 2.5   Life in Wikuk (Gulu District)   23
Box 2.6   Everybody Has Horror Stories to Tell   24
Box 3.1   No Time for Health   28
Box 3.2   A View from the Top   29
Box 3.3   Ties That Bind   30
Box 3.4   Women and Legal Reform   31
Box 3.5   Female Labor Time and Efficiency   33
Box 3.6   Differential Incentives: Two Cases from Kenya   34
Box 3.7   Poverty and AIDS   36
Box 3.8   Domestic Relations in the Context of AIDS   37
Box 3.9   Investing in Girls' Education   38
Box 7.1   The "Rwot Kweri"   116

Figures

Figure 4.1   Real Per Capita GDP   44
Figure 4.2   Domestic Terms of Trade   45
Figure 7.1   Primary Education Expenditures   110
Figure 7.2   Primary Health Expenditures   112

Maps

Map 1.1   Districts with the Highest Incidence of Poverty   9
Map 1.2   Districts with the Highest Incidence of AIDS   12

Preface

The last Country Economic Memorandum for Uganda, *Towards Stabilization and Economic Growth* (Report Number 7439-UG), was issued in September 1988. Since that time, despite a severe deterioration in the country's international terms of trade and the exacerbation of the AIDS pandemic, the Government of Uganda has continued to implement a challenging economic reform program, with support from the World Bank, the IMF and the donor community.

This report documents the progress made to date and compliments the Government of Uganda for taking some bold economic decisions. With the restoration of peace and security throughout most of the country, and the improvement in the investment climate, the time is now ripe for the citizens of Uganda to start taking advantage of the new economic environment. While poverty in Uganda continues to be a serious problem, this report suggests that there is some evidence that, as a result of the policies implemented, Uganda is slowly on its way towards "growing out of poverty". The report cautions, however, that there is little ground for complacency. Reinforcing the recommendations of the 1990 World Development Report, it advocates a growth oriented strategy for poverty reduction in Uganda and advises the Government to "stay the course" and continue implementing the set of policies which will augment the country's human capital and enable its citizens to participate equitably in that growth.

This report has been prepared by a team led by Kapil Kapoor (Task Manager, AF2CO) and comprising Emmanuel Ablo (AF2CO), Maurizia Tovo (AFTSP), Lemma Merid (AFTSP), Mark Blackden (AFTSP), Hailu Mekonnen (PHRWD), Elisabeth Shields (EDICD), Mimi Klutstein-Meyer (AF2CO), Aziz Khan (consultant) and Mark Henstridge (Summer Intern). Bonnie Keller (DANIDA) and Carol Carolus (USAID) participated in the main mission and contributed to the preparation of the report. The team worked in close collaboration with a UNDP programming mission on poverty alleviation and rural development, led by Prof. A. Mafeje and the Government's counterpart team led by Keith Muhakanizi (MFEP) and consisting of Joseph Okune (PAPSCA Coordinator), Damon Kitabire (MFEP), Margaret Kakande (MFEP), R.P. Tumusiime (MWIDCY), Moses Bekabye (MFEP), Harriette Mugerwa (MFEP) and Francis Wagaba (MFEP). The peer reviewers were Helena Ribe (PHRPA) and Oey Astra Meesook (AF4CO). The document was produced by a team led by Kathryn Rivera (AF2CO).

The report was discussed with the Government of Uganda in March 1993.

Executive Summary

1.   With a per capita income of under US$170, Uganda today is one of the poorest countries in the world; indeed, it is a living testament of the havoc caused by the political turmoil and economic decline brought about by more than a decade of despotic rule.

2.   At independence (1962), Uganda had one of the most vigorous and promising economies in Sub-Saharan Africa (SSA), and the years following independence amply demonstrated this economic potential. Favored with a good climate and fertile soil, the country was self sufficient in food, with the agricultural sector being a large earner of foreign exchange. The manufacturing sector supplied the economy with basic inputs and consumer goods and was also a source of foreign exchange earnings through the export of textiles and copper. Export earnings not only financed the country's import requirements but also resulted in a current account surplus. Fiscal and monetary management was sound and the domestic savings rate averaged about 15 percent of GDP, enough to finance a respectable level of investment. Uganda's system of transportation was widely regarded as one of the best in SSA and included an effective network of roads, railways, port and air transport.

3.   Uganda's social indicators were comparable to, if not better than, most countries in Africa. The country's health service had developed into one of Africa's best and pioneered many low cost health and nutrition programs. There existed a highly organized network of vaccination centers, and immunization programs reached as much as 70 percent of the population. Although school enrollment was still low, Uganda's education system had developed a reputation for very high quality.

4.   The Amin regime radically reversed the economic and social progress attained since independence, and the ensuing civil strife resulted in a tremendous loss of human life. It is estimated that as many as 500,000 Ugandans lost their lives during Amin's eight-year dictatorship and as many as one million more were internally displaced from their homes and farms. A 1985 estimate by the U.S. Committee for Refugees concluded that in that year one out of every fourteen Ugandans was either a refugee or was displaced; it was estimated that as many as 200,000 Ugandans had fled the country and were living in exile.

5.   Economic mismanagement accompanied the civil war and professional standards deteriorated rapidly as skilled personnel fled the country. Between 1970 and 1980, Uganda's GDP declined by about 25 percent, exports by 60 percent, and import volumes by close to 50 percent. With large increases in defense expenditures, the government budget became increasingly untenable and was largely financed by bank borrowing which resulted in average inflation rates well in excess of 70 percent. Economic mismanagement and abuse of human rights on a massive scale continued during the Obote regime in the early 1980s. By 1985 government expenditure on education and health, in real terms, amounted to about 27 percent and 9 percent respectively of the 1970s levels. When the National Resistance Movement (NRM) Government assumed power in January 1986, it inherited a shattered economy whose social indicators today paint a dismal picture of the quality of life of its citizens and are indicative of the extent of poverty within the country.

6.   Given this legacy, this Country Economic Memorandum focuses on poverty in Uganda. Part I of the report presents a profile of poverty, using data from the recently concluded Household Budget Survey, the Demographic and Health Survey and the Population Census. These data were supplemented by a Rapid Poverty Appraisal conducted by the mission in August, 1992, in an attempt to get a better understanding of the causes of poverty and what it means to be poor in Uganda.

Particular emphasis has been placed on the gender dimensions of poverty, recognizing the fact that poverty affects men and women in different ways because they play different roles, have different needs and face different constraints. Part I of the report also examines the policies that have been implemented by the NRM Government during the past five years and, despite the data-poor situation, analyzes the impact of adjustment policies on the poor. Part II of the report is forward looking and, consistent with the recommendations of the 1990 World Development Report, articulates a two-pronged strategy for poverty reduction. The first prong of the strategy outlines policies designed to increase labor productivity and accelerate economic growth. The second prong recognizes that while economic growth is a necessary condition for poverty reduction, it is, by no means, a sufficient condition. In order to ensure that the poor are able to participate equitably in such growth, it recommends increasing the share of public expenditures on critical social services in order to foster the development of human resources within the country. Although a special case could be made for targeted interventions for the vulnerable groups in Uganda, the report recommends keeping these to a minimum, given the tight budgetary constraint and poor administrative capacity in the country.

A. Poverty Profile

7.   This report has defined two relative poverty lines for Uganda. The first poverty line has been drawn at U Sh 6,000 per capita per month (approximately US$110 per capita per year in 1989/90 prices), which is approximately equal to four fifths of the mean per capita monthly expenditure in 1989/90 (U Sh 7,512). The second poverty line has been drawn at U Sh 3,000 per capita per month (approximately US$55 per capita per year), which is approximately equal to two fifths of the mean per capita monthly expenditure. Ugandans falling below the U Sh 6,000 poverty line have been characterized as the "poor" and those falling below the U Sh 3,000 poverty line as the "poorest", or the core poor.

8.   Preliminary estimates indicate that, in 1989/90, a minimum of U Sh 6,000 per capita per month would have provided a daily intake of 2,200 calories plus some reasonable nonfood expenditures (e.g., clothing, fuel, etc.). This does not mean that people with monthly expenditures higher than U Sh 6,000 in 1989/90 lived comfortably; rather, it means that those with lower monthly expenditures could not satisfy their basic requirements. The lower poverty line of U Sh 3,000 represents the bare minimum for adequate food intake. At U Sh 3,000, if you are adequately fed, you do not have anything else at all, however essential. As the key social indicators discussed below indicate, access to basic social services is very low throughout the country, implying that some Ugandans living above the poverty line could be considered poor.

9.   Using total expenditure as the measure of welfare and a poverty line of U Sh 6,000, 55 percent of Ugandans can be defined as being poor. The poor are disproportionately found in rural areas, where about 57 percent of the population is poor, compared to about 38 percent in urban areas. Ninety-two percent of the poor in Uganda live in the countryside, while only 89 percent of the population is classified as rural. The discrepancy between rural and urban levels of poverty is even greater using the lower or "core" poverty line; 96 percent of the core poor live in rural areas. When the data are analyzed to take into account the depth of poverty, it turns out that not only is poverty more widespread in rural areas, but that it is *deeper*. In other words, rural people are more likely to be poor than urban dwellers, and their poverty is more severe.

10.   Poorer households in Uganda tend to be larger, have older and less educated household heads, and are more likely to be headed by a woman. Not surprisingly, the dependency ratio, which is calculated as the proportion of the household population younger than 18 and older than 55, is quite high and increases for poorer households. The difference in average per capita expenditure between

urban and rural areas is significant, with rural people spending about 60 percent as much as urban dwellers. Accordingly, indicators generally associated with poverty have higher values for rural Uganda: larger household size, higher dependency ratio, higher illiteracy, etc.

11.   The highest incidence of poverty is in the northern part of the country. In the rural areas of the north, 81 percent of the population have a real per capita monthly expenditure of less than U Sh 6,000 and 42 percent have a real per capita monthly expenditure of less than U Sh 3,000. Such high incidence can be ascribed for the most part to the ravages of the civil war. As persistent insecurity prevented the hardest hit northern districts from being included in the Household Budget Survey, it can be assumed that the actual poverty incidence in the north is higher.

Social and Nutritional Indicators

12.   Life expectancy at 47 for men and 50 for women is one of the lowest in the world, and it is difficult to see how the situation could improve in the near future with the AIDS pandemic threatening not only the adult population but also infants. AIDS has emerged as a significant cause of death and illness among young children. Thus, the already high infant and child mortality rates (respectively, 117 and 180 deaths per 1,000) can be expected to rise. Areas where peace has not yet been completely restored are at a greater risk of HIV infection because of the presence of both regular and rebel armies.

13.   Not surprisingly, insufficient access to health and sanitation services is also reflected in the general mortality and morbidity patterns. Uganda's crude death rate, at 20 per 1,000, is about twice the level of the average low-income country (e.g., neighboring Kenya) and considerably above the SSA average. While such high rates can be partly explained by civil strife and AIDS, it is undeniable that poor health conditions are part of the explanation. Malaria has been found to be the principal killer among adults admitted to hospitals, far ahead of AIDS. Diarrhea, pneumonia and anemia are almost as common as AIDS as reported primary causes of death. Among children under five, who account for over half of hospital deaths, the main killers are malaria, pneumonia, diarrhea and malnutrition. Available information on morbidity, as measured by outpatient statistics and surveys of mothers, confirms a similar pattern. Thus, the main causes of mortality and morbidity, with the exception of AIDS, appear to be related to a generally unhealthy environment and a lack of routine medical intervention.

14.   The Demographic and Health Survey (DHS) conducted in 1988/89 found that 45 percent of children aged 0-60 months had stunted growth, as shown by their height-for-age. Severe growth retardation occurred in 20 percent of the sampled children. Stunting reflects the cumulative effect of chronic malnutrition over a number of years, and it is typically associated with poor economic conditions (as illustrated above). Although it is conceivable that some families will fail to provide adequate nutrition to their children out of ignorance or neglect, it is very unlikely that this would be the case for the majority. This assumption is supported by the fact that stunting is almost twice as common in rural than in urban areas, that is, in areas that where the incidence of poverty is much higher. Thus, we can conclude that, when the effect of insufficient access to social services is combined with that of limited economic resources, the percentage of Ugandans living in poverty appears to be higher than what a poverty line at U Sh 6,000 would suggest.

15.   There are, of course, regional variations. The DHS found the prevalence of stunting to be considerably higher in the southwest (54 percent), while Kampala had the lowest percentage of stunted children (22 percent). The northern districts could not be surveyed because of the insecurity in the area, but medical personnel in Gulu and Kitgum estimate malnutrition rates to be at least 60

percent. Acute malnutrition (i.e., wasting) is only 2 percent according to the DHS, but in Gulu, Kitgum and Karamoja it is estimated to be as much as 30 percent.

Impact of Adjustment on the Poor

16.   Against this backdrop, and the seemingly overwhelming problems facing them, the NRM Government must be complimented for their tenacity and determination to improve the lot of Uganda's citizens. During the past five years, the Government has implemented a far-reaching economic reform agenda which has today transformed Uganda into one of the most liberal economies in Sub-Saharan Africa. With the liberalization of the exchange and trade regime, the abolition of the Industrial Licensing Act, the promulgation of a new investment code, and the gradual liberalization of agricultural pricing and marketing, the Government has succeeded in establishing some of the fundamental preconditions that are essential for sustainable growth.

17.   *Rural and Urban GDP Per Capita.* Since poverty in Uganda is largely a rural phenomenon and most of the poor are engaged in multicrop and mixed production, the trend in real agricultural GDP closely reflects the pattern of rural living standards. Moreover, since most rural land falls under the customary tenancy system where access to land is fairly open, and since over 85 percent of the farming population operates on less than two hectares of land, the benefits of agricultural growth are likely to be evenly distributed among the rural population. Thus, average trends are expected to be a fair reflection of changes in rural living conditions. Aggregate real per capita GDP, which had declined steadily between 1983 and 1986, increased significantly between 1987 and 1991. Real GDP per capita in rural and urban areas essentially followed the same trend. On average, the welfare of the rural and urban poor, in real terms on a per capita output basis, has improved by between 14 and 16 percent respectively during the past five years, maintaining the rural-urban income gap at around 5.2:1 over the second half of the 1980s. Compared to the early 1980s, some income redistribution in favor of the rural areas seems to have occurred. It is important to note, however, that averages mask the existence of wide intraregional differences, particularly in urban areas.

18.   There is considerable uncertainty in determining whether these improvements were entirely a result of adjustment policies, other extraneous factors, or some combination of the two. Given that peace and security were regained at a time that the structural adjustment policies were put in place, causes serious difficulties in disentangling the effects generated by the macroeconomic policies per se. The problem is also compounded by the difficulties in isolating the effects of the price reforms (i.e., changes in the exchange rate, interest rates and product pricing) from the impact of the injection of large amounts foreign exchange support accompanying the reform program. To isolate, at least partially, the effects of the "peace dividend" from the effect generated by policy measures, the domestic barter TOT for cash crops (traded), food crops (nontraded), and the agriculture sector as a whole have been calculated. These prices are influenced, in one way or another, by such policy measures as the changes in the exchange rate, price and trade liberalization, and the elimination of marketing monopolies.

19.   The terms of trade for cash crops fluctuated considerably during the 1981-86 period and experienced a sustained deterioration between 1986 and 1989. However, there was a dramatic improvement in the cash crops TOT in 1990 and 1991. Food crop TOT improved steadily between 1981 and 1987, largely as a result of insecurity, which prevented adequate supplies of food from reaching the market. Since 1987, with the restoration of peace throughout most of the country, there has been a significant revival in agricultural output and in the marketed surplus causing the TOT for food crops to decline. Given the dominance of the food crop sector, this has resulted in the aggregate TOT shifting against agriculture. This somewhat surprising result probably warrants further research

which present data limitations do not permit, i.e., a closer examination of farmers' incomes and expenditures per capita. The key implication of the decline in agriculture TOT is that increases in gross domestic incomes have tended to be smaller than the increases in gross domestic product in agriculture. It must also be pointed out that the improvement in the security situation has resulted in a decrease in the farmers cost of production and so the decline in TOT probably overstates the loss in incomes.

20.   *Macroeconomic Policy and Its Implications*. A poor macroeconomic environment, in addition to providing the wrong market signals and thereby stifling economic growth, hurts the poor by indirectly taxing the resources that they possess. An enabling macroeconomic environment, on the other hand, removes production disincentives, encourages optimal resource allocation, and improves income distribution. The impact of macroeconomic policies, particularly those focusing on taxation and the exchange rate, is particularly pronounced in largely agricultural economies such as Uganda and thereby warrants careful consideration. The exchange rate, in particular, produces the most pervasive impact that often outweighs the other effects of crop-specific policies.

21.   Through a series of changes in the foreign exchange allocation system, the Ugandan shilling has depreciated significantly since 1987. In 1987, the US dollar was officially exchanged at an average rate of U Sh 44.7 and the spread between the official exchange rate and the free market exchange rate amounted to about 266 percent. Starting in 1988, the Government began implementing an aggressive program of adjusting the official exchange rate with a view to compressing the gap between the official and the foreign exchange bureau rate and in July 1990 it legalized the operation of the foreign exchange bureaus. By 1991, the Government had adjusted the official exchange rate to an average of U Sh 750 per dollar, i.e., over a 17-fold depreciation. When the differential had declined to about 15 percent, the Government decided to cease setting the official exchange rate administratively and introduced a foreign exchange auction in January 1992.

22.   It is important to note that real devaluation, by itself, cannot provide positive incentives and stimulate the supply response unless it is complemented by price and market liberalization which allows market-determined or border prices to be transmitted to the producers and reduces the monopoly rents enjoyed by marketing boards. Recognizing this, the Government of Uganda has overhauled the system of marketing, pricing and taxing coffee. Starting with the 1991/92 coffee year (October-September), the Government has moved to a system where only an indicative floor price for coffee is announced and the actual producer price is determined by market forces. The export monopoly of the Coffee Marketing Board has been eliminated and coffee exporting has been opened to competition. To counteract the adverse impact of the decline in the international price of coffee, the Government has virtually abolished all taxes on exports; the remaining export tax only applies to Arabica coffee which commands a premium price on the international market. The Government has further eliminated the export monopoly of the Uganda Tea Authority and the Produce Marketing Board, although the Lint Marketing Board still enjoys a monopoly for exporting cotton. These changes have gone a long way in altering relative prices in favor of cash crops (tradables), and have had a beneficial impact on the poor, to the extent that they are involved in the production of such crops.

23.   The over 50 percent decline in the international price of coffee, as a result of the collapse of the International Coffee Agreement, has caused major foreign trade, fiscal and price instability, inimical to the rural as well as to the urban poor. As a result of the actions mentioned above, particularly since 1990, the Government has been able to protect the price received by producers. Although the real producer price of Robusta coffee declined in the early years of the program with the deterioration in the international environment, in 1991 the price was about 7 percent higher than

the price in 1987, the year when the Government commenced implementing the ERP. The farmers' share of the international price of coffee in 1991 and 1992 was more than double their share in the mid 1980s. As a result of the adjustment measures implemented by Government, relative prices, particularly since 1989, have changed in favor of coffee as compared to the prices received by farmers for growing food crops such as plantain (matoke), cassava and maize, which compete with coffee for farmer's resources, particularly labor. It is therefore apparent that, through macroeconomic and agricultural pricing policies, the Government has been largely successful in preventing the coffee industry from virtually collapsing which would have occurred in the absence of the structural reforms implemented.

24.   *Implications for Household Welfare.* To keep real incomes rising in the face of the overall decline in the TOT of the agricultural sector, various strategies are being adopted by farmers. As recent experience in several areas shows, monetization of the agricultural sector is gradually on the increase as farmers shift resources, particularly labor, from less paying crops to crops commanding higher prices at the farmgate level. In particular, incomes are being supported, in some areas, by the introduction of some high-paying export crops into the production mix. These encouraging developments are also being affected by changes in the labor market. In recent years, labor shortages have started manifesting themselves, particularly in the estate sector, as a result of which real rural wages have risen. Among the reasons for the labor shortage, particularly during peak season, is the decline in the supply of migrant labor from neighboring countries and the impact of the AIDS crisis on the productive segments of the population. Although this labor shortage has adversely affected the up-keep of the coffee trees, a relatively labor-intensive activity, it has helped to supplement the income of net-labor supplying households further improving rural welfare.

25.   *Inflation and Its Impact on the Poor.* While adverse weather conditions and the frequent adjustments to the exchange rate and to interest rates have all contributed to the escalation of prices, the imbalance between government revenues and expenditures, and the link between the fiscal deficit and monetary expansion has been the primary cause for the high rate of inflation in Uganda. The tax effort in Uganda is still among the lowest in SSA, and total revenues are sufficient to finance only about 50 percent of government expenditures. While external loans and grants have traditionally financed a large part of the fiscal deficit, borrowing from the domestic banking system has been an extremely important source of financing for the Government, at least until 1988/89. Consequently, until 1988/89, the large-scale monetization of the deficit resulted in triple digit inflation levels, thereby severely eroding real incomes in Uganda.

26.   In order to stem this erosion, one of the key objectives of the stabilization component of the adjustment program in Uganda has therefore been to keep prices in check by mobilizing incremental fiscal revenues and restricting expenditures to budgeted amounts. Bringing inflation down to levels comparable with those of major trading partners is a declared objective and a continuing challenge for the Government. Since 1990, the Government has embarked upon a concerted program aimed at mobilizing incremental revenues and controlling expenditures. The tax and tariff regime has been rationalized, the rate structure has been greatly simplified, and tax exemptions minimized. With the establishment of the Uganda Revenue Authority (URA) in September 1991, the Government has taken a bold step forward in overhauling its system of tax administration. Furthermore, the Government has instituted a strict program aimed at keeping expenditures in line with the budget and has started paying back its arrears to the banking system. As a result of these measures, Uganda has been successful in reducing the average rate of inflation from over 200 percent in 1986/87 to about 42 percent in 1991/92. The average monthly inflation rate between July 1992 and February 1993, has been -0.2 percent.

27.   *The Provision of Social Services.* Another channel through which adjustment policies impact on the poor is through the restructuring of public expenditures such that an increased emphasis is placed on the provision of economic and social services which increase human capital. Expenditures in areas such as primary health, primary education services, agricultural research and extension, etc. empower the poor, raise their productivity and augment their earning potential in the long run. While Uganda still spends far less on economic and social services than do most countries in the world and in SSA, the adjustment program in Uganda has nonetheless emphasized the need for and resulted in a visible change in public expenditure priorities with expenditure allocations increasing in favor of social sectors in general and on education and health care in particular. Given the extremely low revenue effort mentioned above, the Government plans to continue increasing these allocations steadily, keeping in mind the macroeconomic implications of the constraints imposed by the tight resource envelope.

B. A Strategy for Poverty Reduction

28.   Despite the progress achieved to date, the unfinished economic agenda is large and there should be little cause for complacency. If the Government's overarching objective is to make a serious dent in poverty over the next decade, it will have to vigorously implement the two-pronged set of policies alluded to earlier, i.e., (i) policies which will accelerate economic growth; and (ii) policies which will deliver key services to the poor and, by investing in human capital, ensure that the poor are able to participate equitably in that growth. While there is broad ownership of these policies within Government, the principal challenge ahead lies in building the capacity to ensure that policy changes can be implemented efficiently. Furthermore, there is an urgent need to strengthen the database and develop a poverty monitoring system which can provide policymakers with regular information on the impact of economic and social policies on the lives of the poor.

Policies for Accelerating Growth

29.   Experience from other countries has shown that macroeconomic stability, a high rate of investment backed by domestic savings, and high rates of literacy and numeracy are vital for rapid economic growth. Uganda continues to do poorly in each of these three areas. Inflation continues to be high and savings and investment continue to be low as do rates of literacy and numeracy. The key to achieving macroeconomic stability is to get firm control over the government budget. Despite the rationalization of the tax and tariff regime and the establishment of the Uganda Revenue Authority, the Government's revenue effort remains one of the lowest in the world. In the coming years, it will be imperative to further tighten tax administration and to broaden the tax base. The Government has made remarkable progress in keeping expenditures in line with the budgeted amounts and such discipline has to be maintained. However, given the low revenues, the Government will probably continue to be a dissaver for several years to come thereby necessitating that the private sector generate the large increases in savings that will be necessary to finance the investment needed for rapid economic growth. Experience of countries like China, India, and Kenya has shown that poor countries are capable of saving 20 percent of GDP or more. This places a premium on the development of the financial sector, because the key to higher rates of saving is an efficient financial system capable of mobilizing small savings from a large proportion of the population.

30.   *Policies for Accelerating Agricultural Growth.* At the heart of its growth strategy will have to be the transformation of agriculture. The agricultural sector has the potential to feed the country, to supply food to the regional market, to export horticultural products in addition to the traditional export crops, to produce industrial raw materials (sugarcane, cotton, etc.) and generally to act as the engine of growth. The key to realizing this potential is increasing yields by raising the productivity

of the farmer. That means security of land tenure, investment in research and extension, control of plant and animal diseases and rural feeder roads. For some crops high-yielding varieties are available from local research stations or foreign stations. What remains is to adapt them as necessary, and propagate and disseminate them. An effective extension service is needed to ensure rapid adoption of improved varieties by the farmers. Many countries in Asia have shown that rapid and sustained improvements in yields are possible. The key question is one of timing, i.e., how quickly can Uganda put in place the infrastructure needed to raise yields. The answer partly lies in targeting incremental national and donor resources towards agriculture, particularly research and extension and rural feeder roads. Raising agricultural productivity, along with increased access to basic health and education, must take priority in the Government's spending program. Markets, with the associated infrastructure of storage and refrigeration, also matter a great deal. This is a matter for private investors rather than Government except with regard to government support for the collection and dissemination of market intelligence.

31.   In addition to raising yields, Uganda must pay more attention to the working of the domestic markets in agricultural products. This is not an invitation to Government to intervene in the affairs of producers, processors and traders. Rather, it is to draw attention to the need to use public policy and public expenditure to facilitate the proper functioning of markets in agricultural products. Poor rural roads, for example, can place producers of certain crops, or producers in a particular region, at a disadvantage vis-a-vis producers in other regions or producers of the same or other crops. Or the way truck operators are licensed or regulated may have adverse effects on the markets for agricultural commodities. In Uganda there is anecdotal evidence of very low farmgate prices for some crops relative to final consumer prices. It is the legitimate responsibility of Government to find out whether the gap between farmgate and final prices is broadly reflective of costs or whether it is indicative of a malfunctioning market.

32.   Rural feeder roads constitute an essential element of Uganda's strategy for accelerated agricultural growth. Roads are needed to bring in agricultural inputs and implements, facilitate the work of extension staff, bring access to manufactured goods, create access to basic social services such as education and health and, most important of all, provide access to markets for farm goods. During the early phase of the ERP the Government placed emphasis on the rehabilitation of the major trunk roads and much progress has been achieved in this area. The Government has recently shifted attention to rural roads and the donors have responded enthusiastically with funds, equipment and technical assistance. However, progress with the rehabilitation of rural roads has been slow. The main reason for this is the weak implementation capacity of the Ministry of Local Government and the district authorities upon which falls the responsibility for the construction, repair and maintenance of rural roads. This is a task which will be gradually shifted to the districts, in parallel with the necessary financial and trained manpower resources. The decentralization of responsibilities will probably start with feeder roads maintenance.

33.   In the drive towards greater reliance on market forces and on the private sector, Uganda has moved quickly to dismantle the monopolies in the agricultural sector. These monopolies were the Coffee Marketing Board for coffee exports, the Uganda Tea Authority for tea exports, and the Produce Marketing Board for the export of food crops. In all three areas the emergence of competition is acting as a spur to further market development. In food crops, for example, private traders have been the driving force behind the penetration of the European and Middle East markets in simsim. Unfortunately, Uganda is not entirely rid of monopolies. The Lint Marketing Board still has the right to purchase all cotton for export. Ginneries are free to sell lint to the domestic cotton-processing mills. However traders in cotton lint and seed must be licensed by the Lint Marketing Board. The Cotton Act, last revised in 1964, provides for the zoning of cotton production, the setting

of fixed seed and cotton lint prices, restrictions on the importation of, or trade in cotton and for the licensing of ginneries and restrictions on the siting of the same. As a result the cooperative unions have a de facto monopoly of cotton ginning. There has been much talk of amending the Cotton Act and the Lint Marketing Board Act with a view to introducing more competition into the cotton industry but little action so far. Given the potential for fast growth of a once-thriving industry, Government must set itself monitorable targets for removing the institutional factors constraining the revival of cotton.

34.   Ineffective and inefficient financial intermediation hurts all sectors of the economy, including agriculture. At present agriculture does not depend much on purchased inputs and implements, whether locally made or imported; nor is the bigger proportion of agricultural output marketed or processed. The heaviest demand for credit in the agricultural sector has come from the agencies responsible for the procurement, processing and marketing of the traditional export crops, particularly coffee. Apart from the Rural Farmers Scheme that has been operated by the Uganda Commercial Bank, institutional credit has generally not been available to the smallholder. As a result not enough is known about the capacity of the smallholder to absorb and repay loans. The usual presumption is that credit is a constraint on production. This may well be true in Uganda but it does not follow that rushing credit to the farmer would translate into increased production. The first priority should rather be to get a better understanding of the different factors limiting the smallholder's ability to expand output.

35.   *Policies for Accelerating Industrial Growth.* Although import-substitution, certainly the old-fashioned, state-directed kind, is out of favor, it must be said that Uganda has substantial scope for replacing imports, provided this is done efficiently. A wide range of basic products are still imported, including cement, paints, biscuits, processed milk, garments, blankets, tomato paste, and tinned fruit juices. Import-substitution is more likely to succeed if it is part of an outward-oriented development strategy than one focused entirely on the domestic market. The Republic of Korea, China, and other fast-growing countries have demonstrated the superiority of outward orientation. Thus, Uganda must exploit, to the full, the opportunities for entering export markets. As far as manufactured exports are concerned, there are no obvious winners on the horizon but these cannot be ruled out. It is private investors, not governments, who pick winners (or losers). The government's role is to ensure that the investment climate is conducive to attracting investors who can produce a wide range of manufactured goods for the local and export market. In this regard, the great success achieved by Mauritius in identifying and exploiting an export market niche (in this case, wearing apparel) provides an indication of the opportunities that Uganda can seize.

36.   Given the dearth of long-term finance, modern technology, knowledge of foreign markets and management skills in Uganda, foreign investment has a crucial role to play as the catalyst for the transformation of the economy. In some countries minorities from a particular foreign country or region have performed this role. In Uganda the Asians fit the bill. A significant number of the Asians expelled by Amin in 1972 have become successful entrepreneurs in Britain, Canada and other countries. The courageous decision of the NRM Government to return the expropriated properties to the owners opens the way for these entrepreneurs to invest in Uganda. Having been dispossessed once, they will most likely exercise maximum caution in committing resources to Uganda. Nevertheless, the early signs are encouraging and a number of Asians have embarked upon a major rehabilitation of their properties once these were returned to them. Uganda needs to be forthright about the catalytic role that investors can play in the economy and it should mount investment promotion exercises directed at Asian and other foreign investors.

37. *Employment and Labor Market Policies.* The central objective of employment and labor market policies for the reduction of poverty in Uganda should be to increase the earnings of labor in agriculture. From the objectives of the land reform legislation proposed by the Agriculture Policy Committee, it appears that the Government rightly wishes to pursue a strategy of rural development which promotes a system of smallholder agriculture by further consolidating the de facto universal access to land. For this strategy to work, the proposed land reform legislation must find ways of guaranteeing tenancy rights to all the existing users of land and by improving the land endowment of the very small farmers. To encourage the small farmers to overcome the absence of the advantage of economies of scale, steps should be taken to facilitate their access to an appropriate technological package. As has been stated throughout the report, Ugandan agriculture operates under primitive conditions and the knowledge of farming systems and crop husbandry practices is rudimentary.

38. *Labor Mobility.* The operation of the rural labor market will continue to be constrained due to the absence of a large and mobile rural labor force. This is not by itself a problem as long as the concentration of labor in smallholder agriculture is not artificially promoted by inappropriate incentives. Improved systems of information and infrastructural facilities, along with the steady improvement of productivity in smallholder agriculture, is likely to make as much labor available to the rest of the economy as it can efficiently employ.

39. *Government Role in the Formal Sector.* Regulation of employment and wages in the formal sector has traditionally been kept low in Uganda and the Government has rightly resisted pressures to regulate formal sector wages, through such measures as the legislation of minimum wages. As long as there is a healthy growth of earnings in the primary sector of the economy, the market might be trusted to ensure that the formal sector of the economy pays a price for labor that is adequate for living above the poverty threshold. Creating too great a differential between earnings in the primary sector and the earnings in the formal sector often leads to a lower than optimal rate of industrialization, an unwarranted influx to urban areas leading to an overcrowded informal sector, and a rising differential in the earnings between the formal and informal sectors.

40. *Education and Training.* Education and training facilities must adjust to make the allocation of labor more efficient. Improved productivity of agricultural labor hinges critically on the expansion of primary education. Urban educational services would be better advised to reduce the focus on general higher education and instead increase the emphasis on technical training. Clearly the entire system of pricing of educational services is in need of a basic reappraisal. At present a primary school student in Uganda is charged a tuition which is often a significant proportion of the cash income of an average rural household whereas university education continues to be free of tuition, often with access to additional subsidies.

41. *AIDS.* The effects of the AIDS pandemic on employment and the labor market in Uganda cannot be determined with any precision. It is however clear that AIDS, which disproportionately strikes people in their prime, will increase the dependency ratio and make the task of poverty reduction more difficult. The pessimistic prognosis is heightened by the fact that measures to prevent the spread of HIV infection—critically important though they are—will have little effect on the incidence of AIDS during the next decade. The Government of Uganda deserves credit for dealing with the AIDS issue in an open manner. Besides concentrating efforts on containing the further spread of the HIV infection, e.g., by promoting the use of condoms, the Government, working with the NGO community, should explore the need to make targeted interventions in order to reduce the extreme effects on households whose labor endowments have been depleted by AIDS.

42.   *Public Sector Employment.* Expansion of public sector employment is not an effective method of poverty reduction. Indeed an expansion in public employment almost certainly hurts the cause of poverty reduction by appropriating resources that might be used to expand employment more productively elsewhere in the economy. The number of persons employed in the public sector has grown too rapidly over the years from the standpoint of the actual expansion of public services and the capacity of the Government to protect real wages of public employees from serious erosion. The result is widespread resort to corrupt and fraudulent practices (e.g., bribery, keeping "ghost" workers on the payroll) and moonlighting and second informal jobs. On the whole, the effective labor time spent in public employment may have declined at the same time that there has been a steady rise in the number of persons on payroll. Recently the Government has succeeded in reversing the trend and reducing the number of persons on payroll. The task is incomplete and should continue. To the extent that the reduction in government employment comes through the elimination of ghost workers and attrition (i.e., not replacing the low priority retirees) the process does not impose any burden on the current budget. A further opportunity may become available if the increase in capacity utilization in formal sector enterprises provides a leeway for productive expansion of employment. In that event positions in these enterprises might be filled by the redundant government workers. However, a reduction in public employment is by itself a rather minimal measure. A central objective of the presently underway civil service reform program must be to introduce a culture of improved job performance, matched by higher real earnings commensurate with skill levels. This in turn means that a way must be found to prevent employment in public sector to be determined by the supply of high school and university graduates in a system of irrational relative costs of different forms of education.

Policies for Gender-Responsive Growth

43.   The strategies adopted by the Ugandan Government to reduce poverty and to foster sustainable economic growth need to take explicit account of the gender dimension. In this respect, they must recognize and seek to address the asymmetries in the respective rights and obligations of men and women, and pay particular attention to the gender division of labor, and differential incentives and opportunities facing men and women, as the country embarks on monetization, diversification, and productivity enhancement in the critically important agricultural sector. It is, in particular, necessary that gender-responsive actions be undertaken as an interconnected package of measures which are mutually reinforcing. The priority areas requiring attention if Uganda is to enable both men and women to break out of poverty, and to contribute more fully to economic and social development, are:

(i)   to promote, through literacy and education, and in conjunction with the vigorous pursuit of the gender-responsive legal (and customary) reform efforts underway, the *legal rights and protections* enabling women to benefit from their own labor and to have greater access to and control of economically productive resources, including capital and land, thereby raising the status of women to enable more equal participation in household-level, community, and national decisionmaking;

(ii)   to raise the productivity of women's *economic* (paid) labor through investment in education aimed at overcoming social, financial, and cultural barriers to female participation, including at the post-primary level; through investment in basic, accessible, and affordable health care responsive to the wide range of women's health needs; and through targeted actions aimed at raising women's access to information, technology, inputs, credit, and extension services;

(iii)   to alleviate the *domestic* labor constraint through substantially increased attention to and investment in labor-saving technologies, in infrastructure (especially transport, feeder roads, and markets), and in water supply and woodlots, that take explicit account of female users' needs in design and implementation;

(iv)   to provide maximum political and financial support to the efforts, spearheaded by UNICEF, to *reduce AIDS risk among young girls*; and to protect the rights of children, including through institutional measures in the RC system to ensure appropriate representation and articulation of children's needs.

C. Policies for the Delivery of Social Services

44.   *The Public Expenditure Agenda.* The Government recognizes that, since the single most important asset owned by the poor is their labor, the central element of its poverty reducing public expenditure strategy should be to accord highest priority to developing their human capital. Human capital, more than any other factor, increases the income earning opportunities of the poor and contributes both to individual and national productivity. Accordingly, during the past two years, the Government has been attempting to foster such development in human capital by restructuring government expenditures in favor of the social sectors and rural infrastructure. Notwithstanding the severe resource constraints, the Government must continue to ensure that these priority programs remain protected. Not only should more resources be channelled towards primary education and primary health care, but the efficiency of these expenditures should also be improved by ensuring that money is spent on high impact programs and that the combination of expenditures within and across sectors are optimal. The Government needs to critically review its portfolio of investment projects in order to ensure that it is responsive to the country's changing needs. In other words, Government needs to ensure that expenditures are made on a rational basis rather than the allocated on the basis of historical levels. The combination of capital and recurrent expenditure also needs to be improved.

45.   Both the quantity and quality of desired social services is adversely affected by a lack of sufficient funds. In the medium-to-long run, mobilization of domestic resources, through improved efficiency in tax collection and also through the judicious adoption of cost recovery schemes in appropriate sectors, will be essential. This will need to be augmented by shifting funds from relatively unproductive areas such as defense, state farms, teacher training colleges, universities, curative health, etc. to areas where the economic and social returns are the highest, i.e., primary health, primary education, agricultural research and extension, rural feeder roads and rural water supply.

46.   *Policies to Control the Growth in Population.* Uganda needs to slow down population growth in order to reduce poverty within the shortest possible time. At present, the Government of Uganda does not have an explicit population and family planning policy and lags far behind other SSA countries in encouraging its citizens to have small, manageable families and informing them of methods of doing this. In addition to aggravating poverty, the growing population has adversely affected the environment by increasing the encroachment on forests and by intensifying farming, resulting in soil erosion and stagnating yields. It is therefore imperative that the Government develop a national family planning program and closely monitor progress towards decreasing presently high fertility rates.

47.   *Institutional Issues and the Provision of Safety Nets.* Although a strong case could be made for this in the Ugandan context, targeting the poorest and most vulnerable is far too expensive an option for the Government of Uganda to consider at present, given the extremely low revenue effort and the weak administrative capacity. Instead, the focus should be on providing fundamental services in rural areas: primary education, primary and preventive health care, rural feeder roads, safe, easily accessible water, agricultural extension, and marketing assistance. Communities can help provide

some of these services themselves, with assistance from Government and NGOs. Government, donors and NGOs need to develop a tripartite system to support self-help projects, and to ensure that priority investments are undertaken. If Government wishes NGOs to follow Government leadership in a scenario in which Government formulates policy and sets standards, NGOs, including Ugandan ones, should be involved in policy formulation. For the tripartite system to work, it must be "owned" by a substantial portion of the three sets of actors (Government, NGOs and donors). The policy development process in the areas of AIDS and child welfare could become a model for other sectors.

48.   The program of decentralization being adopted by the Government offers a unique opportunity to support community and NGO initiatives, particularly in light of the fact that the Government lacks the capacity to deliver much needed services to most of its citizens. For this new model to work, it will be imperative for the Government to educate the population and to reorient and educate civil servants towards its changing role. The District Community Action Trust (DCAT), which should be designed as a social investment fund which disburses funds quickly for projects generated by self-help groups, could emerge as an important instrument to address poverty on a broad scale.

Part I

A Profile of Poverty

A Profile of Poverty

"There are three distinct components to the measurement of poverty. First, we have to specify what we mean by the standard of living. Second, we have to delineate a critical level of the standard of living below which there is poverty, by definition. Third, we need to compress information on the standards of living below the critical level into an index of poverty." (Ravi Kanbur, Poverty and Development, PPR Working Paper 618, World Bank, 1991, p. 3.)

Background

1.1   With a per capita income of under US$170, Uganda today is one of the poorest countries in the world. Having seen better days at the time of gaining independence, it is a living testament of the havoc caused by the political turmoil and economic decline brought about by several years of despotic rule.

1.2   At independence (1962), Uganda had one of the most vigorous and promising economies in Sub-Saharan Africa (SSA), and the years following independence amply demonstrated this economic potential. Favored with a good climate and fertile soil, the country was self sufficient in food, with the agricultural sector being a large earner of foreign exchange. The manufacturing sector supplied the economy with basic inputs and consumer goods and was also a source of foreign exchange earnings through the export of textiles and copper. Export earnings not only financed the country's import requirements but also resulted in a current account surplus. Fiscal and monetary management was sound and the domestic savings rate averaged about 15 percent of GDP, enough to finance a respectable level of investment. Uganda's system of transportation was widely regarded as one of the best in SSA and included an effective network of roads, railways, port and air transport.

1.3   Uganda's social indicators were comparable to, if not better than, most countries in Africa. The country's health service had developed into one of Africa's best and pioneered many low cost health and nutrition programs. There existed a highly organized network of vaccination centers, and immunization programs reached as much as 70 percent of the population. Although school enrollment was still low, Uganda's education system had developed a reputation for very high quality.

1.4   The Amin regime radically reversed the economic and social progress attained since independence, and the ensuing civil strife resulted in a tremendous loss of human life. It is estimated that as many as 500,000 Ugandans lost their lives during Amin's eight-year dictatorship and as many as one million more were internally displaced from their homes and farms. A 1985 estimate by the U.S. Committee for Refugees concluded that in that year one out of every fourteen Ugandans was either a refugee or was displaced; it was estimated that as many as 200,000 Ugandans had fled the country and were living in exile.

1.5   Economic mismanagement accompanied the civil war and professional standards deteriorated rapidly as skilled personnel fled the country. Between 1970 and 1980, Uganda's GDP declined by about 25 percent, exports by 60 percent, and import volumes by close to 50 percent. With large increases in defense expenditures, the government budget became increasingly untenable and was largely financed by bank borrowing which resulted in average inflation rates well in excess of 70 percent. Economic mismanagement and abuse of human rights on a massive scale continued during the Obote regime in the mid 1980s. By 1985 government expenditure on education and health, in real terms, amounted to about 27 percent and 9 percent respectively of the 1970s levels. When the National Resistance Movement (NRM) Government assumed power in January 1986, it inherited a shattered economy whose social indicators today paint a dismal picture of the quality of life of its citizens and are indicative of the extent of poverty within the country. The following sections present a brief profile of poverty in Uganda.

Defining Poverty

1.6   Being multidimensional, poverty cannot be reduced to a single indicator. However, in order to estimate the distribution and depth of poverty, it is generally considered acceptable to use real per capita expenditure as a proxy for welfare. A yardstick is then needed to determine who is poor and who is not and, for this purpose, a poverty line is drawn which defines the cutoff living standard below which a person is classified as being poor. Two approaches are frequently used. An absolute poverty line can be calculated on the basis of the income needed to satisfy minimal nutritional requirements and a non-food component. Alternatively, a relative poverty line may be used, whereby a percentage of households at the bottom of the income distribution is considered poor, e.g., the bottom 40 percent. The advantage of using a relative poverty line is that it avoids complex, and often controversial, calculations of a minimum food or commodity basket, while still providing essential information for policy action and targeting of special programs.

1.7   This report has defined two relative poverty lines for Uganda. The first poverty line has been drawn at U Sh 6,000 per capita per month (approximately US$110 per capita per year), which is approximately equal to four fifths of the mean per capita monthly expenditure in 1989/90 (U Sh 7,512). The second poverty line has been drawn at U Sh 3,000 per capita per month (approximately US$55 per capita per year), which is approximately equal to two fifths of the mean per capita monthly expenditure. Ugandans falling below the U Sh 6,000 poverty line have been characterized as the "poor" and those falling below the U Sh 3,000 poverty line as the "poorest" or the core poor.

1.8   Preliminary estimates indicate that, in 1989/90, a minimum of U Sh 6,000 per capita per month would have a daily intake of 2,200 calories plus some reasonable non-food expenditures (e.g., clothing, fuel, etc.).[1] This does not mean that people with monthly expenditures higher than U Sh 6,000 in 1989/90 lived comfortably; rather, it means that those with lower monthly expenditures could not satisfy their basic requirements. The lower poverty line of U Sh 3,000 represents the bare minimum for adequate food intake. At U Sh 3,000, if you are adequately fed, you do not have anything else at all, however essential (see also para 1.11). As the key social indicators discussed

---

[1]   An average intake of about 2,200 calories per day would allow an adult to maintain reasonable health and performance standards, according to the standard established by the World Health Organization. People of different ages, sizes, and occupation may require different levels of caloric intake to be adequately fed. An "equivalence scale" is therefore often used in order to transform the number of people in a household into an "adult-equivalent" number of people. For example, women and younger members of the household are often counted as having consumption requirements that are less than that of an adult male. In the analysis presented in this chapter, such equivalence scales have not been used and the data have been presented on a per capita basis. While equivalence scales can be derived from household expenditure data, this can be a complex and time consuming process. The imposition of a scale from another country, or a made-up equivalence scale is often considered unnecessarily arbitrary. Work is presently underway to estimate a Uganda-specific equivalence scale. It is important to point out that the per capita measure presented here may lead to larger households with more children appearing to be poorer than they actually are which is of particular significance in assessing relative rural/urban poverty. It is expected that the analysis presently underway will shed further light in this area.

Table 1.1: Selected Characteristics of Ugandan Households

Average	All Uganda	Non-Poor	Poor	Poorest	All Rural	All Urban	Female Headed	Male Headed
Real Per Capita Household Expenditure	7,512	11,810	3,485	1,845	6,885	11,760	7,491	7,517
Household Size	5.4	4.8	6.1	6.4	5.6	4.5	4.5	5.7
Dependency Ratio (%)	44	38	51	52	46	37	45	44
Average Age of Household Head	42	40	43	43	43	35	44	41
Female Headed Households (%)	22	21	23	25	21	31	100	0
Household Heads Literate (%)	77	80	74	70	74	93	69	79
Percent Shares in Total Expenditure:								
Food	67	66	67	58	67	61	70	66
Drink and Tobacco	5	6	5	3	5	6	2	6
Clothes	6	6	7	10	6	7	6	6
Rent	3	3	4	7	3	3	4	3
Fuel	2	2	2	3	2	3	2	2
Transport	0.3	0.4	0.2	0.2	0.4	0.2	0.1	0.3
Health	1	1	2	2	2	1	2	1
Education	1	1	1	2	1	1	1	1
Food Expenditure, as Share of Total Expenditure:								
Market Purchases	26	30	23	19	23	53	29	26
Own Production	40	36	44	39	45	8	41	40

Source: Staff calculations based on HBS data.

below demonstrate, access to basic social services is very low throughout the country, implying that some Ugandans above the poverty line could also be considered poor. The role of the poverty lines defined in this report is not to present a precise definition of poverty in Uganda but rather to illustrate where the poor are and what their characteristics are (see Annex III for a brief description of the adjustments made to the Household Budget Survey data to arrive at these poverty lines).

1.9   Table 1.1 shows mean per capita expenditure per month and a number of household characteristics estimated on the basis of a Household Budget Survey (HBS) conducted in 1989/90.[2] The table reveals that the poorer households tend to be larger, have older and less educated household heads, and are more likely to be headed by a woman. Not surprisingly, the dependency ratio, which is calculated here as the proportion of the household population younger than 18 and older than 55, is quite high and increases for poorer households. The difference in average per capita expenditure between urban and rural areas is significant, with rural people spending about half as much as urban dwellers. Accordingly, indicators generally associated with poverty have higher values for rural Uganda: larger household size, higher dependency ratio, higher illiteracy, etc. (additional discussion on female-headed households is presented in the following two chapters).

---

[2]   Data in the 1989/90 HBS conducted by the Statistics Department of the Ministry of Finance and Economic Planning consist of a stratified sample of 4,500 households across Uganda, except for eight districts in the North and East which were not sampled due to insecurity. Expenditures were calculated adding the value of purchased goods and the estimated value (at market prices) of the goods consumed out of own production.

Table 1.2: Poverty Indicators for Uganda

	Population Share	P_0	$P_\bullet$ Indicator P_1	P_2	Contribution to National Poverty P_0	P_1	P_2
For a Poverty Line of U Sh 6,000							
All Uganda	1.00	0.55	0.03	0.01	1.00	1.00	1.00
Urban	0.11	0.38	0.02	0.01	0.08	0.07	0.06
Rural	0.89	0.57	0.04	0.01	0.92	0.93	0.94
Towns	0.07	0.38	0.02	0.01	0.05	0.04	0.04
Central Urban	0.01	0.48	0.03	0.02	0.01	0.01	0.01
Central Rural	0.29	0.49	0.03	0.02	0.26	0.23	0.20
North Urban	0.01	0.55	0.03	0.02	0.01	0.01	0.01
North Rural	0.09	0.81	0.06	0.03	0.15	0.18	0.19
East Urban	0.01	0.30	0.02	0.01	0.01	0.01	0.01
East Rural	0.21	0.70	0.05	0.03	0.28	0.32	0.34
West Urban	0.01	0.30	0.01	0.00	0.01	0.01	0.01
West Rural	0.31	0.47	0.03	0.01	0.23	0.21	0.20
For a Poverty Line of U Sh 3,000							
All Uganda	1.00	0.19	0.01	0.01	1.00	1.00	1.00
Urban	0.11	0.08	0.00	0.00	0.04	0.04	0.03
Rural	0.89	0.21	0.01	0.00	0.96	0.96	0.97
Towns	0.07	0.07	0.00	0.00	0.02	0.02	0.02
Central Urban	0.01	0.14	0.00	0.00	0.00	0.00	0.00
Central Rural	0.29	0.10	0.00	0.00	0.15	0.15	0.12
North Urban	0.01	0.15	0.00	0.00	0.00	0.00	0.00
North Rural	0.09	0.42	0.02	0.01	0.21	0.21	0.20
East Urban	0.01	0.04	0.00	0.00	0.00	0.00	0.00
East Rural	0.21	0.30	0.02	0.01	0.35	0.41	0.42
West Urban	0.01	0.04	0.00	0.00	0.00	0.00	0.00
West Rural	0.31	0.17	0.01	0.00	0.24	0.20	0.23

Source: Staff calculations based on HBS data.

1.10   Scattered evidence suggests that the high dependency ratio estimated here is likely to be only one side of the coin, although available national data do not allow further analysis. The other (hidden) side is that, as a result of civil strife and the AIDS pandemic, there are now entire households made up of "dependents". These are grandparents taking care of their grandchildren, or minors and elderly people living on their own (see following chapter for further discussion). While the phenomenon is probably more pronounced in areas heavily affected by AIDS and civil war, under present circumstances we can expect the dependency ratio to grow, putting an increasingly heavy burden on the shoulders of surviving responsible adults.

Box 1.1: Poverty Indicators

The simplest measure of the incidence of poverty is the proportion of individuals, in each area, which fall below the poverty line, or the "head-count index" (P_0). This is equal to the number of individuals falling below the line divided by the population of the area under consideration.

However, as a measure of the incidence of poverty, the headcount ratio does not show the depth of poverty. Although we know how many fall below the poverty line, we do not know by how much the poorest fall below this line. This can be captured as the total proportional shortfall where, for each individual, the difference between per capita expenditure and the poverty line is calculated, i.e., the extent to which each falls below the poverty line, and this is then divided by the poverty line in order to make the measure proportional to the line. Aggregating these up gives the total proportional shortfall, also known as the "poverty gap index" (P_1). For comparability between different areas, this total is then divided by the population in that area. If we simply add up the difference between the expenditure measure and the poverty line for all those who are below the line, we have the total sum of money required, assuming the possibility of perfect targeting, to eliminate poverty, as defined by the line used, at a stroke.

Neither of the two measures mentioned above reflects the degree of inequality among those who fall below the poverty line. If there is a transfer from someone below the line to another person even worse off, we would like our indicator to register an increase in poverty. Such concerns are met by taking the proportionate shortfall for each individual or household, as described above, and squaring it. If we then add up the squared proportionate shortfall for all those falling below the line, and, again, normalize by dividing by the population of the area in question, we have an indicator of poverty which reflects concerns regarding the distribution of welfare among those falling below the line. This indicator is described in the literature as the "Foster-Greer-Thorbecke Index" (P_2).

A particular strength of the P_α indicators, discussed above is that they are "decomposable". This means that the P_α indicators for the whole of Uganda can be calculated as a population-weighted average of the P_α indicators for each district. As a result, it is also possible to calculate the "contribution" each area makes to overall national poverty.

1.11   The share of food in total expenditure increases, as expected, from the non-poor to poor households. The increase is small, however, perhaps because the share of food for the "non-poor" is also fairly high by international standards, suggesting that many of the households above our upper poverty line are also struggling. The food share for the poorest is less than that for the poor indicating that the poorest have to do without food to have any non-food consumption. Clothes have a fairly constant share of expenditure for different segments of the population, but the share spent on fuel grows as incomes decline. A disturbing finding is that expenditure on drinks and tobacco is almost as high or higher than on essential items such as clothing and rent. While the poorest spend proportionally less than the others on such luxuries, they still spend a distressingly high 3 percent on drinks and tobacco compared to under 2 percent on milk, cheese and eggs, which are arguably the most important sources of proteins for young children. Worse still, the share spent on education and health combined is about half of the amount spent on drinks and tobacco.[3]

---

[3]   As paras 1.24-1.30 show, it can *not* be assumed that expenditures on health and education are low because such services are available free of charge.

Table 1.3: Expenditure on Different Food Items
(As a Percent of Total Expenditure)

	Central Rural	Northern Rural	Eastern Rural	Western Rural
Bread and Cereals	7.1	17.6	15.1	8.2
Meat and Poultry	4.8	6.5	8.6	4.5
Fish	4.2	5.4	4.5	2.1
Milk, Cheese & Eggs	2.5	1.1	3.0	3.0
Oils and Fats	0.8	1.0	0.9	1.1
Fruit and Veg.	15.2	18.4	19.0	14.4
Matoke	13.1	0.9	9.1	13.4
Potatoes and Tubers	12.3	20.4	13.5	11.2
Salt	1.9	1.2	2.4	1.0
Sugar	0.7	1.5	1.1	0.8

Source: Staff calculations based on HBS data.

Poverty Indicators and the Regional Variation in Poverty

1.12   At a poverty line of U Sh 6,000, 55 percent of Ugandans can be defined as being poor (see Table 1.2). As one would have expected from differences in average per capita expenditures, the poor are disproportionately found in rural areas, where about 57 percent of the population is poor, compared to about 38 percent in urban areas. The head count ratio (P_0—see Box 1.1 for definition) indicates that 92 percent of the poor in Uganda live in the countryside, while only 89 percent of the population is classified as rural. The discrepancy between rural and urban levels of poverty is even greater using the lower or "core" poverty line; 96 percent of the core poor live in rural areas. Optimistic inferences about the welfare of urban dwellers, however, should be tempered by the realization that life in the towns is more expensive than in rural areas, so that at equivalent expenditure levels, urban dwellers will face a harsher existence. The higher cost of securing decent housing and sanitary conditions is a case in point. Also, homeless people are more likely to be found in urban centers, but they are not included in the Household Budget Survey.

1.13   When the data are analyzed to take into account the depth of poverty, it turns out that not only is poverty more widespread in rural areas, but it is also *deeper*. In other words, rural people are more likely to be poor than urban dwellers, and their poverty is more severe. Thus, while the "contribution" to national poverty shown by the head count ratio (P_0) for rural areas is 0.92, the poverty gap index (P_1—see Box 1.1), which measures both the incidence and the depth of poverty, is 0.93. The fact that the P_2 measure (see Box 1.1), which places even greater emphasis on how far people fall below the poverty line, is 0.94 shows that poverty is deeper in rural areas. In other words, the very poorest are in rural areas.

1.14   The poverty gap index also allows for the calculation of the amount of money that would be necessary in order to eliminate poverty if perfect targeting were possible (see Box 1.1). The amount of money needed to bring everybody up to the U Sh 6,000 poverty line, if there were no leakages, was U Sh 3,840 million per month in 1989/90 prices or about US$5.8 million per month at the 1989/90 average exchange rate. However, this number needs to be interpreted with caution. While

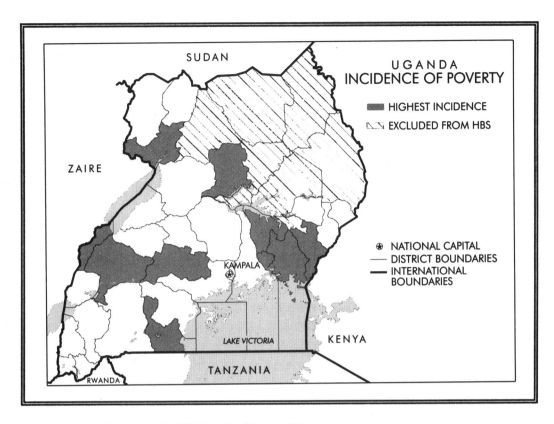

Map 1.1: Districts with the Highest Incidence of Poverty

a monthly transfer of US$5.8 million in 1989/90 would have enabled all Ugandan citizens to spend a minimum of U Sh 6,000 per month, this would still not have been sufficient to provide everyone with access to basic social services. For example, since about 80 percent of adult women had not completed elementary school in 1989,[4] this implies that many of the women above the U Sh 6,000 poverty line did not have adequate access to education and therefore providing such a transfer to Uganda would still have been insufficient to finance the primary education of all its women.

1.15   As Table 1.2 reveals, the highest incidence of poverty is in the northern part of the country (see Map 1.1 for districts with the highest incidence of poverty). In the rural areas of the north, 81 percent of the population have a real per capita monthly expenditure of less than U Sh 6,000 and 42 percent have a real per capita monthly expenditure of less than U Sh 3,000. Such high incidence can be ascribed for the most part to the ravages of the civil war. As persistent insecurity prevented the hardest hit northern districts from being included in the Household Budget Survey, it can be assumed that the actual poverty incidence in the north is higher (data from other sources support this assumption, as discussed in the following chapter).

1.16   Table 1.3 shows the regional variation in the patterns of food expenditures for the rural areas of each region. The variation reflects both different diet patterns and different levels of expenditures. Hence, expenditures on matoke are highest in the central region, where matoke is the staple food,

---

[4]   Emmanuel Kaijika, Edward Kaija, Anne Cross and Edilberto Loaiza, *Uganda Demographic and Health Survey 1988/89*, Ministry of Health, Entebbe, Uganda, October 1989.

while expenditures on cereals are highest in the north, where millet is the staple food. The share of expenditure on cheap and filling foods (e.g., bread, cereals, matoke and tubers) is generally consistent with the regional distribution of poverty as shown in the Pα indicators.

Intrahousehold Inequality

1.17   The choice of household expenditures as an indicator of individual welfare, and therefore of poverty, assumes that resources within the household are distributed equitably among all members. In the case of Uganda, there is some evidence that this might not be true and that men, particularly in certain regions, consume a disproportionately high share of household resources, often at the expense of women and children.

1.18   It was noted earlier (see para 1.11) that the share of household expenditures on drinks and tobacco is higher than on any other basic necessity, with the exception of food, and that this holds true at any expenditure level. Children do not generally consume any tobacco or alcohol; which leaves women and men. The fact that female-headed households spend about half as much on drinks and tobacco than male-headed households is telling (see Table 1.1). From the HBS data, as well as information provided by NGOs and district offices, it appears that men's drinking is often a problem and that men spend much of the little cash they have on alcohol.

1.19   As pointed out by a number of NGOs, the most troublesome aspect of intrahousehold inequality, however, is the inequitable distribution of food among family members. In many traditional families, the man is presented with all the food, and only after he has taken as much as he wants will the other members of the household be served. Nutritional studies in Kamuli district show that the man usually takes (or is given by his wife) half of the food, irrespective of how much food is there to begin with and how many other people have to eat.[5] Older boys eat second, some times sharing their father's dish. Women, girls and small children eat last. It is clear that this practice could be detrimental to small children and women, particularly in times of weather-induced food scarcity. The resulting poor nutritional status of women has serious implications for maternal mortality, low birth weight babies, problematic lactation, and infant and child mortality. When mothers do not eat well, breast milk may not be enough and therefore may need to be supplemented by cow's milk. But poor people can ill afford to buy milk and they will water it down, thus starting the malnutrition and diarrhea cycle.

Nutritional Indicators

1.20   Nutritional indicators are both a measure of health and of wealth. Unlike economic indicators, which are more open to subjective interpretation, nutritional indicators are better indicators of poverty because they represent the result of insufficient food intake and/or inadequate access to health care, and also reflect sanitary conditions and (to a minor extent) mother's education. For example, food intake may become insufficient because of the onset of diarrhea which prevents the body from absorbing some of the food. Diarrhea, in turn, is often the result of unsanitary living conditions, especially lack of access to potable water. The inability to obtain appropriate medical care, either because doctors and medicines are not available within a reasonable distance or because they are

---

[5]   Louise Sserunjogi, *"Vitamin A Intake among Children below Six - Kamuli District"*, Child Health and Development Center, Mulago Hospital, Kampala, March 1992.

unaffordable, will delay the return to a healthy state. Mothers' ignorance of simple actions to limit damage (e.g., administration of safe fluids) may make things worse.

1.21   The Demographic and Health Survey (DHS) conducted in 1988/89 found that 45 percent of children aged 0-60 months had stunted growth, as shown by their height-for-age.[6] Severe growth retardation occurred in 20 percent of the sampled children. Stunting reflects the cumulative effect of chronic malnutrition over a number of years, and it is typically associated with poor economic conditions (as illustrated above). Although it is conceivable that some families will fail to provide adequate nutrition to their children out of ignorance or neglect, it is very unlikely that this would be the case for the majority. This assumption is supported by the fact that stunting is almost twice as common in rural than in urban areas, that is, in areas that where the incidence of poverty is much higher. Thus, we can conclude that, when the effect of insufficient access to social services is combined with that of limited economic resources, the percentage of Ugandans living in poverty appears to be higher than what a poverty line at U Sh 6,000 would suggest.

1.22   There are, of course, regional variations. The DHS found the prevalence of stunting to be considerably higher in the southwest (54 percent), while Kampala had the lowest percentage of stunted children (22 percent). The northern districts could not be surveyed because of the insecurity in the area, but medical personnel in Gulu and Kitgum estimate malnutrition rates to be at least 60 percent. Acute malnutrition (i.e., wasting) is only 2 percent according to the DHS, but in Gulu, Kitgum and Karamoja it is estimated to be as much as 30 percent.

1.23   Seasonal variations in agricultural production, and therefore in income or expenditures, are also important. Hospital admission records and field interviews suggest that malnutrition increases dramatically in the preharvest season. This has important bearings for the interpretation of data on household budgets, as the following example illustrates. If rural households have expenditures of U Sh 2,000 for three (preharvest or dry) months a year and of U Sh 7,000 for the remaining nine months, the frequency distribution will show 25 percent of households falling below the poverty line of U Sh 6,000. However, all households fall below the poverty line for three months of the year.

Social Indicators

1.24   As the above suggests, data on mean per capita expenditures are not enough to understand poverty. When expenditures on health are very low, for instance, does it mean that people are on the average quite healthy, that the state offers very cheap medical services, or that people can not afford to spend money on doctors and medicines however much they need them? Social indicators provide at least a partial answer, because they measure effective use of social services (e.g., immunization, school attendance, etc.) and/or the result of the accessibility and quality of such services (e.g., maternal and child mortality rates).

1.25   The extremely low level of Uganda's social indicators makes it abundantly clear that optimistic interpretations of low per capita expenditures in health and education would be inappropriate. Life expectancy at 47 for men and 50 for women is one of the lowest in the world (Table 1.4), and it is difficult to see how the situation could improve in the near future with the AIDS

---

[6]   Stunting is said to occur when height-for-age is two or more standard deviations below the mean of the reference population.

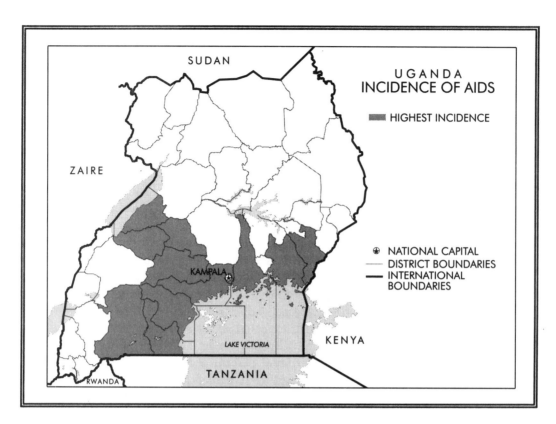

Map 1.2: Districts with the Highest Incidence of AIDS

pandemic threatening not only the adult population but also infants.[7] AIDS has emerged as a significant cause of death and illness among young children. Thus, the already high infant and child mortality rates (respectively, 117 and 180 deaths per 1,000) could possibly rise. Areas where peace has not yet been completely restored are at a greater risk of HIV infection because of the presence of both regular and rebel armies.

1.26   Not surprisingly, insufficient access to health and sanitation services is also reflected in the general mortality and morbidity patterns. Uganda's crude death rate, at 20 per 1,000, is about twice the level of the average low-income country (e.g., neighboring Kenya) and considerably above the SSA average. While such high rates can be partly explained by civil strife and AIDS, it is undeniable that poor health conditions are part of the explanation. Malaria has been found to be the principal killer among adults admitted to hospitals, far ahead of AIDS. Diarrhea, pneumonia and anemia are almost as common as AIDS as reported primary causes of death. Among children under five, who account for over half of hospital deaths, the main killers are malaria, pneumonia, diarrhea and malnutrition.[8] Available information on morbidity, as measured by outpatient statistics and surveys of mothers, confirms a similar pattern. Thus, the main causes of mortality and morbidity, with the exception of AIDS, appear to be related to a generally unhealthy environment and a lack of routine

---

[7]   For a detailed discussion of AIDS in Uganda see *Uganda: The Economic Impact of AIDS*, Population and Human Resources Division, The World Bank, 1992.

[8]   See *Uganda: Social Sector Strategy*, Population and Human Resources Division, Eastern Africa Department, World Bank, 1993.

Table 1.4: Uganda Social Indicators

Poverty Lines				1990
Upper Poverty Line (U Sh)				6,000
Head Count Index (%)				55
Lower Poverty Line (U Sh)				3,000
Head Count Index (%)				19
GNP Per Capita (US$) - 1991			170	
	1965	**1970**	**1980**	**1990**
Gross Enrollment Ratios				
Primary, Male	83	46	56	80
Primary, Female	50	30	43	63
Infant Mortality	119	109	116	117
Under 5 Mortality	..	..	..	180
Immunized for Measles (%)	..	..	..	60
Immunized for DPT (%)	..	..	..	60
Child Malnutrition (%)				45 Stunting
Prevalence (%)				2 Wasting
Life Expectancy:				
Male (yrs.)	47	50	48	47
Female/Male Ratio	1.05	1.03	1.04	1.02
Total Fertility Rate	7.0	7.1	7.3	7.3

Source: Data provided by government authorities.

medical intervention.

1.27   In the absence of a data set with information about both health indicators and per capita expenditures, it is difficult to determine to what extent the poor differ in their mortality and morbidity patterns from the non-poor. Scattered evidence appears to confirm what common sense would suggest: poor people suffer from higher levels of morbidity and mortality (with the possible exception of AIDS). To begin with, they often cannot afford to pay for treatment, as even in public health centers and clinics it is difficult to see a health professional or obtain needed medicines without paying a "fee". To the direct medical costs, one must add travel costs, which tend to be higher for poorer people, since they are more likely to live far from health centers and hospitals. Even when treatment is absolutely free, as in the case of a number of pediatric nutrition centers, mothers may be reluctant to take their malnourished children because they will then not be able to feed themselves while their children are hospitalized. Medical personnel report that it is not uncommon for mothers to end up eating part of the rations destined to their malnourished children because otherwise they have nothing to eat.

1.28   It is well known that maternal education is a major determinant of good child health, especially among the poor who cannot afford paying (literally) for the consequences of ill-advised child care practices. For example, it is widely believed that pulling off the roots of the lower canines of an infant at the first occurrence of fever will guard against future occurrences. The infections resulting from this operation can cause not only more fever, but also serious nutritional problems. Taboos related to nutrition, more common among the uneducated poor, may have deleterious effects on health. The widespread belief that chicken and eggs cause barrenness and therefore are not suitable food for women means that women and girls are deprived of a main source of protein. Uneducated people are also more likely to seek the assistance of self-appointed medical specialists and traditional doctors, whose practices are often questionable if not outright dangerous.[9]

1.29   But just how uneducated are the poor? The DHS found that about 38 percent of the women had no education at all, while 43 percent had received some primary education and only 19 percent of the women surveyed had completed primary school. Since according to our core poverty line 19 percent of Ugandans can be classified as poor, it is very likely that almost all poor women are illiterate. The negative relation found between education and expenditures confirms this hypothesis. Low educational attainment among the adult population, however, is more an indicator of past levels of access to education than of the present. Enrollment ratios, especially in primary school, therefore represent a better measure of current access to education.

1.30   Government as well as private sources agree that official data on school enrollment are inflated in response to incentives for over-reporting. Knowing that the official enrollment for primary school is 80 percent for boys and 63 percent for girls, therefore, allows us only to say that the true enrollment is lower. How much lower is impossible to say. Reported rates in the poorer northern districts, for example, are as high as 80 percent. But interviews conducted by the mission with local school authorities and with parents suggest that the true rate may be close to 40 or 50 percent, with between one fourth and one third of the children never attending school at all. The estimates of teachers and government officials in Gulu and Kitgum put it at about 30-40 percent; in Karamoja, enrollment is believed to be as low as 20 percent. Needless to say, enrollment drops between grades P1 and P7, and it is significantly lower in secondary school. The gender gap widens following the same pattern.

The Voice of the People

1.31   Thus far, poverty has been measured and described above on the basis of criteria defined by various experts, that is, by people who study poverty but have no direct experience of it. But how do the poor themselves see poverty in Uganda? What are the criteria *they* use to determine who is poor and who is not? What are the causes of poverty, in *their* opinion? This section tries to present poverty from the point of view of the poor. What follows, therefore, is highly subjective and it could not be otherwise. It is based primarily on evidence gathered in the field by the mission during a "rapid poverty appraisal", listening to what peasants living in remote villages had to say and observing the conditions in which they live. Because evidence from participatory rural appraisals shows that children are more likely to offer unbiased information than adults, rural schools were also visited to obtain the views of children. Older ones were asked to write and/or discuss their thoughts, and little ones to draw pictures of the poor (see Annex II for how children in Uganda view poverty).

---

[9]   In some instances, traditional doctors have apparently treated AIDS by bleeding all adult members of the village, using the same blade for the incision. The consequences can be easily guessed.

The understanding of people who have been working with the poor and listening to them for years, such as missionaries and NGO workers, supplements information collected first hand.

1.32   As a broad generalization, the poor were identified as those unable to pay for school fees, and/or to buy soap on a relatively regular basis. Shoes were of course out of question, sugar was a rare luxury and so was meat. The average poor would have one set of clothes for every day wear, often in quite poor condition, and a better set for special occasions, e.g., going to church or to funerals. Some peasants thought that a poor family may be as rich as to own one or two heads of cattle.

1.33   In spite of the fact that Uganda is blessed by fertile land and a good climate, several people mentioned that they did not get enough to eat, particularly in the northern districts. People in villages often identified the poor as having to skip meals more or less on a regular basis, and indeed during field work very seldom was anybody seen eating or cooking during the day.[10] In the poorest districts, skipping lunch is normal for the majority of rural people.

1.34   During field work, it was not uncommon to detect an element of personal blame attached to poverty. More than once it was reported that poor people are lazy, that they drink instead of working hard, that their compound is poorly kept, or that they make foolish choices (e.g., planting the wrong type of crop). Ubiquitous was the blame on the civil war and a feeling that life today was harder than before.[11] A number of farmers, many of them RC1 members, also felt prey of middlemen who take advantage of the situation by offering very low producer prices, which have to be accepted for lack of any alternative.

1.35   While there might have been some disagreements in identifying the poor (e.g., can somebody who owns a bicycle be considered poor?), there were no doubts in determining who were the poorest, neither in terms of their characteristics nor in terms of their identity. In this sense, the comment of an NGO using a participatory approach is telling: "Why do you want to waste time coming up with specific numerical indicators? If you go to a village, everybody will be able to tell you immediately who are the poorest and where they live. We have done spot checks, and we have found that the communities are much better than we can be in identifying the desperately poor" (see Chapter 8).

1.36   Interestingly enough, the poor were also identified as people who worked on somebody else's land. Only under extreme duress would the average farmer consider working as a day laborer for wages; conversely, being able to hire someone is a sign of wealth. It appears, for example, that at least in some cases it would have been conceivable for a family to scrape together enough money to send a child to school if the father had "lowered" himself to work for someone else in order to have

---

[10]   A nutritionist at Mulago Hospital explained why studies may portray a much rosier picture than the reality: "When you go for a nutrition survey, you ask people what they ate the day before at lunch, and they will describe for you a healthy meal. But then you look around and you notice that it is lunch time and there's no sign of eating—not a speck of fire, no dirty pots or dishes, not even smoke. They told you what they know they should be eating, not what they ate. Yet, the average enumerator will simply record the answer without realizing that it is inconsistent with what she sees." (Louise Sserunjogi, personal communication, August 1992).

[11]   However, it appears that in most cases people were comparing their life now with their life in the pre-Amin era. When pressed for a comparison with the more recent past, many admitted that at least now there were things available to buy, even though they were expensive.

cash for the school fees (the mother generally would have no time for such extras). But the social stigma attached to working on somebody else's land would have been too much. Opinions were divided over whether it was more disgraceful to work on someone else's field or to be unable to send one's own child to school. One way or another, it was agreed that poverty takes a heavy toll on pride and self respect.

The Poor and the Vulnerable

"In this village, we are all poor. There are times when everybody goes to bed hungry and few of us can afford to send our children to school. Having sugar in the house or a bar of soap is a sign of wealth. But it is true that some are poorer than others. You can tell because they are dressed in rags and their houses have no door and a leaking roof. These people use banana leaves for blankets because they cannot even light a fire." (A poor farmer in Akworo village in Kitgum district, as narrated to the World Bank mission, August 1992.)

Who are the Poor and Vulnerable?

2.1   Given Uganda's legacy of nearly two decades of civil strife and the severe abuse of human rights, the poorest segments of Ugandan society are the ones who were unable to escape the devastation of war and who, if they were lucky to come out alive, lost all sources of livelihood and had to scratch a living from subsistence agriculture. While they are now able to feed themselves, given Uganda's fertile soil and favorable climate, the resurgence of preventable diseases like malaria and diarrhea has meant that their bodies are usually not able to retain the calories they consume. Moreover, the AIDs pandemic has intervened to further exacerbate the situation. The following sections are devoted to the various groups of people who comprise the bulk of the poor in Uganda and the causes of their poverty.

2.2   *Orphaned, Displaced and Abandoned Children.* Results from the 1991 census identify about 784,000 orphans,[12] or 10 percent of all children below the age of 15. The majority of the orphans are believed to have resulted from AIDS and civil strife and are concentrated in the war-ravaged and in the areas with the highest incidence of AIDS, such as the districts of Masaka and Rakai (see Annex I, Table IX.1). The situation is expected to deteriorate further, and according to projections provided by the Director General of the National AIDS Commission, the number of orphans due to AIDS is expected to increase five fold in the next five years.

2.3   The situation appears even more dramatic considering that children who have already lost one parent can expect to lose the other within a few years. Thus, although cases of families headed by a minor are still relatively rare, they are likely to multiply, as dependency ratios climb to figures unmanageable by the surviving adults (Box 2.1). In addition, in some instances children are advised to stay "in possession" of their parents' property, rather than to move in with relatives or neighbors, for fear that unscrupulous kin would misappropriate their inheritance.[13]

2.4   Parental death is not the only reason for children living on their own. According to NGOs working with street children, economic hardship is the main reason for the apparent increase in their numbers, with certain societal attitudes making things more difficult. For instance, it is common for women who divorce to have to leave behind their children as a condition for remarrying (Box 2.2). If they can afford it, the children are put in a boarding school or in the care of relatives. However,

---

[12]   Defined as individuals below 15 years of age missing one or both parents.

[13]   Misappropriation of inheritance is also common when the mother is still alive because of the inferior legal status of women. Thus, children who lose their father are generally more at risk than those who lose their mother. Legal issues are further discussed below and in Chapters 3 and 7.

Box 2.1: Orphans on Their Own

There are five of them, three girls and two boys aged 14, 12, 11, 10 and 9 years. They live in an isolated house on the edge of the village. Their parents died of AIDS two years ago. The house remains half completed, without windows, the kitchen has collapsed to the ground and the remains of an old car stand in the area behind the house. The children have a small plot measuring 20 by 30 metres on which they grow some tomatoes and onions. These they sell to generate income. For food they maintain a small patch of bananas and they also grow beans and potatoes. As soon as their parents died, they dropped out of school because there was no money. The only relative they know is a maternal uncle who lives in another country. They are fond of him but he is not dependable because he drinks excessively.

The children are rarely at home. They have made themselves indispensable by helping with the funeral rites of their community. The three elder children take turns in sleeping at wakes to keep company with the relatives of the deceased, while during the day they all go to help with the additional household chores associated with the presence of visitors. Neighbors admire their courage, diligence and hard work. They are checked upon by neighbors, receive gifts or food and an agricultural officer has encouraged them to start a small horticultural enterprise to bring in some cash. Their level of life compares favorably with that of other non-orphan children of the same age and circumstances in the area. Their growth is not stunted from malnutrition and they do not have to beg for food.

Source: Tony Barnett & Piers Blaike, "AIDS in Africa", 1992, Grifford Press, London.

---

these solutions are often not available and the children are left to fend for themselves.

2.5   Other children may actually be sent to the streets by their parents or guardians to earn their living. For example, young girls (6-10 years old) are sent from city slums to the market to pick beans that might have fallen from lorries or under the stalls, which are then resold at a lower price; profit for a day's work averages U Sh 800-1,000 (about US$0.75), but may be as high as U Sh 1,500. A small survey of street children in Kampala revealed that about two thirds of them were in regular contact with at least one parent (generally the mother) or a guardian/relative, and often contributed money to the household; only 37 percent were completely on their own and slept in the streets.[14]

2.6   Children on their own are a common phenomenon in post-war (and war) situations. Finding themselves violently separated from their family and not knowing where to go, displaced children head for the cities in search of a way to survive. More than twenty orphanages were opened in the Kampala area during the civil war (1981-86) to shelter children escaping from the atrocities of the Luwero Triangle.[15] Now that peace has returned to most of the country, displaced minors tend to be concentrated in the northern region, where there are still pockets of insecurity. It has been estimated[16] that there are about 2,000 street children in Mbale, most of whom have fled there to escape violence in Karamoja, Kumi and Soroti; it is also believed that large numbers of displaced children have sought refuge in Lira. In Kampala it is estimated that there are over 800 children living

---

[14]   David Muyayisa, *"Street Children in Kampala"*, unpublished manuscript, August 1992.

[15]   Hon. A. Bwanika-Bbaale, *"The Role of the Ugandan Government in National Strategy Formulation"*, paper presented to the Working Group on Children Orphaned by AIDS in Africa, undated.

[16]   By representatives of the Ministry of Labor and Social Welfare at the district level in collaboration with Friends of Children Association.

Box 2.2: A Woman Who was an Orphan

"My father died before I was born. My mother looked after me until I was four and she married another man. He told my mother that he would marry her only if she left me behind.

"My only other relative was my grandmother, an old woman who died when I was six. I was then left on my own with a plot of land about two acres large, so I was forced to start working for a living. I worked as a baby sitter or housegirl wherever a neighbor was willing to employ, clothe and feed me.

"When I was 17, some friends advised me that if I married, my husband would look after me, and I could end my so-far miserable life that I had led since my mother left me. So I got married to a man who lived nearby, and very soon I was pregnant. Unfortunately, I delivered twins. Among my people (the Baganda) there are certain ceremonies that one has to carry out in respect of the ancestors in thanksgiving for twins. Failure to do so leads to the whole family being cursed. As I did not have any parents and knew nothing about worshipping my ancestors, I could not carry out the required ceremonies. My husband was afraid he would be cursed so he sent me and our children away.

"I tried to get a job, but because I have no formal education whatsoever, there seems to be no job for me. I had no choice but to return to the land that my grandmother had left me. I was very disappointed and was sure that I would be cursed by my ancestors. I started growing some food on my land and selling off some so as to maintain my children. Nobody in the neighborhood could look after me in exchange for my services as a housegirl as they used to, because now I had children to look after too. Now the twins are four years old and I am pushing on in the same way as before, selling excess food from my garden. Survival is tough for us, and so far I have no hope of ever sending my children to school.

"A few men have approached me, wanting to marry, but I am afraid something will go wrong again."

Source: "Children and Women in Uganda, A Situation Analysis", UNICEF Kampala, 1989, p.72.

---

on the streets.[17]

2.7   *The Handicapped.* Partly a legacy of the civil war, but also the result of inadequate access to health care, the number of handicapped people in Uganda is very large, although no firm estimates are available.[18] In 1977, WHO estimated that 10 percent of the Ugandan population was disabled, but continuing violence and the breakdown of immunization programs are likely to have caused an increase. The National Union of Disabled People of Uganda (NUDIPU), an umbrella organization for NGOs operating in this area, estimates the percentage to be close to 15-17, excluding the emotionally disabled. Yet it is easy to imagine that the horrors of the civil war have seriously traumatized large numbers of people, who are now unable to lead normal productive lives. It is possible that the number of the disabled could be as high as 1 to 1.5 million.

---

[17]   Charles Tuhaise, "Need for Foster Care in Uganda" in *The Vulnerable Child* (UCOBAC Newsletter), January 1992, p.4.

[18]   The 1990 Census contained a question on disabled people, but findings are likely to be unreliable because the definition used was vague ("unable to support himself") and the enumerators were not properly trained, e.g., they were instructed to rely on observation or on questions to the head of household.

Box 2.3: I Used to Crawl

"I was born healthy, but when I was two years old I got polio. My family thought it was a curse. Just looking at me made them uncomfortable, and they did their best to pretend—to themselves and the world—that I simply was not there. Then one day, when I was fourteen, my father's boss came unexpectedly to the house and saw me crawling on the floor. 'What is this?' he asked my father. Reluctantly my father had to admit that I was his son. 'And what are you doing to help him?' insisted the boss. That saved my life. I was taken to the hospital, where it turned out that all I needed to walk was some practice and a simple brace. That's all I needed to be like the others, but until I was fourteen I spent my days segregated at home, crawling on the floor.

Look at me now. I studied, I got a job, I got married, I can support myself and my family. I can even help out my parents from time to time. And they used to be ashamed of me! I have become their favorite son, and even my wife's relatives have started to accept me. Her sisters used to think she was crazy to have married me, and they pitied her. But now they see that we have two healthy children, that I don't drink and I'm kind to her, that I can provide for her and the children. They envy her."

Source: Rapid Poverty Appraisal, August 1992.

2.8   What makes the handicapped particularly vulnerable is not their disability, but the attitude of people. According to traditional beliefs in several parts of Uganda, disability has a supernatural origin. Disability symbolizes a curse which has struck a particular person but is most likely weighing on the whole family. As a result, those afflicted by disabilities tend to be shunned by society, while their families try to keep them hidden to avoid the shame and possibly the ostracism of the community (Box 2.3). Often, physical disability is assumed to go hand in hand with mental deficiency, so little effort is made to educate handicapped children or even to treat them as persons. Should the attitude of the family be positive, assistance may still be lacking because of the multiple demands on the time of women, who traditionally are responsible for the care of the disabled.[19] Poverty compounds constraints to the provision of even the most basic assistance. For example, handicapped people, and children in particular, need to wash more often because they spend much time on the ground, but soap is a luxury item to be used sparingly for the poor. The situation of disabled women is even worse. It is probably not an exaggeration to say that they are likely to represent the most miserable group of society, doubly discriminated against because of their gender and because of their disability.

2.9   *Female-Headed Households.*[20] In both industrial and developing countries, female-headed households are disproportionately represented among the poor. In the case of Uganda, while the HBS data reveal that approximately one fifth of all households are female-headed, it is difficult to test this hypothesis, as cultural norms discourage women from considering themselves without a partner even if that is the situation de facto. Polygynous relationships further complicate the issue. It is estimated that as many as a third of all marriages are polygynous; it is not uncommon that men would have an official wife in one village and other "wives" in other villages. Because of the general level of impoverishment in the country, only the richest men are able to provide adequate financial, let alone

---

[19]   Herbert Muyinda and Tom Barton, "*Socio-Economic Influences on the Health and Rehabilitation of Physically Handicapped Rural Children*", unpublished manuscript, Child Health and Development Center, Makerere University, February 1992.

[20]   For a comprehensive discussion on women's issues, see Chapter 3.

Box 2.4: Meet the Core Poor

It was difficult to guess how old she could have been, and she did not know. All her ten children were grown up, with their own children. Some might even have grandchildren, but she did not know, because she had not seen any of them in years. What she did know was poverty. Absolute poverty.

When asked to define a poor person, she simply said: "Look at me and look at what I have". She was very old, blind and only partly covered by rags. Her belongings in the run down hut consisted of a papyrus mat to sleep on. Nothing else. No clothes, no blankets, no tools. To keep herself warm at night she uses banana leaves. Because she is blind and weak, she cannot fetch wood or keep a fire, so she cannot cook. In any case, she would not have pots in which to cook. The neighbors bring her cooked food, but in the pre-harvest season, when food is scarce for everybody, she may go for days without anybody coming to see her with something to eat. She does try to grow some millet, using a sharp piece of wood as a hoe (she cannot afford a hoe), but in her condition there is little she can do. Fortunately a youth association created by the RC comes to help her from time to time, bringing her water and working on her field. If it were not for them, she probably would be dead.

Source: Rapid Poverty Appraisal, August 1992.

---

emotional, support to more than one family. Most women in polygynous marriages are, for all practical purposes, heads of their household, in the sense that they are principally—and often solely —responsible for the welfare of the family.

2.10   Widowed and divorced women can confidently be assumed to be at risk because of legal and cultural traditions, which in many cases effectively deny them access to the resources once controlled by the household. Whether these women are allowed to keep their children or not, their situation upon separation from their husbands tends to be critical. In the case of widows, relatives of the husband (generally his brothers) will claim rights on the household property, often evicting the widow and her children from their home. In some areas, widows are "inherited" by brothers-in-law along with property, thus affording women the possibility to maintain the usufruct of their household property and providing them the protection and status deriving from a husband. This practice, however, appears to be dying, certainly in part because of the AIDS pandemic. Unclear inheritance laws and the attitude of the courts are a formidable obstacle for the few women who dare to challenge their in-laws. In the end, the big losers are the children, who find themselves not only without a father, but also destitute.

2.11   *Older People and Their Dependents.* There is general agreement that the elderly have become a particularly vulnerable group. Base-line studies conducted in a number of districts by various NGOs using different methodologies, all arrive at the conclusion that older people—alone or with dependents—are disproportionately at the very bottom of the socio-economic ladder, barely eking a living (Box 2.4). How many of them are in a desperate situation is impossible to say, as counting all heads of household above a certain age would undoubtedly produce an overestimate. It is clear, however, that this is not a negligibly small group, that its size is growing, and that uncertainty about prevalence should not be an excuse for inaction.

2.12   Traditionally, older people have been cared for by their children, thus making specific assistance for the elderly unnecessary (of course, an argument can be made for the opposite, as the lack of reliable pension schemes has made high fertility rates the only form of insurance for old age). But the situation is changing as a result of the AIDS pandemic that is claiming most of its victims among the middle aged who are generally supposed to provide for the welfare of the elderly, therefore effectively wiping out their "pension scheme". To make things worse, many old people find themselves with the added burden of having to take responsibility for their orphaned grandchildren. Already too weak to take care of their own needs, they are obviously unable to provide adequately for the needs of their grandchildren—both materially and psychologically.

2.13   *Landless Peasants.* Common wisdom has it that land in Uganda is fertile and in abundant supply. While this may be true in general, there are areas of high population density, especially in the east and near the Rwanda border, where shortage of land has become a serious concern. Unfortunately, it is difficult to estimate precisely how many people suffer from land shortages, as land tenure is not always clear and sometimes small plots under cultivation may be the result of insecurity or labor scarcity rather than lack of access to land.[21]

2.14   Nevertheless, there are sufficient indications of distress related to land scarcity to warrant special attention to this issue. District authorities in Mbale report that crimes in connection with land disputes (mostly homicides) have shown a dramatic increase in recent years. A participatory poverty appraisal conducted by Action Aid in Mubende district found landless and semi-landless peasants to be a sizable group in the poorest of six categories identified by villagers.[22] Given current demographic trends, the situation could worsen in the future. It is worrisome, for example, that school children interviewed in a land-scarce area near the Kenyan border showed full awareness of the adverse consequences of landlessness, but had firm plans to have at least six or seven children "because it is good to have large families".

2.15   Because land shortage is a limited problem, the solution should be at hand, as families could relocate (or be helped to relocate) to scarcely populated areas. Two factors, however, make the solution not as straightforward as it would seem. To begin with, it is difficult for landless people to even know about areas where land would be available, let alone to actually get there. If a trip to the county health post is only undertaken for very serious illnesses because it is too expensive, moving a whole family hundreds of kilometers away (presumably up north) is definitely out of reach. To put it in economic terms, the rural labor market is plagued by information and mobility imperfections, due partly to a weak road and transport infrastructure.[23]

2.16   Second, relocating is a very risky move for a poor farmer. Interviews with peasants in Bulambuli county, Mbale district, where the average plot size is three fourths of an acre for a six-person household, made it clear that moving away from the village is considered close to suicide, because it means losing the safety net provided by the extended family (see Chapter 7). Since poverty is perceived as having both an economic dimension (no resources) and a social dimension (no relatives), it makes little sense to try to escape one of its aspects by embracing the other.

2.17   *The North.* Identifying a whole region as poor and vulnerable is somewhat of a generalization, as not all of its inhabitants are destitute. But the difficult conditions in which the

---

21   For a discussion of the land tenure system, see the *Uganda: Agriculture Sector Memorandum,* Agriculture and Environment Operations Division, Eastern Africa Department, World Bank, 1993.

22   Action Aid, *Analysis of Results of Participatory Poverty Assessment in Mityana County, Mubende District,* mimeograph, July 1992.

23   Alison Evans, *A Review of the Rural Labour Market in Uganda,* University of Sussex, May 1992.

Box 2.5: Life in Wikuk (Gulu District)

"The rebels came last week. They took everything we had left, that is everything they had not already taken. When they came the time before, they took what the NGO had given us, their resettlement package: blankets, a sauce pan, two hoes. Actually, maybe that's why they came. They might have been watching when the NGO came, so they knew there were things to loot. That's why they came. Twice the NGOs gave us something, and twice the rebels came and took it away. Now some people are afraid of taking things from the NGOs, because it will attract the rebels.

This last time when the rebels came, we had very little, but they still took it. They take our food, so now we just keep a little bit in the granary, because if they don't find anything they get angry. Otherwise, we harvest only what is needed for one meal. Since March we have been feeding on millet and wild greens (dodo), but there isn't enough for the whole family. Luckily, groundnuts are getting ripe.

They even took my wife's dress--that's why she's half naked, just wearing a sack. They come and take. Even our women. Young girls of 10-14 do not sleep any longer with their families. They are afraid that the rebels will come and take them away to their camps as they have done with many. So they sleep in the bush, far from the homes."

Source: Rapid Poverty Appraisal, August 1992.

---

majority of the population in this region appear to live warrant this generalization. While the rest of the country is fast recovering from the ravages of wars and insecurity, parts of the north are still struggling to satisfy even the most basic needs. Large scale numerical data are missing,[24] but there is enough information from NGO reports, church missions and field interviews to piece together an overall picture. It is a picture of suffering of people who in many cases have been left with nothing (Box 2.5).

2.18   To be sure, the Government should be commended for having been able to curb violence and restore peace and security through most of the country in a very short period of time. However, there continue to remain pockets of insecurity where reports of abuses committed by rebels and soldiers continue, taking a heavy toll on both physical and mental health. The resulting insecurity disrupts the regular production cycle of peasant households.

2.19   For example, the raids of Karamojong cattle rustlers have resulted in much looting and violence, causing many people to move away from their fields to the relative safety of military camps and towns. District officials identified victims of cattle rustlers as the most desperate cases in their jurisdiction, at times on the verge of starvation; a large number of displaced families living in dire poverty is also believed to be in Lira. Although government forces have managed to contain the raids, and efforts are presently underway to promote peace talks between the two main conflicting groups of Bokora and Matheniko, there is still ample evidence of armed thugs taking advantage of the situation and perpetuating acts of common criminality. The violence of the past few years has left a large number of mutilated or otherwise disabled people (Box 2.6).

---

[24]   It will be recalled that the north and northeast were not included in the two national surveys, which form the basis of the poverty profile, because of security problems. Results from the Integrated Survey conducted under PAPSCA are not yet available.

Box 2.6: Everybody Has Horror Stories to Tell

"I have been a missionary in the North for over twenty years, and in the past few years I have seen a lot of suffering. Everybody has horror stories to tell. Last year the rebels kidnapped 43 girls from the Sacred Heart School in Gulu; one was killed, 40 were raped. Rapes have become so common. Almost all the girls working with us have been ruined. They rape men as well, but mostly women. You can imagine what this does to the spread of AIDS!

A couple of years ago the rebels started mutilating people. "You don't want to give us your millet? We'll cut your hands". They have cut so many arms and legs. They did horrible things. They cut the ears, noses and lips of girls. Now these girls cannot eat, because they have no lips. There was a room full of them at Lacor Hospital. Certainly these atrocities have caused the rebels to lose a lot of support from the local population. Why have they done it? What did they have to gain out of cutting people. Nobody understands.

It is difficult to bring the situation under control. For one thing, people do not even know if those looting and raping are rebels or soldiers, because they all look the same and have the same weapons. In any case, complaining does not help and may even make things worse. They are caught in the crossfire, they have nobody to turn to and nowhere to go."

Source: Rapid Poverty Appraisal, August 1992.

2.20   Because of this insecurity, farmers in the north have not been able to go to the fields, and food shortages are chronic in some areas. At Lacor Hospital, the largest hospital in the north, 89 percent of children's admissions are for malnutrition (up from about 20 percent before the war); at Kitgum's St. Joseph Hospital, they are 80 percent. Medical personnel estimate a malnutrition rate of 60-65 percent, with about 30 percent being acute malnutrition (wasting). Needless to say, malnutrition increases dramatically during the preharvest season. In Karamoja, the nutritional situation deteriorates during the dry season, as young adults migrate to more fertile lands with the cattle, leaving behind the weak—women with young children, the sick, the elderly. Recurrent droughts and the insecurity which prevented many herdsmen from bringing back the cattle prompted local politicians to request (and obtain) the establishment of an emergency nutrition center.

2.21   Many people find themselves without even the most basic commodities, and therefore unable to become self-sufficient. There is a great need for hoes. At U Sh 3,000 or more, their cost is prohibitive for most farmers, yet without them it will be difficult to increase production even if security were to improve. Cattle rustling and looting have basically destroyed people's ability to support themselves. The threat of HIV infection is also likely to result in rising morbidity, thus further eroding people's self-sufficiency. In Karamoja, intratribal fighting, cultural traditions and a general lack of infrastructure are exacerbating the situation in what is arguably the poorest area of the country. It is clear that without extra help, people in the north may not be able to pull themselves out of extreme poverty.

3

The Gender Dimension

The essence of women's distinctiveness lies in the multiplicity of their roles. Most men can confine themselves mainly to being producers. Most women, in addition to being heavily involved in economic production, take prime responsibility as home managers, child bearers, and carers of the children and elderly.... In consequence, women work longer hours than men, usually with smaller resources, fewer opportunities, and lower rewards. Inequities, in fact, typify gender differences." (Mary Chinery Hesse, et al, Engendering Adjustment for the 1990s, Report of a Commonwealth Expert Group on Women and Structural Adjustment, Commonwealth Secretariat, London, 1989, p. 3.)

3.1   The preceding chapters have addressed the economic and social dimensions of poverty in Uganda. The analysis of the incidence and depth of poverty in Uganda suggests that it is essential to distinguish between various types of households, to assess different expenditure patterns and the issue of intrahousehold inequality, and to recognize that people are affected by poverty in many different ways, as the portrayal of the lives of poor people in the country has shown. These various factors illustrate, in short, the gender dimension of poverty in Uganda. Furthermore, as this chapter will argue, gender is important not just in the assessment of poverty, but in the formulation and design of poverty reduction and economic growth strategies for the country.

3.2   While it may seem self-evident to state that, in Uganda as elsewhere, poverty, economic change and structural adjustment affect both men and women, what is often not recognized by policymakers—and certainly not explicitly—is that they affect men and women in *different* ways, because men and women play different roles, have different needs, and face different constraints in responding to economic policy changes and to shifts in incentives.[25] This combination of differences arises from fundamental imbalances, or "asymmetry",[26] in the respective rights and obligations of men and women, and translates into men and women having highly differential economic capacities, as reflected in their access to, use of, and control over, economically productive resources. These differences have implications not only for economic equity, but also, and much more importantly, for economic efficiency and foregone economic output and income.

3.3   By analyzing the gender dimension of poverty and economic change in Uganda, this chapter aims to illustrate the asymmetry in rights and obligations of men and women and its effects on the country's economic and social development. Since development interventions tend to be at best "gender blind", the chapter does shift the focus of attention toward women and emphasizes the roles, needs, and constraints of women. This is not to ignore the fact that our chief concern is with the socially structured (gender) relations of women and men, for, as Hilda Tadria has argued, "household gender and economic relations are interconnected in the wider economic sphere.... There are many

---

[25]   This is the conceptual rationale for addressing "gender" as a critical dimension of development. See, Caroline O.N. Moser, "Gender Planning in the Third World: Meeting Practical and Strategic Gender Needs", *World Development*, Vol. 17, No. 11, 1989.

[26]   Ingrid Palmer, *Gender and Population in the Adjustment of African Economies: Planning for Change*, Women, Work and Development Series No. 19, International Labor Office, Geneva, 1991, p. 12.

problems ... men and women experience together. Their activities can only be understood in relation to each other."[27]

3.4   From the outset, it is important to stress three factors that limit the analysis in this chapter. The first is that Uganda is a country of some diversity, and any generalizations must necessarily be treated with caution. In particular, notwithstanding many similarities, men's and women's respective responsibilities and burden-sharing arrangements do vary to some degree across the country, in particular as a function of the broad distinctions that can be made between the Bantu societies in the south of the country and the Nilotic, Nilo-Hamitic and Sudanic peoples of the north. The second is that many of the phenomena we observe, especially the economic survival strategies such as increasing reliance on sales of food crops to meet household needs for cash, have changed in scale if not in nature in recent years; it is therefore too early to reach any firm conclusions on the trends that are emerging. The third is that data are scarce, and sex-disaggregated data all the more so. It is therefore necessary to combine qualitative and quantitative data, and case study evidence, to substantiate the analysis.

Profile of Women's Roles and Constraints

3.5   The situation of women in Uganda has been described in various documents.[28] What follows is a brief summary of women's multiple roles and constraints, in relation to those of men, which are of particular relevance to understanding the dimensions of poverty, and to the formulation of poverty reduction and economic growth strategies for the country.

3.6   *Agriculture.* Women are responsible for producing 80 percent of Uganda's food, and provide about 70 percent of total agricultural labor.[29] They are principally but not exclusively confined to the unpaid subsistence sector, and carry out their agricultural tasks without benefit of technological innovation, inputs, or finance. Many of these problems, of course, also apply to poor male farmers in rural areas, though not in the same way, since men provide only around 30-40 percent of the country's agricultural labor, and men are not constrained by competing claims on their labor time. Evidence from the north suggests that basic agricultural implements (hoes, for example) are scarce and costly for the poorest farmers.[30]

---

[27]   H. M. K. Tadria, "Changes and Continuities in the Position of Women in Uganda", in *Beyond Crisis: Development Issues in Uganda*, Paul Wiebe and Cole Dodge, Eds., Makerere Institute of Social Research, Kampala, Uganda, 1987, pp. 79-80.

[28]   See, in particular, Eva Jarawan, *Women in Development: Current Issues and Agenda for Further Research*, Population and Human Resources Division, Working Paper, June 1991; UNICEF, *Women and Children in Uganda: A Situation Analysis*, Kampala, Uganda, 1989; UNICEF/ACFODE, *Uganda: Women's Needs Assessment Survey 1988*; *Agricultural Sector Memorandum*, Agriculture and Environment Operations Division, 1992; *Social Sector Strategy*, Population and Human Resources Division, 1992, World Bank.

[29]   Data on women's time allocation, and especially in relation to the agricultural division of labor, are scarce. The figures cited here are in Jarawan (op. cit. p. 20). The *Situation Analysis* (UNICEF, 1989, p. 77) cites survey data indicating that women provide 68 percent of the labor for food crops and 53 percent of the labor for cash crops. Interestingly, the same survey indicates the disparity of women's control over the income from their labor, as women sell only 30 percent of foodcrops and 9 percent of cash crops.

[30]   "In many homes there are not enough agricultural tools for each adult to have a hoe.... In as many as 4 percent of rural households, there may be no agricultural tools at all." *Women and Children in Uganda: A Situation Analysis*, UNICEF, Kampala, Uganda, 1989, p. 21.

3.7   *Household Management.* Women have primary responsibility for household management, child rearing, food preparation, care of the sick and elderly, and family health and welfare. These tasks are also carried out without benefit of labor-saving technology (for example, in the north, it can take two hours to grind sufficient millet for a normal family meal), or adequate social service and transport infrastructure. Women's primary responsibility for these tasks is difficult to document in the absence of time-use data, or data on how long it takes to perform certain critical tasks (such as fetching water or wood). Survey data reinforce the asymmetry of male/female obligations with respect to household tasks, where the greater share of household tasks is performed by women/girls: cooking (86 percent); fetching water (70 percent); collecting firewood (73 percent); child care (62 percent); washing clothes (88 percent); care for the sick and elderly (62 percent).[31]

3.8   *Workload.* This combination of responsibilities means that women have a very heavy workload: women work longer hours than men, between 12 and 18 hours per day, with a mean of 15 hours;[32] there are no comparable data on average male working hours. In Kenya, it has been shown that women work half as many hours again as men on both agricultural and nonagricultural tasks (12.9 hours compared with 8.2 hours).[33] Interviews with district officials and NGO representatives confirm a prevalent view that the time women devote to work is considerably greater than that of men—indeed, some argue that women are essentially working throughout their waking hours. Women are, therefore, if anything, *overemployed*, not an economically idle resource awaiting supply response incentives. This reinforces the argument made in Chapter 6 that a more accurate picture of labor force participation is made by including in the labor force those who are predominantly engaged in "household activities." If "leisure time" is a valid indicator of well-being, women are very poor indeed.

3.9   *Health.* As a result of women's heavy workload and time burden, women's own ill-health is especially significant. The Needs Assessment Survey established what it described as an "alarmingly high" morbidity rate for rural women—at 76 percent—in the two weeks before the interview.[34] This has particular significance when viewed in conjunction with the high total fertility rate at 7.3 live births (see Table 1.4 for selected social indicators). Contraceptive use is constrained to a low level (5 percent among women of reproductive age), because of lack of access, and generally unfavorable male attitudes. With the high fertility rate, most of a woman's reproductive years are dominated by pregnancy, childbirth, and child care, leading to health problems. Women's low health status greatly constrains their capacity to provide for the health of their families (which is principally the responsibility of women), as well as their economic productivity and potential. Women's health, not just maternal health, and nutrition, thus deserves particular attention. Women's lack of time and their lack of minimum education and information are further important factors negatively affecting the health and well-being of children (Box 3.1).

---

[31]   UNICEF/ACFODE, ibid, pp. 28-29.

[32]   UNICEF/ACFODE, ibid, p. 17.

[33]   Katrine Saito, "*Raising the Productivity of Women Farmers in Sub-Saharan Africa*", Vol. I, Overview Report, PHRWD, September 15, 1992, p. 26. Her conclusion is also pertinent. "An average of 13 hours' work a day is debilitating to body and spirit and cannot be expected to [lead to] satisfactory results for either farm output or household management."

[34]   UNICEF/ACFODE, ibid, p. 3.

> **Box 3.1: No Time for Health**
>
> A typical Ugandan child starts life in a large family in a rural area. Like most of her relatives, she is delivered at home by an older neighbor. As a small baby, the child is likely to be healthy and grow well, as long as she has her mother to care for her and breastfeed her. After six months, however, the protection she obtains from breast milk will wane, and the child will begin to suffer from repeated bouts of infectious diseases, especially diarrhea, because her mother does not have the time to carry enough water from two kilometers away to keep the house, kitchen, and utensils as clean as she would like. Each episode of diarrhea or other illness leaves the child a little thinner and weaker, because she cannot regain the weight lost when she was ill. She is undernourished not because her village lacks food, but because her mother does not have the time or firewood to cook frequent small meals or to coax her to eat when she does not feel well.
>
> *Source: "Children and Women in Uganda: A Situation Analysis", UNICEF, Kampala, Uganda, 1989.*

3.10   *Education.* Women's low levels of literacy as adults and the increasing gender inequity at different levels of the education system compound the difficulties they face in meeting their multiple responsibilities; despite being the principal providers and promoters of good health at the household level, many are illiterate[35] and have very little knowledge of health, nutrition, and hygiene. More importantly, women are also poorly informed about other issues of importance to them and their families, notably their legal rights—see paras 3.17-3.19 below.

3.11   *Isolation.* Characteristic of women's lives in rural areas is their relative isolation. There are few channels of communication to and in rural areas, and women seem largely excluded from them. Women have low rates of participation and involvement in formal groups or decision fora (18 percent in women's groups; 2 percent in agricultural cooperatives); women receive minimal attention in the form of visits from either extension or health workers (5 percent); they have low access to radio (34 percent), while most external contact arises through RC activities (38 percent). [36]

Gender Issues for Poverty Reduction and Economic Growth

3.12   The above profile of women's multiple roles and constraints amply illustrates the asymmetries in rights and obligations of women and men, as reflected in significantly different workloads, responsibilities, degrees of isolation and autonomy, and access to productive assets. This leads to identification of a number of issues that need to be addressed in defining a gender-responsive poverty reduction and economic growth strategy for Uganda. These are:

(i)   the value (both economic and noneconomic) of women in Ugandan society, and how this affects women's capacity to fulfill their multiple roles, and by extension reinforces the impoverishment of women and children in Uganda;

(ii)   the extent to which laws and customs constitute a greater obstacle to women than to men in carrying out their economic and social roles, and inhibit poverty-reduction efforts;

---

[35]   According to the HBS, for Uganda as a whole, 26 percent of men are illiterate, compared with 40 percent of women.

[36]   UNICEF/ACFODE, ibid.

Box 3.2: A View from the Top

Sometimes, women are their own worst enemies. We women have been trapped within a web of traditional values which assign a very high value to child bearing and almost none at all to anything else we can do. Our status depends on our success as mothers and on little else. Furthermore, our value increases or decreases according to whether we produce sons and how many. This has been going on for so long that even the women have come to believe and to accept it, to the extent that women even discriminate against their own daughters, in favor of their sons! The feeling of inadequacy and nothingness gets transmitted from mother to daughter, from generation to generation. Consequently, you find, in some cultures, girls eating less if food is scarce, working more hours, getting inferior and inadequate education, and eventually being given away in marriage at an early age in exchange for wealth.

Source: Janet Museveni, Closing Address, Seminar on Women as Providers and Promoters of Health, October 17-19, 1990. Proceedings, ACFODE, Kampala, Uganda, 1991.

(iii)   the diversity in size and composition of households in Uganda, and how this affects both analysis of poverty and design of poverty-reduction interventions, especially as concerns intrahousehold resource allocation and inequality;

(iv)   the gender division of labor, and its implications for poverty alleviation and economic growth strategies; and

(v)   the intersectoral linkages that are particularly important from a gender perspective in addressing multidimensional poverty.

The Value of Women in Ugandan Society

3.13   Uganda's women are principally valued for their role as mothers, which is reflected in the high total fertility rate at 7.3 live births, itself partly attributable to the widespread practice of early sexual activity, early pregnancy, and early marriage.[37] This is not to say that the centrality of women's role in economic activity (especially in food production) is not recognized, only that this role is taken for granted and undervalued (Box 3.2).[38]

3.14   In the economic sphere, men control the cash-based economy, while women remain for the most part in the nonmonetized subsistence sector. Men are so closely identified with the cash sector, to the virtual exclusion of women, that women who earn cash often hand it over to their husbands, and while men are usually paid in cash, women are often paid in-kind, for example, with food, salt, or soap. This makes it difficult to identify possible wage discrimination between men and women, though "distress labor selling" of female labor at less than the village norm has been observed as particularly prevalent during the 1991/92 season, in the face of drought and escalating food prices.[39]

---

[37]   For a discussion of the implications of this in the context of AIDS, see: *New Phase of UNICEF Support for AIDS Control in Uganda*, Summary Document, UNICEF, Kampala, Uganda, April 1992.

[38]   Subsistence agriculture, based on HBS data, is now included in the calculation of GDP, and in this respect, women's economic activity has begun to overcome its invisibility. This cannot yet be said of women's work in the community and around the household.

[39]   See Alison Evans, *A Review of the Rural Labour Market in Uganda*, May 1992.

Box 3.3: Ties That Bind

A woman is bound to obey her husband in everything by virtue of the bride price that her husband's relatives paid to her family. The payment of bride price entitles a man to the woman's labor, her sexual services, and her full obedience. Men who can afford it can practice polygamy. On marriage a woman goes to live with her husband in his home. Traditionally, women were not consulted over the choice of husband and divorce was difficult if not impossible for a woman to initiate because her relatives would have to be persuaded to return the bride price. If a woman was divorced by her husband, she would return to live with her relatives and her husband had no further obligations to her. Her children, irrespective of age, would stay with her husband. If the husband died, she inherited nothing. In fact, she herself would be inherited by other male relatives.

Source: *"Violence Against Women in Uganda", A Research Report by Ms. Veri Wakabi and Ms. Hope Kwesigye, USAID/FIDA, July 1991.*

3.15   Women's exclusion from the cash economy has far-reaching repercussions, both because men's and women's "value" to society tends to be measured as a function of their contribution to the monetized economy, and because of ambivalent attitudes and shifting expectations toward women taking on greater responsibility for cash earning. "The differences between men and women in access to cash produces and maintains significant gender inequities. A man who earns cash is highly regarded even if he cannot feed his family, whereas a woman who is "merely" a subsistence producer is undervalued even if she feeds her family. It follows ... that with the existing division of labor, a man is highly regarded because he is essentially a cash earner (even if he is not earning cash) whereas a woman is underrated because she is essentially a dependent (even if she is earning cash)."[40]

3.16   Women who do earn cash face a particular dilemma in a climate where men are "not keen on women who are economically independent."[41] Even though men are the principal beneficiaries of women's cash earning, they (men) are not supportive of women in this respect. ACFODE, a local NGO, points out that in some cases men abdicate all responsibility for their families when women earn money, so women "are not sure which is better, to remain being looked after by the man however bad this 'looking after' is, or to get money and do everything in the home."[42] This has far-reaching repercussions in the context of a development strategy that emphasizes the monetization of the economy, and particularly of agriculture. If women are to avoid being further marginalized in low-technology and low-productivity subsistence agriculture, Uganda will need to take particular measures to address this cultural dimension of monetization, if the modernization and diversification of agriculture—a key component of the country's growth strategy—is to be undertaken in a manner that enables the majority of (women) farmers to participate in and benefit from it.

---

[40]   Tadria, op. cit., pp. 81-82.

[41]   Action for Development (ACFODE), Background Paper on ACFODE's Objectives and Activities, no date, p. 2.

[42]   Ibid, Action for Development (ACFODE).

Box 3.4: Women and Legal Reform

As part of the constitutional reform process, the Ministry of Women in Development, with DANIDA support, organized seminars throughout the country aimed at giving women the opportunity to voice their opinions about the reform and to influence the framing of the new constitution. Between November 1990 and May 1991, 113 county-level seminars were held in 25 districts of the country, and more than 4,000 women had participated in the consultations. The concerns and priorities of these women are particularly revealing.

- **Constitution as the Supreme Law:** women recommended that all customary laws, practices and religious beliefs that are repugnant, discriminatory, not good for the health of women, or otherwise undermine the status of women and are contrary to the provisions of the constitution as a Supreme Law, should be abolished.

- **Fundamental Rights and Freedoms:** women recommended that every man and woman in Uganda should have the constitutional right to a basic education, and that every man and woman should have the constitutional right to earn a living--particular emphasis was placed on protecting women whose husbands make it their right to decide whether or not their wives work for pay. Rights to education and health included specific recommendations on child spacing and number, as well as the right to practice family planning.

- **Discrimination:** There should be no discrimination on the basis of sex. All discriminatory legislation should be repealed and replaced. The principal areas of the law where women have suffered injustices because of their discrimination are: (i) marriage; (ii) divorce; (iii) inheritance and property rights; and (iv) employment regulations. A majority of participants recommended that monogamous marriages be promoted; some argued that with the present scourge of AIDS, polygynous unions should be outlawed. Customary marriages which confer unequal marital rights on the parties concerned should be considered as unconstitutional and discouraged.

- **Bridewealth:** Those advocating the abolition of bridewealth did so on the ground that bridewealth undermines the status of women and that it often implies that men believe they have the right to treat their wives as slaves, or property or ornaments purchased. They argued that many men who have paid bridewealth subject their wives to inhuman treatment (including wife-beating), contravening the provisions of the 1967 Constitution. Those advocating retention of bridewealth sought to ensure that it be more tightly regulated to avoid exploitation and promotion of a "greedy attitude" by parents. While participants acknowledged that outright abolition of the practice is not realistic, women were optimistic that with the social and economic changes taking place in Uganda the practice would slowly fade out over time.

- **Divorce:** The practice of returning bridewealth in the event of divorce or separation should be abolished. Laws should be amended to treat women as equal partners with men in divorce proceedings, i.e., women, like men, should only have to establish one ground for divorce.

- **Inheritance/Property:** All customary practices that deprive women of their constitutional right to own and acquire properties (cows, land, other fixed assets) should be outlawed. There should be more equal sharing of property of deceased husbands than is presently provided for under the law (i.e., from 15 percent to 25-50 percent). The customary practice of inheriting a woman by a brother or any other near male relative upon the death of the husband should be abolished. Women bitterly complained that men fight to inherit a widow whose late husband left property which they can benefit from. Several cases were also quoted where women were abandoned with their children by the clansmen of their late husbands because the man had died poor.

- **Employment Regulations:** Participants' recommendations in this area included ensuring that women benefit from their contribution to accumulated household income, and that this contribution be legally recognized; that sexual harassment of women in their place of work be a criminal offence severely punishable; and that equal pay, promotion opportunities, and benefits for equal work should be guaranteed.

Source: Recommendations by the Women of Uganda to the Constitutional Commission Through the Ministry of Women in Development, June 1991.

Unequal Before the Law?

3.17   In Uganda, as in many societies, laws and customs impede women to a greater extent than men in obtaining credit, productive inputs, education, training, information, and medical care needed to perform their economic roles. This applies especially in the areas of access to and control of the physical and financial resources they need if they are to play their multiple roles in both economic and social development.[43] Key issues concern property law and land use/tenure rights, inheritance laws and practices, and family law governing marriage, divorce, child custody, domestic violence, and bride price (Box 3.3).

3.18   Asymmetry in the respective obligations of men and women is characteristic of both the legal system and customary practice in Uganda. Indeed, while there are specific instances of sex discrimination in laws and regulations, "most of the laws are gender-neutral, thus giving rise to *de facto* discrimination."[44] While this is an area requiring specific analysis, especially with respect to the impact of such discrimination on women's economic capacity, gender bias exists in a number of areas, and derives from the fact that under customary law (and practice) women are essentially minors, without adult legal status or rights.[45] These include divorce, including definition of and compensation for adultery; inheritance, since women are not their husbands' automatic heirs; and child custody laws, as women do not have custody of their children. There is also bias in property rights, even where no statute prevents women from owning property, since, by custom, property acquired during marriage belongs to the husband.[46]

3.19   To address these recognized biases in law and custom, Uganda is making a concerted effort to reform its legal system, beginning with constitutional reform, and women's groups are actively seeking to ensure that these reforms respond to the needs and constraints of women as well as of men. The most important initiatives concern the redrafting of the constitution, following a grassroots consultative process in which women's groups and the Women in Development Ministry have been very active (Box 3.4), and the work of the Child Law Reform Commission in seeking to articulate and protect the legal rights of children (especially important in view of the number of orphans in Uganda) as the country's laws and statutes are revised.

The Diversity of Households in Uganda

3.20   If the analysis of household welfare and behavior is to take account of gender asymmetries, it must necessarily reflect the diversity of households in Uganda and the different roles played by men and women. The size, composition, and dependency ratios in Ugandan households vary considerably. Evidence from the HBS suggests that about one fifth of all households in Uganda are headed by women. Female-headed households (FHH) are generally smaller than male-headed households (MHH), comprising on average 4.5 people, as compared with 5.7 in MHH. While it is important to look at the education and health status of all household members, the data indicate that the proportion of female household heads among illiterate household heads is, at 30 percent, higher than among literate household heads, where it is 20 percent. Illiterate female heads of households may therefore

---

[43]   The linkage between law, gender, and economic development is explored in Doris Martin and Fatuma Hashi, *Law as an Institutional Barrier to the Economic Progress of Women*; *Sub-Saharan Africa: Gender, Evolution of Legal Institutions, and Economic Development*; and *Women in Development: The Legal Issues in Sub-Saharan Africa Today*, AFTSP Division Working Papers, Nos. 2, 3, and 4, June 1992.

[44]   "*Initial and Second Report by the Uganda Government on the Implementation of the Convention on the Elimination of All Forms of Discrimination against Women*", no date.

[45]   See Jarawan, op. cit., p. 8; and, more generally, the Fatuma and Hashi study cited above.

[46]   See UNICEF, *Children and Women in Uganda: A Situation Analysis*, p. 75.

Box 3.5: Female Labor Time and Efficiency

Family labor efficiency, or more accurately, female labor time and efficiency, is also severely compromised by the almost total absence of basic *domestic technology* in rural areas. In all the villages and households visited, none had access to piped water, most used boreholes anything between 1 and 5 km away. Firewood collection has to be done regularly, often three or four times a week, in some cases daily. Women's lack of transport technology—bicycles, wheelbarrows, pull-carts—makes this task both arduous and extremely time-consuming. When men collect firewood, they frequently have access to a bicycle which significantly reduces the time-costs of transportation. Low-efficiency cooking stoves aggravate the need for frequent trips to collect fuelwood. Limited availability or affordability of simple hand grinders or shellers makes manual food processing, especially of hard grains such as maize and rice, another time-consuming chore for women and female children. The time costs associated with the heavy burden of domestic work place constraints on women's labor time as both family and hired labor. Female labor time, on account of the greater domestic labor overhead, is relatively supply inelastic and less substitutable than male labor. Consequently, the capacity of women farmers to reallocate their labor time to shifts in crop or labor market incentives has to be seen within the context of these wider and continuous demands on their time.

Source: Alison Evans, "A Review of the Rural Labor Market in Uganda", May 1992.

---

constitute an especially vulnerable group of the core poor.

3.21   The importance of examining *intrahousehold* resource allocation cannot be overemphasized. The resource allocation process within households reflects the status, bargaining power, and options of the parties concerned, which in turn are largely a function of control over assets and income. As has been shown in a preceding section, however, women generally do not, and are not expected to, control cash income or economic assets; they remain in the subsistence (noncash) sector, where their economic contribution is not valued but taken for granted. Household expenditure patterns, as revealed in the HBS, confirm that gender inequity within the household is an extremely important dimension of poverty. This was confirmed in the visits to the north where within households women are visibly poorer than men, and where children invariably describe their mothers as being poorer than their fathers. The fact that drink and tobacco comprise more than twice the share of monthly expenditures in MHH than they do in FHH, as discussed in Chapter 1, is one reason why the National Program of Action for Children places emphasis on the need for households—especially poor households—to reallocate their own expenditures away from these commodities and toward meeting the basic education and health care needs of their children.[47]

The Gender Division of Labor

3.22   The gender division of labor is the central manifestation of the asymmetrical rights and obligations of men and women. While both men and women play productive, reproductive, and community management roles in society, women, in contrast to men, must balance simultaneous competing claims on limited time for each of these roles—women's time and flexibility are therefore much more constrained than is the case for men. Account must be taken of two aspects of the gender division of labor. The first derives from women's already heavy workload, the significance of which is that women's labor time is highly inelastic and that female labor availability (whether for economic

---

[47]   Uganda National Plan of Action for Children, *The Way Forward IV: Priorities for Social Services Sector Development in the 1990s*, Ministry of Finance and Economic Planning, Kampala, Uganda, June 5, 1992.

Box 3.6: Differential Incentives: Two Cases from Kenya

Adoption of Tea. A recent study of adoption of tea growing in Kenya found that female-headed households had only half the propensity of male-headed households to adopt tea. Since in Kenya around one third of rural households are female-headed this diminished capacity can be substantial. The case of Kenyan tea is particularly revealing because most of the tea picking is done by females. This is reflected in the effects of the household labor endowment on the propensity to adopt tea. Extra male labor has no effect on the propensity to adopt tea whereas extra female labor leads to a statistically significant increase. In Kenya, the key tea sector is characterized by three apparently incompatible facts. Women do most of the work on tea, households with more women are more likely to adopt the crop, yet households headed by women are far less likely to do so. The implication is that female-headed households face some severe constraints additional to those faced by male-headed households which prevent them from entering what would otherwise be a natural activity for female-headed households.

Maize Weeding. One illustration of asymmetric rights and obligations within the household is given where women work on holdings the output of which is controlled by men. A recent Kenyan sample survey compared the effectiveness of weeding (a female obligation) on maize yields in male- and female-headed households. In both types of household there were two weedings per season and each weeding significantly raised yields. However, whereas in female-headed households these weedings raised yields by 56 percent, in male-headed households the increase in yield was only 15 percent. Since other differences were controlled for, the most likely explanation is a systematic difference in effort due to differential incentives. Thus, the "incentives" argument, so familiar in the World Bank, does not stop at the door of the household. To put this in perspective, if the sample is representative of rural Kenya, the national maize loss from this disincentive effect is about equal to the maize gain from the application of phosphate and nitrogen fertilizers.

Source: Adapted from Analysis Plans for Understanding the Social Dimensions of Adjustment, Chapter 8: "The Impact of Adjustment on Women", Report No. 8691-AFR, World Bank, July 1990, pp. 156, 159.

---

activities or for community-based mobilization for self-help schemes) requires explicit assessment of the opportunity costs involved. This is especially the case in reference to agriculture. Just as important, women's lack of access to labor-saving technology, whether for economic or domestic activities, coupled with the multiple constraints and obligations they face, combine to diminish both the productivity of women's labor time use and the flexibility or responsiveness to economic incentives of their labor allocation (Box 3.5). This means that raising the productivity of Uganda's (women) farmers is a significant and multifaceted challenge for Ugandan policymakers.

3.23   The second aspect is the still pervasive economic division of labor where men largely control the monetized (cash) sector, while women largely remain in the unpaid subsistence sector, as indicated above. The significance of this is that women have extremely limited access to and control of economically productive resources, which is important for two principal reasons. First, women and men face different economic incentives and opportunities—therefore, supply response cannot be assessed in a manner undifferentiated by gender. Specifically, if women continue to have little or no control over the cash income generated from export crops, a strategy encouraging farmers to diversify production away from food crops towards export crops will fail to attract women out of the subsistence sector (Box 3.6). Second, women are increasingly becoming responsible for meeting household cash requirements that were once paid by men's cash income. For example, in 1988, 30 percent of women with children in school paid all or part of their children's expenses.[48] This is one of the contributing factors to the adoption by women of strategies to generate income—such as sale of food crops, alcohol, labor, sex, and other services. These strategies, and the search for alternative and less damaging economic opportunities for women, therefore require special attention both in terms of how women fulfill their multiple roles and in terms of design and implementation of poverty reduction and economic growth strategies.

Intersectoral Linkages

3.24   It is the interconnections, and inevitable trade-offs, among economic production, child bearing, caregiving, household management, and community participation activities that take on particular significance, given the competing claims on women's time. The linkages between poverty, lack of access to and control of economic resources, and survival strategies have particular importance in the context of two emerging demographic and social trends. The first is the growing number of single female-headed households, which are substantially more cash-poor than their male-headed counterparts. The second is the AIDS pandemic, and the attendant increased burden and risk for women. Key issues which need to be addressed are:

  (i) the interdependence of economically productive and social sector investments and programs, all of which affect labor time allocation;

  (ii) the socio-economic implications of AIDS for household survival strategies, poverty reduction, and economic prospects; and

  (iii) the problem of low female participation in education, and the nexus of low education and high fertility in Uganda.

3.25   *The Interdependence of Economically Productive and Social Sector Investments and Programs.* Hesse et al point out that the disproportionate burden on women in the area of household management and family welfare means that women almost always face more severe constraints and harsher choices in their use of time than do men.[49] Uganda provides many poignant illustrations of these harsh choices. e.g., the trade-off between making (principally female) child labor available in the household and sending that child to school. This is illustrated by Evans in her study of rural labor markets, in discussion of strategies adopted by households to address labor shortages.[50]

3.26   A second is in the area of health care. Many studies confirm that while first immunizations reach a relatively good proportion of children (60 percent), follow-up immunizations, and, more generally, routine preventive medical care, are not as successful. If a child is otherwise "healthy" at the time a second or third immunization is due, it is likely that a woman, faced with the competing claims on her time, and given that she probably has minimal mobility, will not be prepared to sacrifice a day or half-day to do something which does not appear on the face of it to be necessary,

---

[48]   Cited in *Children and Women in Uganda, A Situational Analysis*, UNICEF, Kampala, 1989, p. 78.

[49]   Mary Chinery Hesse, et. al., *Engendering Adjustment for the 1990s*, Report of a Commonwealth Expert Group on Women and Structural Adjustment, Commonwealth Secretariat, London, 1989, p. 3.

[50]   Evans, op. cit.

Box 3.7: Poverty and AIDS

A recent study examined the linkages between socio-economic status and poverty in 15 villages in Masaka District in Uganda. It concludes as follows:

> The results from this study suggest that poverty leads to a greater risk of HIV infection for both male and female heads of household. The infection of males and females is obviously interrelated and the vulnerability to infection of the poor men may be linked to the risk of infection in their partners. Such a situation would occur when a woman adopts an income generating strategy such as brewing and selling alcohol coupled with the provision of sexual services to provide a cash income. Our qualitative data suggest that alcohol manufacture is one means by which the poor seek to increase their income and alcohol consumption may keep some men and women in poverty and at increased risk of "careless" sex.

> Among first degree relatives it is the adult daughters belonging to poor households who appear to be at increased risk of HIV infection. The apparent greater risk of the female offspring would seem to support part of the original hypothesis which suggested that poor women, because of the strategies they adopt to survive, are at an increased risk of infection.

> The results of this rural study suggest that both women and men of low socio-economic status in the study area are at greater risk of HIV infection than people of higher status. There is probably no simple association between any one factor of poverty and risk of HIV infection. It is likely, however, that there is a link with an individual's lack of access to resources and the strategies adopted in order to compensate for this.

Source: *"Socio-Economic Status, Gender, and Risk of HIV-1 Infection in a Rural Community in South West Uganda", Janet Seely, et. al, Medical Research Council (UK) Programme on AIDS in Uganda, 1992.*

---

given all the other things she has to do, and the benefits of which she simply does not understand.[51] This time-constraint approach to the issue of access to health care may help to explain why follow-up immunizations are considerably rarer than initial ones, and how interconnected this is with women's education level, knowledge base, and degree of autonomy and control over resources. A time-based view of constraints also helps to explain why a recent assessment in Mulago Hospital reveals that only 1.8 percent of women returned for postnatal check-ups.[52]

3.27   *The Socio-Economic Implications of AIDS.* The socio-economic implications of the AIDS pandemic in Uganda are just beginning to be assessed and understood. The Society for Women and AIDS in Africa (SWAA) has described women as facing "triple jeopardy" given their multiple attributes as individuals, mothers, and caregivers. The relationship between poverty and AIDS is particularly important in view of the fact that women can be characterized, in general and as argued in this chapter, as being "individuals lacking access to resources." In this context, the conclusions of a recent study on AIDS risk among the poor are particularly pertinent (Box 3.7). This, combined with the prevalence of early sexual activity and pregnancy, helps to explain why the statistics on AIDS cases show that young women aged 15-19 are five times more likely to be infected with AIDS than

---

[51]   It should also be noted that even where women do understand, and do want to do more, the burden of responding to immediate needs is still likely to limit their capacity to respond.

[52]   Christine Akiri-Kajeru, Preliminary Assessment of Mulago Hospital Statistics, 1990.

Box 3.8: Domestic Relations in the Context of AIDS

Case A: A man's continuation of sexual involvement after the death of a sexual partner due to AIDS.

Mukasa was married to two women (Rozi and Bess) who lived in separate villages. He was living with Rozi, the senior wife, on a more permanent basis when she developed AIDS and died after about one year of infection.

Mukasa then moved in with Bess, the junior wife. After about fourteen months, Bess's young teenage sister, who was living with them, developed the symptoms of AIDS. In a panic, Bess quickly returned her to her parents where she died of AIDS after six months. Everybody suspected Mukasa to be the sexual contact.

A year later, Joy, a young woman who had also had a brief affair with Mukasa, died. Several months afterwards Mukasa died, followed by the deaths of Bess and their one-year old child. They have left several orphans. Several village men are in a panic as they had sexual encounters with Joy.

Case B: A husband's violence towards his wife.

Recently, on the outskirts of the city center, a husband allegedly assaulted his wife because she refused to have sex with him. She was fearful that his former philandering ways might have afflicted him with the disease.

For almost two years he had totally ignored her until now. But she wanted no part of him. His reaction was to viciously beat her up. Few would condone such behavior. But, then again, as one sympathetic man noted on the incident: "she was his wife. He had every right to sleep with her if he so wished."

Perhaps this is a chauvinistic point of view, but it is important to note the husband's violent reaction is an example of the extreme consequences of "zero grazing". It can be exceedingly frustrating for those men not used to domesticity.

Source: *Cases Cited in Mere Nakateregga Kisekka, "AIDS in Uganda as a Gender Issue", Women's Mental Health in Africa, Eds. Esther D. Rothblum and Ellen Cole, Harrington Park Press, New York, 1990.*

---

young men of the same age group. This greater degree of risk for women persists to the 20-24 age group.[53] The conclusions of the study suggest that exploration of alternative economic survival strategies for women (other than alcohol brewing and selling, or sale of sexual services) to offset their lesser access to economically productive resources should be a high priority.

3.28   The AIDS crisis has far-reaching repercussions for marriage, family life, and care of the sick. The burdens of increased risk of domestic violence, as well as of caring for the sick fall disproportionately on women (Box 3.8). Responsibility for caring for AIDS orphans and other vulnerable children falls principally on women. One study indicated that, among 175 foster children and orphans in 70 households, a consistent pattern of discrimination against these children is apparent, through lower access and attainment in schools, and use of these children as a source of

---

[53]   *"New Phase of UNICEF Support for AIDS Control in Uganda"*, Summary Document, UNICEF, Kampala, 1992.

Box 3.9: Investing in Girls' Education

Economics, with its emphasis on incentives, provides a useful way to understand why so many girls are deprived of education and employment opportunities. And concrete calculations demonstrate that there are enormous economic benefits to investing in women. Over time, the importance of female education will dwarf that of many of the financial issues we more routinely address. Our analysis leads to four conclusions. First, there is a horrifying problem of excess female mortality in many developing countries. It is but the most obvious manifestation of a much broader problem of female deprivation. Second, female deprivation results from a vicious cycle where girls are not educated because they are not expected to make an economic contribution to their families, an expectation which represents a self-fulfilling prophecy. Third, increasing educational opportunities for girls offers the best prospect for cutting into this vicious cycle. Increasing outlays directed at educating girls would yield enormous economic and social benefits. Fourth, the share of the world's girls who go to school can be increased at a relatively modest cost. Over time, increases in girls' education have the potential to transform societies.

When girls are not educated, their labor has little economic value outside the home. They are forced to marry young and are unable to stand up to their husbands. They have more children than they really want and are unable to invest heavily in each child. Poverty is perpetuated.

When girls are educated, they have economic opportunities. Their families have more a stake in their survival and their success. They marry later and are able to take part in household decisions. They choose to have fewer children and can invest more in the health and development of each child. Their daughters and sons have expanded horizons. And often they escape from poverty.

Source: Adapted from Larry Summers, "Investing in All the People: Educating Women in Developing Countries." Remarks prepared for a Development Economics Seminar at the World Bank, September 1992.

---

cheap labor.[54]

3.29   *Barriers to Female Education and the Nexus of Fertility and Education.* The perception that women are less economically valuable than men is reflected in choices with respect to investment in education. Many families face the difficult choice of not being able to send all children to school. While lack of money for school fees is often cited as the principal reason for school dropout, other factors undoubtedly play a part: "parental reluctance, need for the child's labor, lack of interest, pregnancy and marriage, gender bias, and the lack of linkage between primary education and income-generating potential all have a role to play."[55] It is important to note here that negative attitudes towards women and the value of female education are a significant factor in the lower achievement, attainment, and enrollment rates of girls in schools. In the words of one male parent, "[education of girls is a] waste of money as they get married and go away. The girls who are highly educated are

---

[54]   Source: *Socio-Economic Influences on the Health and Rehabilitation of Physically Handicapped Rural Children: A case study in Kayunga Sub-County, Mukono District, Uganda.* Final Report, Herbert Muyinda and Tom Barton, Child Health and Development Centre, Makerere University, Kampala, Uganda, February 1992.

[55]   Anne Fleuret, et. al., *Girls' Persistence and Teacher Incentives in Primary Education in Uganda*, USAID, Kampala, Uganda, March 1992.

arrogant." Or, as one girl put it, "I believe that even if I had the fees [my parents] would not have permitted me to go [to school] simply because I am a girl."[56]

3.30   The benefits of female education are receiving increasing attention among development practitioners, so much so that it has been argued that female education is the single most important investment that a country can make (Box 3.9). Girls' education, apart from any intrinsic advantages it may provide, has the beneficial effect of postponing marriage and first birth, and therefore contributes positively to the reduction of teenage pregnancy and high fertility. However, educating girls in itself is not sufficient, if cultural, legal, and other biases against women in the society at large continue to limit women's economic capacity. Consequently, the need to pursue gender equity *beyond primary school*, and in the society at large outside the school setting, becomes of paramount importance.

Conclusion

3.31   This chapter has sought to explore the particular cultural, economic, financial, and social constraints which women face in carrying out their multiple roles and responsibilities. While it presents a situation facing women that is very difficult, though not unlike many countries in Sub-Saharan Africa, it is important to recognize the progress that has been made, especially since the NRM Government came to power in 1986. The Ugandan Government clearly recognizes the importance of women's role in both economic and social development, and is aware of the critical need to raise women's status. It has taken some significant steps, some of which are unique in Africa, to promote women's participation in the political process, to establish institutional mechanisms aimed at addressing women's issues in public policy and resource allocation, and to begin to tackle an important area of systemic bias against women through legal reform. The extent of women's representation in political bodies and their participation in government and political fora, through the reservation of one position for women at every level of the RC system, and through affirmative appointment of female ministers in key portfolios, compares very favorably with other SSA countries, and constitutes a significant step forward, notwithstanding the difficulties women continue to face in effectively exploiting the opportunities afforded and in making their voices heard.[57] The establishment of a Ministry responsible for Women in Development provides an important institutional focal point for addressing gender issues across a range of government activities, as well as an opportunity to tackle underlying systemic issues, such as legal reform. In fact, as indicated earlier, the Government is particularly aware of legal issues (including issues of custom and practice) affecting women both economically and socially, and is actively engaged in revising its constitution. Women's NGOs and legal organizations have been actively involved in this process.

3.32   While there has been progress, it is clear from the picture of women's status and the constraints they face presented in this chapter that much more remains to be done, if women are to be empowered to fulfill their economic and social roles. As the Government prepares its poverty reduction and economic growth strategy, it will need to address the gender dimension explicitly. While cultural practices and traditions are extremely difficult to change, a key priority for the

---

[56]   Ibid.

[57]   See, for example, the profile of a female community leader in UNICEF, *Children and Women in Uganda: A Situation Analysis*, p. 12; and the discussion of cultural constraints to women taking part in RC meetings, and in public life outside the household in Dodoth County, in Alison Lochhead, *Gender and Development in Dodoth County, Karamoja*, OXFAM, Kampala, Uganda, January 1991.

Government must be to create a level playing field whereby both men and women are afforded equal opportunity to participate in economic growth. This will necessitate that the Government follow through with the legal reform process that has been initiated and ensure that the legal rights of women are protected so that they may benefit from their own labor and have greater access and control of economically productive resources. Through literacy and education, the Government should endeavor to overcome the social and cultural barriers which limit female access to information, technology, credit, and extension services. Given the time constraints faced by women, the Government must pay increased attention to investments in female labor-saving technologies. This would include investments in infrastructure, particularly feeder roads, water supply and transportation. Finally, the Government should provide political and financial support to efforts aimed at reducing the risk of AIDS among young girls.

4

Impact of Adjustment on the Poor

"Any analysis of the effects of structural adjustment on poverty must compare the outcome not with the preceding period, but with the outcomes that could be expected from alternative policies that would have been economically and politically feasible under the difficult conditions ...."(Lyn Squire, "Poverty and Adjustment in the 1980s", The World Bank Economic Review, May 1991, p. 182.)

General

4.1   Adjustment measures can broadly be divided into two categories: stabilization measures which focus on financial disequilibrium within the economy, i.e., in the fiscal and external accounts, and are designed to reduce overall demand; and structural adjustment measures which stimulate supply and are aimed at "restructuring the production capacities in order to increase their efficiency and to help restore growth".[58] It is not always easy to disentangle the combined impact of adjustment measures from those of the preceding crisis and other long term factors and it is therefore critical to have a clear understanding of the economic and political conditions which existed in the country prior to the introduction of the adjustment program. To understand how adjustment policies affect the welfare of the poor, it is necessary to explore in detail the sources and patterns of their income and expenditures, and the changes in factor and product markets through which those policies are mediated.

4.2   The poor in Sub-Saharan Africa (SSA), as in Uganda, are mainly rural and are engaged in a multitude of economic activities of which agricultural production looms large. Since the bulk of the exports of these countries comes from the agricultural sector, structural adjustment policies, with their emphasis on restoring an "equilibrium" level exchange rate and liberalizing agricultural pricing and marketing, are posited to impact positively on the agricultural sector, and thereby, the rural poor. For example, to the extent that the poor participate in the markets for traded (tradable) goods as sellers, exchange rate adjustments are likely to move the terms of trade in their favor, resulting in an increase in incomes. Furthermore, stabilization policies, which dampen the excess demand for goods and services, control fiscal deficits, reduce monetary expansion and thereby control inflation are similarly expected to have a beneficial impact on the poor. However, to the extent that the poor operate outside the monetized economy, and are absent (or left out) from the traded goods sector, their welfare would not be affected by adjustment policies, which tend to change relative prices. Therefore, one needs to know the rate of market participation of the poor, and particularly the extent to which the poor are involved in the production and marketing of tradable commodities.

4.3   The record of adjustment policies in SSA countries indicates that in countries where such policies have been persistently followed, structural imbalances have been removed and reasonable rates of growth have been restored. In addition to the conducive macroeconomic environment created by the adjustment policies themselves, these results have, however, depended on such factors as the gravity of the pre-adjustment situation and the impact of other factors such as changes in international terms of trade; weather conditions; the "adequacy" of external financing; and the emergence of a stable political environment, where this has been lacking. The impact of these policies on the welfare of the poor is however not adequately researched, and the limited findings available are inconclusive.

---

[58]   Ishrat Husain, *Adjustment and the Impact on the Poor, The Case of Africa*, World Bank, mimeo, 1992.

This is due to the weakness of the statistical agencies as a result of which a fairly long series of household data, which are crucial for such purposes, are lacking. Where the data are available, complicated models are often needed to understand what would have prevailed had the adjustment policies not been implemented, given that most of these countries experienced unsustainable macroeconomic imbalances and weak or negative economic growth rates that precipitated the adjustment programs in the first place (i.e., the problem of the counterfactual).

The Ugandan Experience

4.4   As discussed in Chapters 1 and 2, with more than a decade of civil strife, political turmoil, and economic decline up until the mid-1980s, Uganda's historical legacy has been much worse than most of its SSA neighbors that have experienced macroeconomic imbalances and faltering economic growth. Upon assuming power, the key objectives of the NRM Government were to build a broad-based government and restore peace and security in the country; to bring about internal financial stability by lowering the rate of inflation and reducing the imbalances in the economy; and to lay the basis for the alleviation of poverty by promoting rehabilitation and economic growth. Accordingly, starting in 1987, the Government began implementing its far-reaching Economic Recovery Programme (ERP) supported by the World Bank, the International Monetary Fund (IMF), and the donor community.

4.5   To achieve its stated objectives, the adjustment measures implemented by Uganda have contained both sets of policies alluded to above, i.e., stabilization policies, designed to restrict demand to the confines of the overall resource envelope and thereby restore financial equilibrium and structural policies, designed to increase efficiency, stimulate the supply side of the economy and encourage growth. On the stabilization front, the Government has adjusted the value of the Ugandan shilling and moved to a market determined exchange rate; contained the fiscal deficit by implementing numerous revenue enhancing and expenditure controlling measures; and implemented measures to curb inflationary crop financing. On the structural front, the Government has liberalized the trade regime by abolishing export and import licensing; dismantled all price controls, which were few to begin with; repealed the Industrial Licensing Act, promulgated a new investment code, returned properties expropriated by the Amin regime and commenced privatizing public industrial enterprises; made important strides in abolishing export and distribution monopolies; embarked upon a major overhaul of the civil service; restructured the tax system and improved tax administration; and has made an impressive start in restructuring public expenditures towards critical economic and social services. While the economy continues to be plagued by severe capacity constraints which make day-to-day implementation of the reform agenda very difficult and often result in lapses and slippages, the outcome of the adjustment program has, on the whole, been very encouraging. There has been a substantial decline in the rate of inflation since 1986 and the economy has consistently registered a healthy rate of economic growth.

4.6   This chapter analyzes the impact of the adjustment policies implemented by the NRM Government on the citizens of Uganda and, in particular, on the lives of the poor. Data limitations make this an extremely difficult task. From the outset, it should be noted that, like other SSA countries, Uganda lacks a series of household-level data. While Uganda has completed several useful surveys in a short period of time, and others are underway to bridge the data gap, these data have very limited use in capturing the evolution of poverty over time. In the absence of fairly long time series data on the volume and sources of income and expenditures, one can only resort to indirect ways of assessing the changes in living standards. The analysis presented below is therefore partial in nature and is only intended to present the general direction of changes and broad orders of

Table 4.1: Growth and Sectoral Distribution of GDP

	Sectoral Distribution Percent		Growth Rate Percent	
	1981-85	1986-91	1981-85	1986-91
Agriculture	63.2	61.2	2.3	4.2
Industry	7.3	8.4	0.8	11.8
Services	29.5	30.4	2.7	5.8
Cash Crops	6.5	6.7	6.4	7.1
Food Crops	93.5	93.3	2.0	5.1
Aggregate GDP	100.0	100.0	2.2	5.3

Source: Data provided by Government Authorities.

magnitude. In this pursuit, the chapter evaluates Uganda's experience in the recent past by examining the structure and trends in aggregate GDP, and the trends in rural and urban real per capita GDP. These are, in turn, supplemented by an examination of some of the underlying factors that influence changes in real incomes.

Rural and Urban GDP Per Capita

4.7   In order to determine the implications of policy-induced changes in relative prices on the structure of output, it is necessary to assess the degree to which the economy produces traded (tradable) goods, which relative price changes are intended to support.[59] As shown in Table 4.1, the Ugandan economy is dominated by the production of food crops which, although tradable in theory, are mostly grown for subsistence purposes. Consequently, for the analysis in this chapter, the traded goods sector refers to the cash crops sector and the manufacturing sector.[60] Despite the relatively faster pace of growth that the traded goods sector has experienced, the share of traded goods in GDP has remained less than 10 percent.

4.8   Since poverty in Uganda is largely a rural phenomenon and most of the poor are engaged in multicrop and mixed production, the trend in real agricultural GDP closely reflects the pattern of

---

[59]   The degree of tradability, constituting both importable and exportable goods, refers to a hypothetical structure of output that would emerge under conditions where all distortions are removed, and goods and factors are traded freely.

[60]   The so defined traded goods sector is probably underestimated here since only the traditional export crops are counted as cash crops in the national accounts. In recent years, several traditional food crops, such as simsim and beans, have emerged as important sources of cash for the farmers. Nevertheless, the share of the traded goods sector still remains under 10 percent of GDP.

rural living standards.[61] Moreover, since most rural land falls under the customary tenancy system where access to land is fairly open, and since over 85 percent of the farming population operates on less than two hectares of land, the benefits of agricultural growth are likely to be evenly distributed among the rural population. Thus, average trends are expected to be a fair reflection of changes in rural living conditions.

4.9   Figure 4.1 presents the trends in real per capita GDP, broken down into its urban and rural components. Between 1983 and 1986, aggregate real per capita GDP declined steadily, reaching a bottom of U Sh 13,184 in 1986. Starting in 1986, it grew steadily to reach U Sh 15,802 in 1991. Real GDP per capita in rural and urban areas essentially followed the same trend. Real GDP per capita in rural areas increased from U Sh 9,269 in 1986 to U Sh 10,543 in 1991, while real non-agricultural real GDP per capita rose from U Sh 47,236 to U Sh 54,682, respectively. These numbers demonstrate that, on average, the welfare of the rural and urban poor, in real terms on a per capita basis, has improved by between 14 and 16 percent respectively during the past five years, maintaining the rural-urban income gap at around 5.2:1 over the second half of the 1980s.[62] Compared to the early 1980s, some income redistribution in favor of the rural areas seems to have occurred. It is important to note, however, that averages mask the existence of wide intraregional differences, particularly in urban areas.

4.10   There is considerable uncertainty in determining whether these improvements were entirely a result of adjustment policies, other extraneous

REAL PER CAPITA GDP
In 1987 Prices

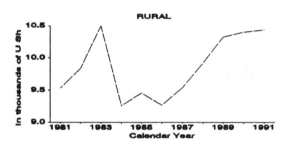

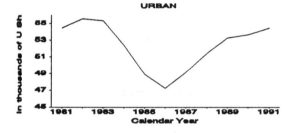

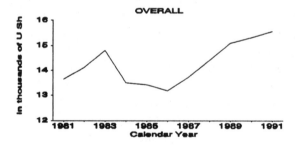

Figure 4.1: Real Per Capita GDP

---

[61]   Real per capita agricultural GDP, used as a proxy for rural real per capita GDP, is arrived at by dividing real agricultural GDP by the rural population. This overstates the rural per capita GDP to the extent that urban farming is important. On the other hand, it will be an underestimate provided that nonagricultural activities are important in rural areas. In this computation, the two sources of bias are assumed to offset each other. A similar reasoning is made for the real per capita GDP in urban areas.

[62]   Two assumptions implicit in this analysis are that agriculture's terms of trade vis-a-vis the nonagricultural sector remained unchanged as did the distribution of income in both rural and urban areas. If agriculture's terms of trade improved (deteriorated) there would be a relative improvement (deterioration) in agricultural income. See the discussion on the trend in the terms of trade below.

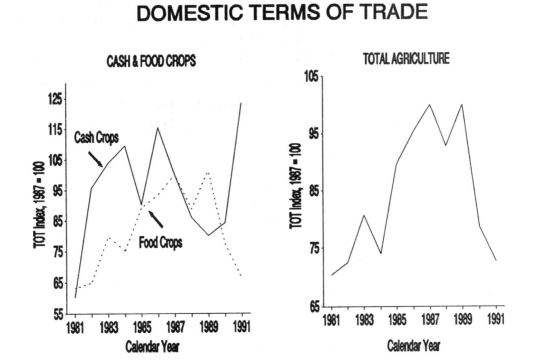

DOMESTIC TERMS OF TRADE

Figure 4.2: Domestic Terms of Trade

factors, or some combination of the two. During the second half of the 1980s, Uganda was just emerging from the political chaos following the Obote II regime, which had brought the urban economy to a virtual standstill. The large-scale destruction and heightened insecurity impacted significantly on rural areas as well; market links were disrupted as marketing institutions and infrastructure collapsed forcing the rural economy to become self-reliant. Thus, given that peace and security were regained at a time that the structural adjustment policies were put in place, causes serious difficulties in disentangling the effects generated by the macroeconomic policies per se. The problem is also compounded by the difficulties in isolating the effects of the price reforms (i.e., changes in the exchange rate, interest rates and product pricing) from the impact of the injection of large amounts foreign exchange support accompanying the reform program.

4.11   To isolate, at least partially, the effects of the "peace dividend" from the effect generated by policy measures, the following section examines some policy-induced determinants of rural and urban income such as the trends in the domestic terms of trade and real wages.

Changes in Domestic Terms of Trade (TOT)

4.12   Figure 4.2 presents the domestic barter TOT for cash crops (traded), food crops (nontraded), and for the agriculture sector as a whole. The TOT have been computed by dividing the cash crop, food crop and agriculture deflators by the nonagricultural GDP deflator in an attempt to compare the prices of the goods that farmers sell to the prices of the goods that farmers buy.[63] These prices are influenced, in one way or another, by such policy measures as the changes in the exchange rate, price and trade liberalization, and the elimination of marketing monopolies.

4.13   As the figure reveals, the terms of trade for cash crops fluctuated considerably during the 1981-86 period and experienced a sustained deterioration between 1986 and 1989. However, there was a dramatic improvement in the cash crops TOT in 1990 and 1991, the reasons for which are discussed below. At the same time, the TOT for food crops, which dominate agriculture, have been on a steady declining trend since 1989. Food crop TOT improved steadily between 1981 and 1987, largely as a result of insecurity, which prevented adequate supplies of food from reaching the market. Since 1987, with the restoration of peace throughout most of the country, there has been a significant revival (the present drought in some parts notwithstanding) in agricultural output and in the marketed surplus causing the TOT to decline. Given the dominance of the food crop sector, this has resulted in the aggregate TOT shifting against agriculture. This somewhat surprising result probably warrants further research which present data limitations do not permit, i.e., a closer examination of farmer's incomes and expenditures per capita. As is discussed below (paras 4.24-4.25) the increase in agricultural output was accompanied by an increase in the real wages in the agriculture sector further corroborating the finding that the benefits of growth were substantially shared by the smaller farmers. The key implication of the decline in agriculture TOT is that increases in gross domestic incomes have tended to be smaller than the increases in gross domestic product in agriculture. It must also be pointed out that the improvement in the security situation has also resulted in a decrease in the farmers cost of production and so the decline in TOT probably overstates the loss in incomes.

Macroeconomic Policy and Its Implications

4.14   Macroeconomic policies, including agricultural marketing and pricing policies, together with external factors, affect both tradable and nontradable crops by influencing the TOT for these crops and thereby have an impact on the structure of incentives and income distribution. The price that a farmer receives for growing a cash (tradable) crop, when it is not arbitrarily fixed by the Government, is generally determined by the international price of the product, costs of transportation from farmgate to processing centers and then to ports of exit, processing and marketing margins, the exchange rate regime, and explicit or implicit export taxes. The farmgate price for food crops, on the other hand, largely reflects domestic demand and supply conditions, including the flow of substitute imported food crops, and marketing margins.

4.15   A poor macroeconomic environment, in addition to providing the wrong market signals and thereby stifling economic growth, hurts the poor by indirectly taxing the resources that they possess. An enabling macroeconomic environment, on the other hand, removes production disincentives, encourages optimal resource allocation, and improves income distribution. The impact of macroeconomic policies, particularly those focusing on taxation and the exchange rate, is particularly pronounced in largely agricultural economies such as Uganda and thereby warrants careful consideration. The exchange rate, in particular, produces the most pervasive impact that often out-

---

[63]   Four variants of the domestic barter TOT were computed. These included TOT computed on the basis of the deflators for industry, services and the nonfood consumer price index in the denominator, respectively. The results from these alternative measures were not significantly different from the analysis presented above.

Table 4.2: Foreign Trade Taxes, Trade Deficit and Exchange Rates

Calendar Year	Nominal Exchange Rate U Sh/US$	REER 1987=100 Index	Export Tax/ GDP (%)	Spread Between Official & Free Market Rate (%)
1981	0.5	3.06	1.2	..
1982	0.9	1.07	2.9	..
1983	1.5	0.84	4.8	..
1984	3.8	0.57	7.2	52.1
1985	7.0	0.74	5.8	145.1
1986	14.2	0.78	3.3	329.0
1987	44.7	1.00	2.0	266.3
1988	106.0	0.90	1.0	289.8
1989	222.0	0.77	0.9	156.2
1990	433.0	0.47	0.9	61.3
1991	750.0	0.36	0.4	24.7
1992[1]	1000.0	0.33[2]	0.0	15.0[2]

[1] Estimated.
[2] Annual average as of June 30, 1992.

Sources: Ministry of Finance and Economic Planning, IMF and staff estimates.

weighs the other effects of crop-specific policies.[64]

4.16   Through a series of changes in the foreign exchange allocation system, the Ugandan shilling has depreciated significantly since 1987 (Table 4.2). In 1987, the US dollar was officially exchanged at an average rate of U Sh 44.7 and the spread between the official exchange rate and the free market exchange rate amounted to about 266 percent. Starting in 1988, the Government began implementing an aggressive program of adjusting the official exchange rate with a view to compressing the gap between the official and the foreign exchange bureau rate and in July 1990 it legalized the operation of the foreign exchange bureaus. By 1991, the Government had adjusted the official exchange rate to an average of U Sh 750 per dollar, i.e., over a 17-fold depreciation. When the differential had declined to about 15 percent, the Government decided to cease setting the official exchange rate administratively and introduced a foreign exchange auction in January 1992.

4.17   It is important to note that real devaluation, by itself, cannot provide positive incentives and stimulate the supply response unless it is complemented by price and market liberalization which allows market-determined or border prices to be transmitted to the producers and reduces the monopoly rents enjoyed by marketing boards. To the extent that the international prices are not passed on to producers but are retained by the state as tax and by marketing boards, the benefits to

[64]   A number of country case studies commissioned by the World Bank have demonstrated that the impact of exchange rate misalignment on agricultural incentives is more severe as compared to direct crop-specific policies. A summary of these case studies can be found in A. O. Krueger, M. Schiff and A. Valdes, "Agricultural Incentives in Developing Countries: Measuring the Effect of Sectoral and Economywide Policies", *The World Bank Economic Review*, Vol. 2, No. 3, 1988.

the farmer are limited.[65] Recognizing this, the Government of Uganda has overhauled the system of marketing, pricing and taxing coffee. Starting with the 1991/92 coffee year (October-September), the Government has moved to a system where only an indicative floor price for coffee is announced and the actual producer price is determined by market forces. The export monopoly of the Coffee Marketing Board has been eliminated and coffee exporting has been opened to competition. In the early years of the program, all exporters were required to surrender their foreign exchange to the Government at the appreciated official exchange rate. The Government now permits all noncoffee exporters to either retain their foreign exchange earnings or sell these to the foreign exchange bureaus at the market determined exchange rate. Coffee earnings, while still sold to the Government, are transacted at the foreign exchange bureau rate. To counteract the adverse impact of the decline in the international price of coffee, the Government has virtually abolished all taxes on exports such that export taxes declined from about 34 percent of total revenues in 1986/87 to less than 2 percent in 1991/92. The remaining export tax only applies to Arabica coffee which commands a premium price on the international market. The Government has further eliminated the export monopoly of the Uganda Tea Authority and the Produce Marketing Board, although the Lint Marketing Board still enjoys a monopoly for exporting cotton. These changes have gone a long way in altering relative prices in favor of cash crops (tradables), and have had a beneficial impact on the poor, to the extent that they are involved in the production of such crops.

4.18   *Impact on the Farmgate Price of Tradable Crops*. Uganda's exports are dominated by coffee which accounts for the bulk of the country's foreign exchange earnings and, until recently, its fiscal revenues. Due to its heavy dependence on a single export commodity, Uganda's macroeconomic performance, and the welfare of the poor, has suffered considerably as a result of the adverse movements in international price of coffee. The over 50 percent decline in the international price of coffee, from US$2.60/kg in 1985 to less than US$1.00/kg in 1992, as a result of the collapse of the International Coffee Agreement, has caused major foreign trade, fiscal and price instability, inimical to the rural as well as to the urban poor.

4.19   As a result of concerted action, particularly since 1990, the Government has been able to protect the price received by producers. Despite the deterioration in the international environment, the real producer price of Robusta coffee in 1991 was about 7 percent higher than the price in 1987, the year when the Government commenced implementing the ERP.[66] The farmers' share of the international price of coffee in 1991 and 1992 was more than double their share in the mid 1980s.

4.20   Table 4.3 reveals that, as a result of the adjustment measures implemented by Government, relative prices, particularly since 1989, appear to have changed in favor of coffee as compared to the prices received by farmers for growing food crops such as plantain (matoke), cassava and maize, which compete with coffee for farmer's resources, particularly labor. The farmer's relative price between coffee and maize, coffee and cassava, and coffee and matoke, for instance, has increased by 227 percent, 272 percent, and 119 percent, respectively between 1989 and 1991. It is therefore apparent that, through macroeconomic and agricultural pricing policies, the Government has been largely successful in preventing the coffee industry from virtually collapsing which would have occurred in the absence of the structural reforms implemented.

---

[65]   Ishrat Husain, ibid.

[66]   Unlike the nonagricultural GDP deflator used earlier, the real price series in this section is computed using the aggregate CPI as the deflator. Recomputing the real prices using the nonagricultural GDP does not change the trend, although the magnitudes are slightly different.

Table 4.3: Index of Real Farmgate Prices
1987 = 100

| | | | | | | | | | Ratio of Relative Prices: Robusta/Food Crops | | |
	Robusta (Kiboko)	Seed Cotton (AR)	Greenleaf Tea	Millet	Maize	Sorghum	Cassava	Plantains	Robust/ Maize	Robust/ Cassava	Robust/ Plant
1982	69.0	69.7	33.1	50.8	77.3	47.1	24.9	30.6	89.3	276.8	225.7
1983	116.0	131.9	111.4	50.6	139.2	45.6	35.9	81.4	83.3	322.9	142.5
1984	176.9	191.6	161.8	163.0	235.9	152.5	121.8	130.7	75.0	145.3	135.4
1985	153.5	132.1	109.8	77.0	196.0	70.3	64.1	102.5	78.3	239.6	149.8
1986	106.1	63.1	149.8	125.5	109.9	89.3	72.8	179.8	96.6	145.7	59.0
1987	100.0	100.0	100.0	100.0	100.0	100.0	100.0	100.0	100.0	100.0	100.0
1988	84.4	142.2	67.5	83.7	84.4	83.7	81.0	103.9	100.0	104.2	81.3
1989	52.3	143.1	73.2	67.0	244.0	67.0	64.5	80.4	21.4	81.0	65.0
1990	78.5	181.9	55.0	66.9	130.9	66.8	64.1	84.6	60.0	122.5	92.9
1991	107.3	219.5	73.6	52.2	153.3	67.0	35.6	75.5	70.0	301.4	142.2

Note: *Until 1990 the Government established producer prices for coffee, cotton and tea which have since been liberalized.*

Source: *Agricultural Secretariat, Bank of Uganda and African Development Indicators (for millet, sorghum and cassava).*

4.21   The real farmgate price of cotton, the other important export crop which accounts for about 5 percent of total exports, registered a much stronger increase, with the price increasing by about 119 percent between 1987 and 1991. While the real farmgate price of tea declined by about 25 percent during the 1987-91 period, tea presently accounts for a very small fraction of Ugandan exports. The upward trend in the TOT for cash crops during the past two years, as illustrated in Figure 4.2 above, is therefore largely the result of the combined impact of coffee, cotton, and a few newly emerging nontraditional exports such as beans and sesame.

4.22   *Impact on the Farmgate Price of Nontradable Crops.* The major nontradable crops in Uganda constitute plantain (matoke), cassava, maize, millet and sorghum. The trend in the real farmgate price of these crops, as shown in Table 4.3, supports the deterioration in food crops TOT. On average, the real producers' price of these five crops dropped by about 25 percent between 1987 and 1992. Since nontradable crops account for about 70 percent of agricultural production, the trend in the real farmgate price of such crops has more than offset the increase in the farmgate price of tradables and resulted in the decline in the overall TOT of the agricultural sector.

Implications for Household Welfare

4.23   While combining the trends in real farmgate prices with existing data on prevailing farming systems can provide some idea of the regional evolution of household welfare on account of agricultural activities, lack of details of agricultural income by district makes this an extremely difficult exercise. For example, in the high rainfall areas around Lake Victoria, where Robusta coffee is predominantly grown and where poverty is comparatively less pronounced, it is likely that household income from cash crop production would have increased in recent years on account of the improvement in the cash crops terms of trade. This would also be true for households of the Teso system in eastern Uganda where cotton is grown and in the mountain areas of the west where Arabica coffee is grown. However, since these households are also engaged in the production of food crops, whose terms of trade have declined, the net results are ambiguous. It, however, bears repeating that with the significant increase in agricultural output in recent years, welfare of the rural poor appears to have improved although, given the weight of nontradable food crops in total agricultural output, incomes probably did not increase as much as did output. What is unambiguous, however, is the fact that policy changes have helped the cause of poverty reduction.

4.24   To keep real incomes rising in the face of the overall decline in the TOT of the agricultural sector, various strategies are being adopted by farmers. As recent experience in several areas shows, monetization of the agricultural sector is gradually on the increase as farmers shift resources, particularly labor, from less paying crops to crops commanding higher prices at the farmgate level. In particular, incomes are being supported, in some areas, by the introduction of some high-paying export crops into the production mix. These encouraging developments are also being affected by changes in the labor market. In recent years, labor shortages have started manifesting themselves, particularly in the estate sector,[67] as a result of which real rural wages have risen (see below). Among the reasons for the labor shortage, particularly during peak season, is the decline in the supply of migrant labor from neighboring countries and the impact of the AIDS crisis on the productive segments of the population. Although this labor shortage has adversely affected the up-keep of the coffee trees, a relatively labor-intensive activity, it has helped to supplement the income of net-labor supplying households further improving rural welfare.

What Has Been Happening to the Incomes of the Poor?

4.25   While there is no direct evidence available of the change in the incomes of the poor households, a look at the trend in real wages of agricultural labor may shed some light on the trend in the living condition of the rural poor. Table 4.4 shows the estimates of real wages of casual, permanent and contract labor in rural Uganda between December 1984 and February 1992. There are obvious question marks about these estimates.[68] And yet the overall positive trend in real wages is strong enough to defy all the doubts and imperfections of measurement. If the obviously questionable observation for December 1987 is excluded, there was a steady and strong increase in real wages of casual labor until 1990. Real wage for contract labor has been more volatile, but an increasing trend continued through 1991. For permanent labor the increase in wages continued through 1992 with the exception of the questionable estimate for 1990.

4.26   Of the three, the trend in the real wage of casual labor is probably the most reliable indicator of the trend in earnings of the poorer households. This is because the permanent workers are not principally drawn from the rural households (see Chapter 6) and the contract wage rate, being

---

[67]   Alison Evans, *A Review of the Rural Labour Market in Uganda*, University of Sussex, May 1992. It should be noted, however, that the estate sector accounts for a very small proportion of Ugandan agriculture.

[68]   In a highly inflationary economy, adjustments for price changes are problematic in any case. In Uganda the difficulty is compounded by the fact that the only available consumer price index (CPI) is for the capital city, Kampala and a few other urban centers. Moreover, there was a change in the weights of the index starting in 1988. We have spliced the old and the new index together. There are also some serious question marks about the nominal wage data. For example, why was there a sudden upward surge in casual and contract wage rates in 1987? Why was there an absolute decline in permanent wage rate in 1990? Why was there a sharp discontinuity in contract wage rate after 1986? Satisfactory answers to these questions are not available.

Table 4.4: Real Wages of Agricultural Workers
(Real Wages in Ugandan Shillings at December 1991 Prices
Money Wages in Current Ugandan Shillings)

Date	Casual Labor Nominal	Daily Wage Real	Permanent Labor Nominal	Monthly Wage Real
Dec 1984	1	48.08	–	–
Dec 1985	3	52.54	90.00	1576.18
Dec 1986	15.00	107.53	–	–
Dec 1987	100.00	259.20	750.00	1944.01
Dec 1988	165.00	165.00	2000.00	2000.00
Dec 1989	300.00	191.31	4000.00	2550.86
Dec 1990	400.00	208.37	3500.00	1823.20
Dec 1991	500.00	197.01	7000.00	2758.08
Feb 1992	600.00	208.99	10000.00	3483.23

Contract Labor (Per Ha)			Kampala CPI (Base Dec 1987)
	Nominal	Real	
Dec 1984	40.00	1923.08	2.08
Dec 1985	100.00	1751.31	5.71
Dec 1986	260.00	1863.80	13.95
Dec 1987	3500.00	9072.06	38.58
Dec 1988	5200.00	5200.00	100.00
Dec 1989	12500.00	7971.43	156.81
Dec 1990	17500.00	9116.01	191.97
Dec 1991	30000.00	11820.33	253.80
Feb 1992	30000.00	10449.69	287.09
May 1992	–	–	359.40

Source: Nominal wage rates are from Agricultural Secretariat, Bank of Uganda. The CPI has been prepared by splicing together the Old Kampala Cost of Living Index for low income groups (1984 to 1988) and the New Kampala Cost of Living Index (1988 onwards). The index has been "rebased" upon December 1988 by dividing each of the two indices by their December 1988 values.

expressed in terms of payment per hectare, is difficult to interpret.[69] Looking at the real wages of casual workers, it appears that the relatively rapid growth of Ugandan agriculture, particularly between 1986 and 1992, was substantially shared by the smaller peasants and that this led to a rise in the supply price of their labor and, consequently, a reduction in rural poverty.

Distortions in Product and Factor Markets

4.27   Distortions in product and factor markets, such as quantitative restrictions on imports and import and export licensing, confer significant income on a favored few, mainly through the creation of rent income. Insofar as this income is derived from unproductive activities, the distortions transfer income to higher income groups. The removal of these distortions, therefore, reallocates resources

---

[69]   For example, contract wage rate is specific to the type of task per ha and nothing is known about the composition of tasks over time and/or the method of weighing the wage rates for individual tasks in arriving at the overall wage rate for contract labor.

Table 4.5: Fiscal and Monetary Performance

	1986/87	1987/88	1988/89	1989/90	1990/91	1991/92
Fiscal Ratios						
Total Revenue/Total Expenditure	52.6	50.9	52.2	54.0	50.8	32.0
Tax Revenue/Total Revenue	83.2	87.4	84.5	91.6	93.7	93.4
Coffee Revenue/Tax Revenue	41.3	32.0	13.3	17.3	9.9	1.2
Total Revenue (incl Grants)/GDPMP	4.6	6.9	7.0	8.3	10.8	13.5
Total Revenue (excl Grants)/GDPMP	4.2	5.4	5.4	6.8	7.1	6.6
Total Expenditure/GDPMP	7.9	10.5	10.3	12.7	14.1	20.6
Capital Expenditure/Total Expenditure	37.5	44.2	33.5	43.8	51.5	44.5
Current Expenditure/Total Expenditure	62.5	55.8	66.5	56.2	48.5	55.5
Current A/C Balance/GDPMP (-= deficit)	-0.8	-0.5	-1.5	-0.3	0.3	-4.9
Overall Deficit/GDPMP (+ = deficit)	3.8	5.5	5.3	6.5	7.6	14.0
Financing:						
Grants/Total Financing	10.7	28.3	30.2	22.6	48.5	49.5
Foreign Borrowing (net)/Total Financing	7.6	37.8	41.3	102.2	45.0	36.2
Domestic/Total Financing	81.7	33.9	28.5	-24.8	6.5	14.3
Monetary Ratios						
Claims on Government/Domestic Credit	50.0	49.2	38.6	11.5	10.7	31.9
Crop Financing/Domestic Credit	18.3	18.7	28.4	30.6	33.6	20.6
M1/GDPMP	5.4	5.8	6.1	5.9	6.1	6.2
M2/GDPMP	6.2	6.4	6.8	6.8	7.2	7.9
M1/M2	88.4	90.3	90.2	86.2	83.8	79.2
Inflation: CPI Kampala	216.5	167.9	130.5	45.4	24.6	42.1

Note: Capital expenditures and total expenditures include net lending.

Source: Ministry of Finance and Economic Planning, IMF and staff estimates.

away from relatively well-off groups, causes increases in productive activity, and therefore benefits a broader cross-section of society, including the poor. Since the introduction of the ERP, the Government has made considerable progress in reducing such distortions within the economy. With respect to the trade regime, the process which began with the introduction of the Open General License (OGL) and the Special Import Program (SIP) has now culminated in a system whereby the Government has abolished all import and export licenses and replaced these with an automatic export and import certification system, subject to a narrowly defined negative list. Furthermore, on the domestic front, the restrictive Industrial License Act has been abolished and the Investment Authority established as a one-stop shop for encouraging private investment and promoting the newly promulgated investment code. All of these measures are expected to have a significant positive impact on the business environment which should lead to productive job creation and an increase in wages and thereby in the overall standard of living.

Inflation and Its Impact on the Poor

4.28   As over 90 percent of GDP in SSA countries goes to consumption, and more so in poorer countries such as Uganda and by the poorer members of the population, bringing inflation into check and reversing the trend is prudent macroeconomic policy and is good for poverty reduction. Inflation essentially taxes all those who participate in the market as buyers of goods and services, and generally distributes the benefits in favor of government. The merits of this inflation tax are questionable on efficiency and equity grounds; particularly since the benefits of the expenditures generated through the inflation tax tend to be narrowly distributed while the adverse effects are more pervasive.

4.29   In Uganda, own-production accounts for about 40 percent of the total consumption of the rural poor. However, to the extent that the poor have to depend on the market for over 60 percent of their consumption needs, their welfare is affected adversely by the high rates of inflation. The negative impact of inflation on the rural poor is further aggravated by the fact that food crops, whose terms of trade have declined, dominate the marketable surplus from the agricultural sector, while a few critical "traded" consumables, such as sugar, soap, vegetable oil, etc., figure large in household purchases. Therefore, the positive impact that inflation has had on agricultural incomes has been far less than its negative impact through expenditures. Furthermore, as a result of infrastructural and transportation bottlenecks, the marketing margins of intermediaries tend to be high, further dampening the incomes of agricultural producers while inflating their expenditures. For instance, between 1987 and 1990, the margin between producers' and consumers' prices for matoke increased from 17 percent to 45 percent, while that of maize increased from 14 percent to 81 percent, over the same period.

4.30   While adverse weather conditions and the frequent adjustments to the exchange rate and to interest rates have all contributed to the escalation of prices, the imbalance between government revenues and expenditures, and the link between the fiscal deficit and monetary expansion has been the primary cause for the high rate of inflation in Uganda. The tax effort in Uganda is still among the lowest in SSA,[70] and total revenues are sufficient to finance only about 50 percent of government expenditures. While external loans and grants have traditionally financed a large part of the fiscal deficit, borrowing from the domestic banking system has been an extremely important source of financing for the Government, at least until 1988/89. Consequently, until 1988/89, the large-scale monetization of the deficit resulted in triple digit inflation levels (Table 4.5), thereby severely eroding real incomes in Uganda.

4.31   In order to stem this erosion, one of the key objectives of the stabilization component of the adjustment program in Uganda has therefore been to keep prices in check by mobilizing incremental fiscal revenues and restricting expenditures to budgeted amounts. Bringing inflation down to levels comparable with those of major trading partners is a declared objective and a continuing challenge for the Government. Since 1990, the Government has embarked upon a concerted program aimed at mobilizing incremental revenues and controlling expenditures. The tax and tariff regime has been rationalized, the rate structure has been greatly simplified, and tax exemptions minimized. With the establishment of the Uganda Revenue Authority (URA) in September 1991, the Government has taken a bold step forward in overhauling its system of tax administration. Furthermore, the Government

---

[70]   In 1990, total revenue to GNP ratios for Malawi, Zaire, Kenya and Sierra Leone have been 23 percent, 12 percent, 23 percent, and 9 percent respectively. *World Development Report, 1992*, The World Bank, Washington, DC.

has instituted a strict program aimed at keeping expenditures in line with the budget and has started paying back its arrears to the banking system.

4.32   While day-to-day implementation problems abound, the overall results of the Government's efforts have been very encouraging. As illustrated in Table 4.5, government revenue efforts have increased from about 4 percent of GDP in 1986/87 to about 7 percent of GDP in 1991/92. During the first three months of 1992/93 (i.e., July to September 1992), the Uganda Revenue Authority has mobilized over U Sh 60 billion in revenues as compared with U Sh 31 billion for the corresponding period in 1991/92, implying an annualized tax-to-GDP ratio in excess of 8 percent. The efficiency of tax collection has also increased greatly with URA's recurrent costs, as a percentage of revenues mobilized, declining to about 5 percent and projected to decline further to 3 percent by 1994/95. While expenditures as a percent of GDP appear to have increased significantly, these largely reflect an effort on the part of the Government to consolidate the budget by including all expenditures which were previously off the budget. As a result of these measures, claims of the banking sector on the Government have continued to decline. Government claims as a percentage of total domestic credit decreased from about 50 percent in 1986/87 to under 11 percent in 1990/91, increasing thereafter to about 32 percent in 1991/92. The increase in 1991/92 was the result of a temporary lapse in fiscal management when the Government failed to cut expenditures in line with the shortfall in import support assistance from the donor community. The Government, however, corrected the situation in the fourth quarter of the fiscal year and its financial program is back on track. Consequently, Uganda has been successful in reducing the average rate of inflation in recent years; inflation declined from 216.5 percent in 1986/87 to 24.6 percent in 1990/91, before it reversed to 42.1 percent in 1991/92, on account of the drought and the temporary slippage in fiscal management. Largely as a result of the renewed financial discipline, the average monthly inflation rate between July 1992 and February 1993 has been -0.2 percent.

4.33   *Seasonality of Inflation and Intra-Year Vulnerability.* The harvest period in Uganda is different depending on the crops harvested and geographic distribution of the farming activity. While crops like matoke and cassava can be harvested throughout the year and there are multiple cropping seasons in several parts of the country, there are areas, particularly in the north and the east, which are characterized by a single yearly harvest. For farming households, harvest is usually rich, and post-harvest can be lean even for those who are otherwise well-to-do. The well-being of net-buying households in rural areas, rural and urban wage earners, and otherwise well-to-do farmers (in the leaner months) suffers when prices swing upwards seasonally on their long-term trend. In addition to the agricultural cycle, seasonal price variability could be conditioned by short-term macroeconomic management such as the seasonality in bank credit including those destined for coffee purchases. Understanding the underlying factors for the seasonal variations in prices can help in facilitating the design of short-term poverty sensitive macroeconomic targets within the perimeters of the annual targets.

4.34   Using monthly data for the decade between 1982-92 (using the old, the new and the combined series), inflation in Uganda appears to follow a tri-modal pattern. In the first cycle, inflation starts to pick momentum in November and reaches an apex in January. After a brief period of lull, the second cycle comes in April and May. The third is a short spell in September. These peaks match the coffee harvesting season well as coffee deliveries rise between November and January and again between July and August. Seasonal fluctuations in aggregate demand caused by coffee crop finance could be partly responsible for the seasonal variations in the aggregate price level. The seasonal fluctuation in prices assumes special relevance given the weak post-harvest storage conditions and the importance of perishable products in the product mix. Household vulnerability to inflation in Uganda would therefore oscillate seasonally, particularly given that the poor have limited assets, liquid or otherwise, serving as a hedge against bad days.

The Provision of Social Services

4.35   Another channel through which adjustment policies impact on the poor is through the restructuring of public expenditures such that an increased emphasis is placed on the provision of economic and social services which increase human capital. Expenditures in areas such as primary health, primary education services, agricultural research and extension, etc. empower the poor, raise their productivity and augment their earning potential in the long run.

4.36   While Uganda still spends far less on economic and social services than do most countries in the world and in SSA, the adjustment program in Uganda has nonetheless emphasized the need for and resulted in a visible change in public expenditure priorities with expenditure allocations increasing in favor of social sectors in general and on education and health care in particular (Chapter 7). Between 1989/90 and 1991/92, there has been a 49 percent real increase in locally funded expenditures on primary education whose share in GDP has increased from 0.4 percent to 0.5 percent. Similarly, locally funded expenditures on primary health increased by about 238 percent in real terms over the same period. Given the extremely low revenue effort, discussed above, the Government plans to continue increasing these allocations steadily, keeping in mind the macroeconomic implications of the constraints imposed by the tight resource envelope.

Conclusion

4.37   Despite severe data constraints, which limit the analysis presented in this chapter, there is no denying the fact that the last five years have seen an increase in production, a decrease in inflation, and a marked improvement in the overall economic and political environment. To that extent, the population of Uganda has benefitted. With the return of peace and security to most parts of the country, Ugandan citizens are once again able to feed and clothe themselves and plan for a better tomorrow. Notwithstanding the "peace dividend", had the Government not embarked upon the adjustment program when it did, it is our conclusion that the economic and social climate would have continued to deteriorate, with the gains from peace being eroded by the continued ravages of triple-digit inflation, resulting from irresponsible fiscal policy. The coffee industry would not have survived the developments in the international market; foreign exchange shortages would have continued thereby stifling agricultural and industrial development; and income distribution would have worsened with significant rents accumulating to the favored few. The Government should therefore be applauded for implementing a courageous and demanding economic reform program.

4.38   It is often argued that there can be severe short-term "social costs" associated with structural adjustment programs which traditionally emphasize the elimination of price controls, severe cuts in fiscal expenditures which are often accompanied by cuts in wages and salaries and the elimination of subsidies. While this might be true in some cases, in the Ugandan context, the adjustment program has not called for wage freezes (instead the emphasis has been on increasing salary levels); reductions in subsidies (which were few to start with); or the elimination of price controls (which were limited and were almost always nonbinding). As has been demonstrated above, there appears to have been a general improvement in the quality if life in Uganda and most Ugandans appear not to have been adversely affected by the social costs of adjustment. While it is too soon to evaluate the results of the recently started civil service retrenchment program, the discussion of labor markets and the salary structure in Uganda (Chapter 6) indicates that the costs associated with such retrenchment will be mitigated by the fact that the recent shortage of labor will enable retrenched civil servants to be absorbed in other sectors of the growing economy and that the household farming sector and/or the urban informal sector is able to provide returns to labor which are comparable to what the retrenched civil servants were receiving from the Government.

4.39   However, having said that, there appears to be very little cause for complacency. Living standards, as was discussed in Chapter 1, are still far below the levels achieved in the 1960s and the early 1970s. While the Government is on the right track, it is imperative that the Government "stay the course" and continue vigorous implementation of the adjustment program which is designed to transform the subsistence economy into a strong, monetized economy. The poor in Uganda are located in areas with little access to roads, transport, communication, agricultural services and marketing facilities. Overhauling the incentive system and allowing the markets to operate may be necessary conditions for restoring incomes, but these are not sufficient. To the extent that infrastructural bottlenecks prevent Ugandans from participating in an increasingly monetized economy and the majority of the people continue to eke out a living in the subsistence economy, the benefits of adjustment will, for the most part, only have an indirect impact on their existence. Adjustment policies can only have a beneficial impact if the people are empowered to participate in the new economic environment which results from the policies implemented. As the Government continues implementing its adjustment program, it is imperative that it also devote adequate resources to develop and maintain a poverty monitoring system which will enable it to quantify and measure the impact that the adjustment policies are having on the lives of the poor on a continuing basis. The Integrated Survey presently underway is an excellent example of the kind of data that needs to be collected on a fairly regular basis.

4.40   The following chapters of this report are forward-looking and present a vision for the future economic development of Uganda together with a set of policies designed to make that vision a reality. At the heart of the vision is the overarching objective of reducing poverty through sustained economic growth.

Part II

A Strategy for Reducing Poverty

5

Accelerating Economic Growth

"The countries that have been most successful in attacking poverty have encouraged a pattern of growth that makes efficient use of labor and have invested in the human capital of the poor. Both elements are essential. The first provides the poor with opportunities to use their most abundant asset—labor. The second improves their immediate well being and increases their capacity to take advantage of newly created possibilities." (World Development Report 1990, World Bank, p. 51.)

Introduction[71]

5.1   In almost every country reducing poverty is a key objective, if not the raison d'etre, of development policy. For a country like Uganda, whose GNP per capita is estimated at under US$170, making it one of the poorest countries in the world, the imperative of reducing poverty cannot be overemphasized. Experience from a cross-section of countries has demonstrated that economies that have achieved high rates of growth (e.g., Botswana, Mauritius, Thailand and Indonesia) have been most successful in reducing poverty. Overall economic growth results in a rise in incomes, which is a necessary but not sufficient condition for reducing poverty. Poverty in Uganda is largely a reflection of the fact that the economy has failed to achieve sustained growth for a quarter of a century (1965-1990). During this period Uganda's GDP per capita declined at an average annual rate of 2.4 percent, compared to a weighted average annual growth of 1.7 percent for low-income countries.[72] It must be added that Uganda was not alone; only a handful of SSA countries bucked the trend towards economic retrogression.[73]

5.2   The pattern of economic growth also matters and this means that incomes which are rising as a result of economic growth must also be accompanied by a reduction in income inequality. International experience has shown that the growth that benefits the largest number of people is that based on labor-intensive methods of production. Labor is the most important asset, sometimes the only asset, owned by the poor. To enable the poor to participate and share in the growth, labor and product markets have to function efficiently. Public policy affects the way these markets work and, at a broader level, determines the rate and pattern of growth. Policy has an even more critical role to play in improving the social conditions of the people, principally through meeting basic needs, particularly in health and education.

5.3   This chapter advocates a growth-oriented strategy for reducing poverty in Uganda. It reviews Uganda's recent performance on the growth score, suggests alternative growth scenarios and examines the sectoral sources of growth. In doing this one must bear two points in mind. The first point is that there has been a general slowdown of growth throughout the world. In the 1965-1980

---

[71]   This chapter draws on *Uganda: Agricultural Sector Memorandum*, Agriculture and Environment Operations Division, World Bank, 1992 and *National Agricultural Research Strategy and Plan, Vol. II: Priorities and Programs*, Government of Uganda.

[72]   Unless otherwise specified, the comparative data used in this chapter come from the *World Development Report*, World Bank, 1992. Also, wherever the expression low income countries appears in this chapter it excludes China and India.

[73]   The notable exceptions are Botswana, Mauritius, Burundi, Lesotho, Cameroon and Congo.

period 42 of the 78 low and middle income countries for which data are available achieved average annual GDP growth rates of 5 percent or higher. During the next decade (1980-1990) only 15 out of 86 low and middle income countries managed growth rates of that magnitude. Clearly, the global recession and the international debt crisis of the 1980s have taken their toll. The second point is that growth actually accelerated in East Asia and the Pacific and in South Asia during the 1980s. This suggests that, in spite of the odds, rapid growth is attainable, provided certain basic conditions are met (paras 5.6-5.10).

5.4   While the imperative of reducing poverty in Uganda calls for rapid growth, the past failed efforts directed at promoting growth and alleviating poverty in SSA seem to argue for a long-term perspective on poverty reduction in Uganda and other SSA countries. Skepticism regarding the ability of Uganda and other SSA countries to break out of the low or negative growth conundrum does not seem to be entirely misplaced. Still, as will become clear later, Uganda stands a good chance of following the fast track to poverty reduction. Moreover, there is encouraging evidence from a number of countries to the effect that the development process can be telescoped into a much shorter time frame. The outstanding examples are the Republic of Korea and China which, in recent years, more or less doubled per capita output in just a decade. Two SSA countries have done just as well. Botswana and Mauritius also virtually doubled per capita output within the short space of ten years. This helps to counter the view that SSA countries are condemned to slow growth. Still one must raise the question: why have a few countries been so successful in increasing output while so many others have failed miserably? There is obviously no blueprint for rapid growth but a number of ingredients for success can be identified. These are discussed below.

5.5   Before turning to the prerequisites for rapid growth, it is useful to ask: is the performance of the fast-growing countries explained by special factors, i.e., small or large population, more or less homogeneous population, small land area, a vast mineral endowment, etc.? Obviously, there are circumstances and conditions peculiar to each country and it is to be expected that these would come into play as a country tries to grow and develop. However, special factors by themselves cannot explain rapid growth. After all, special factors can be as easily squandered as taken advantage of. Take one example. Rapid growth in Botswana has been built upon diamond exports while many SSA countries similarly endowed with mineral wealth have failed to prosper. Moreover, special factors can be adverse rather than favorable. Thus, Botswana has achieved rapid growth in spite of being a land-locked country and being buffeted, until recently, by apartheid related turmoil in the region.

Prerequisites for Accelerated Economic Growth

5.6   The experience of the economically successful developing countries shows that three factors namely macroeconomic stability, high rate of investment backed by domestic savings, and a high rate of literacy and numeracy, are absolutely necessary for achieving rapid growth over the long term. *Macroeconomic stability* is needed to give people the confidence to undertake long-term investments, particularly those involving technological change in industry and agriculture. The main indicators of macroeconomic stability are low fiscal deficits (or budget surpluses), low and stable inflation and a stable exchange and trade regime. Countries like Botswana and Mauritius have been constant in their pursuit of policies that ensure the maintenance of macroeconomic stability. In Table 5.1 inflation is used as a proxy for macroeconomic balance. In the earlier period (1965-1980) the world economy experienced generally low inflation and Uganda's average inflation rate was not far above the average of 17.3 percent for the low-income countries. In the ensuing decade (1980-1990) Uganda clearly failed to achieve macroeconomic stability and inflation surged, while the successful comparator countries either reduced or kept inflation low.

5.7   Another fundamental prerequisite to rapid growth is a *high rate of investment*. That means investment in farms, factories and other productive assets as well as investment in human capital and in economic and social infrastructure. Such investment must in turn be backed up by high rates of domestic savings by either the public sector or the private sector or both. Of course, foreign savings and investment have an important role to play in development, both in the rich countries and the poor ones. But in general, foreign investment often follows, rather than leads, domestic investment. Table 5.2 shows that Uganda lags well behind the successful comparator countries on the saving and investment score.

5.8   *High rates of literacy and numeracy* are also fundamental to the achievement of rapid and sustained growth. Literacy and numeracy have important externalities which justify investment in these programs. But on the narrower grounds of promoting growth there is a strong case for heavy investment in education, particularly primary education. The ability to read and write is crucial to the acquisition and application of modern production and marketing skills. In agriculture, for example, the farmer's capacity to adopt yield-raising innovations depends on his or her ability to at least read the messages directed at him or her. This is why countries that have made rapid growth a key objective of national development policy have invested heavily in education at an early stage of their development. Table 5.3 shows that Uganda again does poorly on this score.

Table 5.1: Annual Rates of Inflation Uganda and Comparator Countries (Percent)

	1965-1980	1980-1990
Uganda	21.4	107.0
Ghana	22.9	42.5
Botswana	8.4	12.0
Mauritius	11.8	8.8
Indonesia	35.5	8.4
Thailand	6.2	3.4

Table 5.2: Domestic Investment and Savings Uganda and Comparator Countries (Percent of GDP)

	Domestic Savings		Domestic Investment	
	1965	1990	1965	1990
Uganda	11	5	12	11
Ghana	18	15	8	11
Botswana	6	40	-13	30
Mauritius	17	30	13	21
Indonesia	8	37	8	37
Thailand	-2	37	19	34

5.9   However, lessons from international experience show that the three fundamentals discussed above are also not enough. Five additional ingredients for accelerating economic growth are highlighted here:

(i)   *Transformation of Agriculture*. This involves the modernization of agriculture through the introduction of new technology, accompanied by the provision of adequate infrastructure and in some cases, land reform. The transformation of agriculture offers many advantages. It results in growth that is egalitarian, except where land ownership is highly concentrated; it initiates the process of diffusion of modern production skills to large numbers of people; and it creates a ready linkage between agriculture and industry. The conventional wisdom has been that agricultural sector growth tends to be limited by factors such as the slow growth of domestic demand for food, the protectionist policies of the rich countries and the slow pace of diffusion of agricultural technology. While this is true to some extent, this type of pessimism can be overdone. It has been partially disproved by the experience of a number of countries. China, for example, registered an average annual growth rate of 6.3 percent in agriculture during the 1980-1989 period. Other countries which are much smaller than China (Morocco, Togo, Bhutan and Burkina Faso) achieved comparable rates of agricultural output growth during the same period. For a country that is heavily dependent upon agriculture for employment, exports and growth it makes sense to invest in agriculture as a prelude to industrialization.

Table 5.3: School Enrollment Uganda and Comparator Countries (Percentage of Age Group Enrolled)

| | Primary | | Secondary | | Tertiary | |
	1965	1989	1965	1989	1965	1989
Uganda	67	77	4	13	0	1
Ghana	69	75	13	39	1	2
Botswana	65	111	3	37	..	3
Mauritius	101	103	26	53	3	2
Indonesia	72	111	12	47	1	..
Thailand	78	86	14	28	2	16

(ii)   *Technical Education.* General education is essential but it is not enough; it does not equip the work force with the abilities needed to master modern production techniques which are critical to raising productivity. Rapid growth demands more and more technically trained people, with training in mathematics, engineering and the sciences. The experience of the Republic of Korea, Malaysia, Thailand and other fast-growing countries confirms this.

(iii)   *Exports.* The fast-growing countries have also emphasized exports, and have adopted a vigorous program of export promotion, supplemented by specific government interventions (export processing zones, fiscal incentives, the provision of business-friendly public service, etc.). While government interventions have no doubt played a role in the export expansion of the Newly Industrialized Countries, one must take care not to exaggerate the range and efficacy of these interventions. International experience shows that rapid export expansion can be based upon minerals, agriculture, manufactures or, more often, some combination of these. In some cases (for example in the Republic of Korea and Mauritius) rapid export expansion has meant dramatic rates of growth of manufactures. However, in many cases rapid export expansion has been resource-based (Malaysia, Thailand and Indonesia, to name a few). With regard to agricultural exports, the trick to success involves three elements: modernize traditional export crop production; diversify export crops; and increase domestic value added through the production of high value crops and increased processing of agricultural commodities.

(iv)   *The Catalytic Role of Foreign Investment.* This role can be played or supplemented by particular communities of settlers (for example, the Asians in East Africa and the Chinese in Southeast Asia). The foreign investor often brings with him or her capital, technology, management techniques, skills, quality standards and markets. As partners, competitors or suppliers, local investors therefore benefit from the presence of foreign investors.

(v)   *Problem-solving Partnership Between the Public and Private Sectors.* Fast growing economies have been characterized by an effective, problem-solving partnership between the public and private sectors as opposed to an adversarial relationship between the two. Such a partnership is built on the premise that the Government is willing and able to help individuals and businesses to grow and become rich.

5.10   Uganda fares poorly on the prerequisites and the other essential ingredients for accelerating growth, discussed above. First, although within sight, macroeconomic stability has yet to be achieved. The key to achieving macroeconomic stability is firm control of the government budget. Second, saving and investment rates are very low. For the domestic savings rate to improve significantly there must be in place a financial system capable of mobilizing savings from the vast majority of the people, which does not yet exist in Uganda. Third, illiteracy rates are too high, especially for women; in 1990 adult illiteracy was 52 percent for the total population and 65 percent for women. Only an accelerated program of universal primary education can remove this handicap. Fourth, there is insufficient technical education. Deliberate efforts need to be made to reorient education towards the technical subjects. Five, as will become clear later, agriculture is still very backward. High-yielding crop varieties are yet to be introduced; few modern inputs are used; only the simplest of implements are used; and the rural road network is in an appalling state of disrepair. Six, the export base is too narrow and fragile, dependent as it still is on coffee for about 75 percent of export earnings. A determined push to expand exports is called for. Seven, although investor interest appears to be on the rise, only a trickle of foreign investment is coming into the country. The Government needs to address systematically the problems of poor infrastructure and bureaucratic impediments to investment. Finally, there is no effective partnership between the public sector and the private sector. There is a need for a partnership which provides a forum for problems to be aired, followed up and solved.

How Did Uganda Fare?

5.11   Uganda's overall economic growth record is compared to that of a number of countries in Table 5.4. The table shows that while countries like Uganda and Ghana missed the opportunity to grow for the greater part of the past quarter century, others raced ahead. This comparison is not entirely fair to Uganda, given the fact that for much of this period the country was engulfed in chaos. Indeed, it can be argued that Uganda's capacity to grow has not really been tested up to now. Performance under the ERP over the long term will provide such a test. So far the results have been encouraging; the past five years of adjustment

Table 5.4: Average Annual GDP Growth Rates Uganda and Comparator Countries (Percent)

	1965-1980	1980-1990
Uganda	0.6	2.8
Ghana	1.3	3.0
Botswana	13.9	11.3
Mauritius	5.2	6.0
Indonesia	7.0	5.5
Thailand	7.3	7.6

have witnessed an average annual GDP growth rate of 5.3 percent. Admittedly, there were some special factors behind this achievement. The growth resumed from a depressed base and the return of peace and security to large parts of the country after more than a decade of civil war made it possible to bring idle capacity, be it an industrial plant or farm land, back into production. However, the high rates of growth recorded over this period cannot be wholly ascribed to these special factors. The policies and measures implemented under the ERP, with their emphasis on greater reliance on market forces, have played an important part in stimulating the growth of production. Other measures include the injection of more foreign exchange in the form of import support into the economy and the rehabilitation of the infrastructure, particularly roads. Growth during the 1987-1992 period, in fact, came in a spurt of an average of 7.2 percent over the first three years, followed by a slowing down to 4 percent during the next two years. The recent deceleration of growth is indicative of the fact that the impact of the special factors on production has started to wear off. But the lower rates of growth recorded in 1990 and 1991 can also be explained to some extent by poor rainfall in those

Table 5.5: Average Annual Sectoral Growth Rates
Uganda and Comparator Countries
(Percent)

	Agriculture 1965-80	1980-90	Industry 1965-80	1980-90	Manufacturing 1965-80	1980-90	Services 1965-80	1980-1990
Uganda	1.2	2.5	-4.3	5.5	-3.7	5.2	1.1	3.3
Ghana	1.6	1.0	1.4	3.3	2.5	4.0	1.1	5.7
Botswana	9.7	-4.0	24.0	13.0	13.5	5.3	11.5	11.9
Mauritius	..	2.6	..	9.2	..	10.8	..	5.1
Indonesia	4.3	3.2	11.9	5.6	12.0	12.5	7.3	6.7
Thailand	4.6	4.1	9.5	9.0	11.2	8.9	7.4	7.8

years, since Ugandan agriculture is entirely rainfed. Except in the drier, semi-arid areas of the north and Karamoja, rainfall is normally adequate for growing crops but once in a while the rains have been known to be inadequate, late or poorly distributed.

5.12 Uganda's record on sectoral growth is compared to that of five other countries in Table 5.5. Uganda's performance in agriculture and industry during the 1965-1980 period was dismal. In this period agricultural production failed to keep pace with population growth while industry declined by over 4 percent each year. The following decade saw an improvement on the past 15 years but even then agricultural output barely kept pace with population growth. Ghana was in the same league as Uganda and their performance contrasts sharply with that of Indonesia and Thailand which together provide a good example of rapid and broad-based growth.

5.13 The main reason for the poor performance of the various sectors in Uganda (and hence the economy as a whole) during the period under review is the general instability that the country went through. Insecurity disrupted agricultural production and shut down markets while industrial plants were looted or abandoned. The country was isolated from the rest of the world for many years. Fortunately, starting in 1986, Uganda has largely returned to normality. Improved security and law and order, together with other factors, have had a positive impact on the performance of all the sectors. In reflection of these developments agriculture grew during the 1986-1991 period by an average of 4.2 percent, industry by 11.8 percent and services by 5.8 percent (Table 5.11).

The Link Between Growth and Poverty Reduction in Uganda

5.14 Each successive Policy Framework Paper (PFP) that Uganda has negotiated with the IMF and the World Bank has targeted GDP to grow by 5 percent per annum. There appears to be really no basis for this growth rate other than that, if attained, it would permit a modest increase of about 2 percent per annum in per capita output.[74] Looked at in relation to Uganda's growth record over the long term (minus 2.4 percent during 1965-1990) a growth rate of 5 percent seems robust. But when viewed in the context of poverty reduction, 5 percent is low (see below). Uganda can choose to stick to the PFP growth scenario of 5 percent per annum for the next 10-15 years. Alternatively, it could

---

[74] This growth assumption finds common usage in Sub-Saharan Africa PFPs.

lower its sights in line with the recent slowdown in growth to around 4 percent. Although not ruled out, the scenario involving a GDP growth target below that incorporated in successive PFPs is not discussed in this report. Rather, what the report tries to do is to challenge policymakers in Uganda to aim higher; the higher growth scenario presented here is a target and not a prediction.

5.15   How high can Uganda aim? This report suggests that Uganda should aim to push the average annual growth rate towards about 8 percent by the end of the projection period. The choice of 8 percent is bound to be largely arbitrary. It has, however, been dictated by the imperative of reducing poverty in Uganda in the shortest possible time. Countries such as Thailand, Botswana, Mauritius and the NICs generally have consistently achieved growth rates of 8 percent or higher for long periods. Can Uganda do the same? The initial conditions (literacy rate, economic and social infrastructure, population growth rate, macroeconomic policies, etc.) were not more favorable in the comparator countries than in Uganda today. It must, however, be admitted that the case for high rates of growth in Uganda depends largely on the speed with which agriculture can be technologically transformed. The natural resource endowment is so favorable as to give cause for hope that rapid growth is possible in Uganda.

5.16   The base GDP growth rate (5 percent) and the high growth rate (8 percent) have very dramatic implications for poverty reduction. Attaining the former would mean that per capita output rises by 2.5 percent per annum while achieving the latter would cause per capita output to increase by 5.5 percent per year, assuming the 1980-1991 intercensal population growth rate of 2.5 percent holds for the next decade or longer. There is significant difference between the two growth scenarios when it comes to the number of years it would take to double GDP per capita (Table 5.6). With the

Table 5.6: Years Required to Double GDP (Per Capita)

Population Growth Rate (%)	GDP Growth Rate	
	5%	8%
3.0	35	15
2.7	31	14
2.5	29	14
2.3	27	13
2.1	25	12

economy growing at 5 percent it would take Uganda 29 years to double GDP per capita which would still leave it below today's average GDP per capita for low-income countries. Were Uganda to achieve a growth rate of 8 percent per annum it would cut in half, to 14, the number of years it would take to double GDP per capita. Doubling GDP per capita by the year 2005 (or approximately US$340 GNP per capita) would still leave Uganda a very poor country but it would begin to make a dent on the difficult issue of reducing poverty.

5.17   *The Population Question.* The number of years needed to double GDP per capita is sensitive to the population growth rate used. Table 5.6 shows that, assuming population grows at 3 percent instead of 2.5 percent, with the economy growing at 5 percent per annum, it would take 35 years, as opposed to 29 years, to double output per capita. Conversely, reducing population growth to 2.1 percent while the economy grows at 5 percent would shave four years off the time it would take to double GDP per capita. The calculation is less sensitive to the population growth rate at the 8 percent (or higher) GDP growth rate than at the 5 percent growth rate. With GDP growing at 8 percent it would take just three years more to double per capita GDP if the population were to grow at 3 percent instead of 2.1 percent. The lesson to draw from this is not that at the higher GDP growth rate Uganda can afford a rapidly-growing population. On the contrary, Uganda needs to slow down population growth in order to reduce poverty within the shortest possible time. In this regard, it bears repeating that, even if Uganda is able to double GDP per capita (resulting in about US$340 GNP per

Table 5.7: Distribution of GDP
(Percent, in Current Prices)

	Agriculture		Industry		Manufacturing		Services	
	1965	1990	1965	1990	1965	1990	1965	1990
Uganda	52	54	13	10	8	4	35	35
Ghana	44	48	19	16	10	9	38	37
Botswana	34	3	19	57	12	6	47	40
Mauritius	16	12	23	33	14	24	61	55
Indonesia	51	22	13	40	8	20	36	38
Thailand	32	12	23	39	14	26	45	48

Note: Botswana is a drought-prone country where rainfall can fail almost totally, thereby wiping out crops.

capita) within the next 12 to 15 years it would remain one of the poorest countries in the world. There can therefore be no trade-off between economic growth and population growth.

Structure of Production

5.18   Before examining future sources of growth in Uganda it is necessary to review briefly the present structure of production. A country's structure of production is expected to change during the process of economic development. The universal pattern is for the share of agriculture in GDP to decline over the long term, with corresponding increases in the contribution of industry and services. This kind of structural change has been delayed in Uganda and other countries that have stagnated or actually declined over the past quarter century. In contrast, in the fast-growing economies, the transition to less dependence on agriculture proceeded smoothly (see Table 5.7).

5.19   As Table 5.7 shows, the Ugandan economy is still predominantly agrarian. While the contribution of agriculture to GDP increased from 52 percent in 1965 to over 60 percent in the mid-1980s, it has now started to come down; in 1991 it was 51 percent. It is hard to say whether or not this is the beginning of the expected structural change. The structural adjustment that Uganda has been undergoing since 1987 has probably started to have an effect but it is too early to measure the effect of this on something as fundamental as the structure of production. As can be seen from the table, the fast-growing economies followed the normal pattern; i.e., the contribution of agriculture to GDP declined during the course of economic development. In Thailand the share of agriculture fell from 32 to 12 percent between 1965 and 1990; in Indonesia from 51 to 22 percent during the same period. It also implies that the share of food crops, which have accounted for 35-45 percent of GDP in recent years, will have to decline. Future GDP growth will involve such intersectoral as well as intrasectoral output shifts.

5.20   The share of industry in GDP is exceptionally low for Uganda and the contribution of industry to GDP actually declined from 13 percent in 1965 to 10 percent in 1990. For low-income countries the average share of industry was 34 percent in 1990, having risen from 20 percent in 1965. The manufacturing subsector in Uganda underwent the same sort of contraction as industry as a whole, with its share of GDP falling from 8 percent to 4 percent. This means that Uganda would embark upon a strategy of rapid growth with an extremely small manufacturing base; this presents challenges as well as opportunities.

5.21   The share of services in Uganda's GDP was unchanged (at 35 percent) between 1965 and 1990. From international experience the general tendency is for the contribution of services to increase as economic growth proceeds. This tendency is confirmed by the data for Indonesia and Thailand, although Botswana and Mauritius buck this trend. In the case of Uganda, some services, especially commerce, actually increased but growth in this and other areas was cancelled by the effects of the collapse of commodity production in the industrial sector and the growing retreat by the farmers into subsistence food production.

Sources of Future Growth

5.22   The following section presents a projection of the future sources of growth for the Ugandan economy. The basic aim of the exercise is to provide a sense of the rates at which individual subsectors would have to grow in order for Uganda to aspire to an overall growth rate of 8 percent. There is no pretense that the actual outcome will correspond to this projection; rather, this section presents a vision of pushing Uganda's production possibility frontier to the limit and the policies needed to transform this vision into a reality. In agriculture, estimates have been made regarding future area expansion and gains in yields, based on recent performance and expectations about the development of a particular crop. There is very little hard knowledge about the industrial sector; consequently, in this case, the projections assume that, as private investment picks up, the industrial sector would return to the high growth rates seen at the beginning of the ERP. Even less is known about the services sector. Nevertheless, the assumption made here is that as growth picks up in the commodity-producing sectors, the demand for more and better services would increase. Services are therefore projected to grow at much higher rates than in the recent past.

5.23   The review of the present structure of production serves to highlight the centrality of agriculture in any development strategy for Uganda. To achieve an overall average rate of growth of 8 percent a year over the next 10-15 years Uganda would have to raise agricultural growth rates well beyond its long-term historical average of about 2 percent per annum. Since this is a relatively short period (less than a generation) in the life of a nation, expectations regarding economic and social change within this time frame have to be tempered with realism. However, the economically successful countries have shown that per capita GDP can be doubled within the space of ten years and significant progress made in reducing poverty. The sections below explore the question of whether Uganda is capable of achieving this kind of progress. The discussion of sources of future growth centers largely on the agricultural sector for three reasons. The first, obvious, reason is that agriculture is the dominant sector; given Uganda's resource endowment that is where, in absolute terms, the potential for rapid increases in output lie, at least over the time horizon considered in this report. The second reason is that even where industry is concerned the best prospects are to be found in agro-processing. The third reason is a practical one: a great deal more is known about the agricultural sector than any other sector. The emphasis on agriculture, however, should not be interpreted to mean that Uganda should not push for industrialization. The only caveat to be sounded is that this should not be done at the expense of agriculture.

Agriculture

5.24   *Importance and Salient Features*. Agriculture is, and will remain, the mainstay of the Ugandan economy for a long time to come. The sector now accounts for 51 percent of GDP, generates about 90 percent of export earnings and employs 80 or more percent of the labor force. It also provides the base for a number of manufacturing and processing industries. Agriculture therefore represents a potent force for poverty reduction in Uganda. There are a number of reasons for this claim. Firstly, 85 percent or more of the population live in the rural areas where they are engaged wholly or predominantly in agriculture. Secondly, smallholders account for practically the entire agricultural output; it is estimated that there are 2.5 million farm households, of which 80 percent cultivate less than 2.5 hectares of land each.[75] Thirdly, landlessness is not a major problem in Uganda. Fourthly, smallholder agriculture relies primarily on labor-intensive methods of production. In view of the preponderance of smallholders, the absence of landlessness on a large scale and the labor-intensity of production, the benefits of rapid agricultural growth should in principle be equitably distributed. Unfortunately, such a benign outcome cannot be taken for granted because there are other factors at work. The distribution of the benefits of agricultural growth are affected by such things as the functioning of product and labor markets, the allocation of research and extension resources to different types of crops and the regional distribution of physical infrastructure, particularly roads.

5.25   *The Composition of Agricultural Output.* Uganda is endowed with a wide range of soils, rainfall and altitudes which enable it to produce a diversity of crops and livestock. It also has large fish resources in Lake Victoria and other lakes. The country has a total land area of 19.4 million hectares which are distributed as follows: 4 million ha for annual crops, 1.5 million ha for permanent crops, 5 million ha for pastures and grazing land, 6.5 million ha for forests and 2.4 million for very marginal use. Crop yields per hectare are very low right across the board (Table 5.8). This is so principally because producers lack access to improved technologies and inputs necessary to increase yields. In spite of the havoc wrought by civil wars and the low yields, Uganda has more or less remained self-sufficient in food. However, occasional food shortages in some parts of the country on account of poor rainfall are not unknown.

5.26   The composition of agricultural output is given in Table 5.10. There are three striking things about the agricultural data. The first is the oversized contribution of food crops to agricultural output; during the 1987-1991 period food crops accounted for between two thirds and three quarters of agricultural output. The slight decline in the food crop share seen over the past two years probably reflects the effect of adverse weather conditions more than anything else. Second, nearly 55 percent of food crop production is considered nonmonetary, i.e., for subsistence. Third, the contribution of cash or export crops to agricultural output is exceptionally low; it ranged between 3 percent and 7 percent during 1987-1991.[76] In Ghana, cocoa alone still accounts for 13 percent of agricultural output despite the sharp decline in the role that this crop plays in the economy.

5.27   The next important subsector of agriculture is livestock. During the past five years livestock contributed, on average, 17 percent of agricultural output. Livestock is an integral part of farming systems in Uganda and about one third of farm households depend on livestock for a major part of their incomes. Data on the numbers of livestock are poor. However, the Ministry of Agriculture, Animal Industry and Fisheries (MAAIF) estimated the 1990/91 livestock population as follows: 4.3 million cattle, 3 million goats, 0.8 million sheep, 0.6 million pigs and 10-12 million poultry. The rest of agricultural output comes from forestry and fishing, with the combined contribution of these two subsectors close to 8 percent.

---

[75]   Large tea and sugar estates and plantations exist but the total number of hectares under these crops is only about 40,000. In addition to these estates, there are a few large cattle ranches, whose herds were decimated by war and disease.

[76]   The national accounts equate cash crops with export crops. As nontraditional exports have started to grow strongly, there has been a tendency to under estimate cash crops. Simsim illustrates the point: it is still classified as a food crop although an increasing proportion is being exported.

5.28   *Past Developments in Agricultural Growth.* A realistic assessment of the growth potential in the agricultural sector must start with a long-term view of past achievements. The average annual growth rate of the sector during the period 1965-1980 was 1.2 percent, which was well below the 2.6 percent achieved by low-income countries (Table 5.5). In the 1980-1990 period the average annual growth rate of agriculture in the low-income countries went up to 3.9 percent, while Uganda only managed to raise the average annual growth rate of agricultural production to 2.5 percent. At 2.5 percent agricultural output growth in Uganda barely kept pace with the growth of population. Uganda's agriculture was no doubt badly disrupted by civil conflict and the attendant economic difficulties.

5.29   In recent years (1987-1991) the agricultural sector has shown signs of a strong recovery. The average annual growth rate during this period was nearly 5 percent (Table 5.11). The rapid growth registered in the sector over the past five years, made possible by the recovery of the food crops subsector, owed a great deal to the improvement in security. It also reflects the fact that output started recovering from a low base. But that is not the entire explanation. The improvement in the underlying conditions needed to spur growth also had something to do with it. As far as agriculture is concerned the most relevant factors have been the rehabilitation of the roads (especially the trunk roads), the rapid increase in the fleet of vehicles on the roads, the dismantling of price and distribution controls and the greater availability of inputs. There is also no doubt that Uganda is in the enviable position of being favored with good rainfall. However, food production is sensitive to the vagaries of the weather. During the past two years, agricultural sector growth decelerated, to less than 3 percent, as production, particularly of food crops, was adversely affected by poor rainfall.

5.30   The increased food crop production in recent years has come almost entirely from area expansion. Fortunately, except for a few heavily populated areas, land availability is not a problem now or in the foreseeable future. It is estimated that, averaging over different soil classes, only 30 percent of the cultivable land was used in 1991.[77] However, yields are very low and have remained so since the early 1970s. If anything, several crops have registered declines in yields during the 1970s and 1980s, mainly on account of the collapse of the agricultural research and extension infrastructure and the lack of technological innovations.

5.31   Although not entirely immune, the food crop subsector proved remarkably resilient during the years of political and military turmoil, in sharp contrast with the virtual collapse of cash crop production during those years. In the case of the tree crops (principally coffee and tea) the area planted remained largely unchanged while for the annual cash crops the cultivated area shrank drastically. Cotton best illustrates the decline in the area under cash crop cultivation: from a peak of 677,500 hectares in 1978 the planted area fell to 67,000 hectares in 1990. Cotton production actually dipped below the 1987 low of 5,800 tons before recovering to that level in 1990. Similarly, coffee production declined from 160,300 tons in 1987 to 147,400 tons in 1991. Although a recovery of cash crop production is underway, the factors that have adversely affected cash crop production include low farmgate prices and delayed payments to the farmers, insecurity, inadequate supply of inputs, poor roads and the general breakdown of the agricultural research and extension services. Cotton has experienced only a weak recovery owing to the severe institutional constraints affecting the production of this crop. The constraints include the virtual monopoly of the cooperative unions on ginning and the export monopoly of the Lint Marketing Board.

---

[77]   See *Uganda: Agricultural Sector Memorandum,* ibid.

5.32   The numbers of livestock of all types declined during the 1980s, with cattle suffering the heaviest losses. The cattle population is estimated to have declined by about one third on account of the breakdown of disease control programs and increased cattle rustling and looting. A slow recovery of cattle numbers has just started. In poultry, however, production has rebounded strongly since 1987, thanks to the improved availability of livestock feed, imported feed additives and new breeding stock.

5.33   *Future Sources of Agricultural Growth.* The source of growth in agriculture has to come from the nontraditional export crops, technology change in food production, and increased demand due to increased incomes from growth in the export and industrial sectors. Over the past five years the growth in urban demand for food has been an important driving force behind increased agricultural production. Based on population and income growth over the next decade or so the domestic market for food is expected to expand by 3-4 percent per annum. Production has concentrated on the traditional low-value, often bulky, crops such as matoke and cassava which suggests that there is room, even as far as domestic consumption is concerned, for production to shift over time towards higher-value or more nutritious crops (beans and vegetables, for example) as well as livestock. The potential for import substitution is already being tapped in sugar, dairy and other areas; it is almost exhausted in tobacco. Further scope for import substitution probably exists but has yet to be identified and exploited. Furthermore, there is now overwhelming reliance on the marketing of unprocessed food, even in the urban areas. This can be expected to change so that increased food processing becomes the cause and effect of further monetization of the agricultural economy.

5.34   As mentioned earlier, the bulk of the increase in agricultural production since the launching of the ERP has come from the expansion of the area under cultivation. Even then the total cropped area is still below the level of the late 1970s. While not a limiting factor on agricultural growth in the country as a whole, land scarcity is a constraint in some parts of the southwest and northeast. However, land availability is not enough. The fertility of the soil is very important. In many parts of the country the natural fertility of the soil cannot be relied upon to produce high yields. This is especially true since high-yielding varieties are presently virtually unknown in Ugandan agriculture. As shown in the annex to this chapter, by any standards, crop yields are very low which in turn suggests that present yields can be raised substantially. To say that is not to underestimate the resources and the commitment needed to raise yields. There are, however, encouraging examples from international experience in this area.

Table 5.8: Present vs Potential Crop Yields (Metric Tons per Hectare)

	Present	Potential
Coffee (Robusta)	0.6	1.5
Cotton	0.3	0.8
Tea	1.4	3.0
Matoke	5.5	8.0
Finger millet	0.3	1.5
Maize	1.5	2.0
Sorghum	0.8	2.0
Rice	1.0	2.0
Cassava	9.0	12.0
Sweet potatoes	5.0	20.0
Irish potatoes	8.5	20.0
Beans	0.8	1.2
Groundnut	0.8	2.0
Simsim	0.4	0.8

Source: Government of Uganda, National Agricultural Research Strategy and Plan, Volume II: Priorities and Programs, 1991 and staff estimates.

5.35   The domestic market has already been alluded to above. Markets are indispensable to any growth strategy in Uganda, whether agriculture-led or not. In agriculture it is not too difficult to envisage a situation of very rapid increases in output based on the widespread adoption of improved varieties and the associated technological packages. Under this scenario, lack of markets could become a major disincentive to production. To augment domestic demand, Uganda will have to look to two outside markets namely, the regional market and the international market. The regional market in agricultural products is presently small but has the potential to grow, based on the growth of incomes, differences in food preferences, the vagaries of the weather, etc. As the country with probably the best agricultural potential in the region, Uganda owes it to itself to be in the forefront of regional integration aimed at opening up markets. The international market offers, in principle, vast opportunities for Ugandan products. However, protection and fierce competition is the name of the game in these markets . Outside of the traditional export crops, Uganda must achieve much higher agricultural productivity in order to be able to compete effectively in the international arena. The focus will be on horticulture, spices and other nontraditional export crops.

5.36   As far as the traditional export crops are concerned, a strong case can be made for a big push into cotton production. Current production is just about one seventh of peak production. Knowledge of the crop and what it takes to grow and process it have survived to some extent in the growing areas. The way forward is to address systematically the problems plaguing this crop (poor quality seed, a weak or nonexistent extension service, ineffective procurement by the cooperative ginneries, etc.). A relatively large domestic processing industry could be built upon the fortunes of this crop. In addition, Uganda could count on exports of cotton and cotton products.

5.37   Over the medium term, with increases in productivity together and with an increase in the area under cultivation and in markets, the agricultural sector can be pushed to grow at an average annual rate of between 4 and 5 percent (Table 5.11). Despite this sustained growth, however, the share of agriculture in GDP is projected to decline from its present level of 50 percent to about 45 percent in the year 2005, in constant 1987 prices.

Industry

5.38   *Industry and Economic Development.* Industry plays an important role in economic development. In fact, hardly any country has "developed" without becoming industrialized. Industrialization is needed to absorb increasing numbers of people released from the land as a result of rising agricultural productivity and it provides the principal vehicle for the diffusion of modern production skills. Furthermore, the experience of the Asian and other NICs has shown that, with the right kinds of policies and adequate market access, very high rates of growth (10 percent or more) can be achieved in industry for long periods. The Republic of Korea, for example, achieved an average annual industrial growth rate of 16.4 percent during 1965-1980, followed by a rate of 12.2 percent during 1980-1990. For Botswana (which started from a very low base) the comparable annual industrial growth rates were 24 percent and 13 percent for the two periods. In Mauritius it was 9.2 percent during the 1980-1990 period. Agriculture has not been known to grow at such high rates on a sustained basis. Developing countries therefore have a justifiable reason for pursuing policies aimed at promoting rapid industrial growth, especially the growth of manufacturing. They realize that rapid growth of overall output (say, in the 6-10 percent range) cannot be achieved without a much faster growth of the industrial sector. The mistake that many developing countries have made is to pursue industrial growth without due regard to the health of the agricultural sector. In Uganda, as in many countries, it is not a matter of either agriculture or industry but how both can be developed.

5.39   *Past Industrial Performance.* Uganda has witnessed a very rapid growth of industrial production since the launching of the ERP, mainly on account of the growth of construction and, to a smaller extent, manufacturing. The index of industrial production has risen strongly from 100 in

1987 to 178.4 in 1991, implying an average annual rate of growth of 13.7 percent, and the share of industry in GDP has risen from about 8 percent to just under 12 percent over the same period. There were special factors behind this high rate of growth. In the first instance it reflected the fact that growth resumed from a depressed base. Secondly, it was relatively easy to reactivate idle productive capacity to meet pent-up demand for basic consumer goods. There has been a mini boom in construction, driven by rehabilitation investments in the public sector and new investments in residential buildings. However, the share of manufacturing in GDP has gone up by less than one percentage point over the past five years which serves to drive home the point that the industrial base in Uganda is too small to be the driving force behind the rapid growth strategy proposed in this report. The developing countries that have achieved rapid growth of manufacturing output in recent years started off with a larger initial base than Uganda's at the present time. In 1965 Indonesia, Mauritius, Thailand and the Republic of Korea, for example, already had manufacturing-GDP ratios of 8, 14, 14 and 18 percent, respectively.

5.40   The current efforts to revive production at the Kilembe copper/cobalt mine notwithstanding, Uganda has no mining subsector to speak of. The output of public utilities also remains tiny as they are confined to the main urban centers which they are not even able to serve adequately. Industry is thus made up largely of manufacturing and construction. As is often true of countries at the early stages of industrialization, manufacturing in Uganda is dominated by the following product groups (with the weights in brackets): drinks and tobacco (26 percent), food processing (21 percent), textiles and clothing (16 percent) and chemicals, paint and soap (12 percent). Together these product groups account for three quarters of manufacturing output.

5.41   Most of the plant and equipment in the industrial sector was installed by the Asians in the 1950s and 1960s. With the expulsion of the Asian owners in 1972 the factories, whether in the hands of the public sector or the private sector, fell into disuse and misuse or were looted during the civil wars. Thus, following the recent rapid growth of industrial output some firms are already reaching the limits of their capacity. This is one source of investment demand. The other is demand for new investment in order to produce goods not presently made locally or to expand the production of those already being produced.

5.42   *Future Sources of Industrial Growth*. Given the structure of output, industrial development in Uganda must initially be agro-based. Uganda needs to step up the processing of agricultural commodities that are produced now and the much larger quantities that it is capable of producing in the future. The demand for processed agricultural products will come from three sources: one, subsistence farmers drawn more and more into the market economy; two, urban consumers whose ranks are growing rapidly; and three, foreign buyers.

5.43   Industry must not only be agro-based; it must also be relatively labor-intensive. This is in accord with Uganda's resource endowment. While there are some indications that labor might be in short supply on account of the civil strife, the AIDS epidemic and the easy access to land which encourages Ugandans to eke out a living from subsistence agriculture (Chapter 6), the bulk of Uganda's labor force is underemployed and inefficiently utilized with substantial scope for redeployment. Only the most basic industrial skills are available in the economy and even these are in short supply. The skills needed to handle advanced technology simply do not exist, even if the importation of such technology made economic sense. Furthermore, the initial thrust of industrial growth is bound to center on the usual list of basic consumer goods requiring simple production skills: food, drinks and tobacco, textiles and clothing and so on. This is the established pattern in all countries that have undergone the industrialization process. In Uganda the situation is made more favorable by the fact that the domestic resource base exists to support such production.

5.44   For a variety of reasons (greater reliance on technology, rapidly changing tastes, etc.) the manufacturing sector is normally the most dynamic sector of the economy. Manufacturing in Uganda is now too small to impart much dynamism to the rest of the economy. To begin to do that it must grow very rapidly. In order to attain the high GDP growth rate (8 percent) postulated in this report, the manufacturing sector would have to grow by at least 10 percent per annum over the next 10-15 years. If this happens, the share of manufacturing in GDP would double every eight years or so. Even so, manufacturing would account for less than 20 percent of GDP two decades from now. The main factors that are likely to constrain the growth of the manufacturing sector are inadequate infrastructure, especially utilities, and the shortage of industrial skills. Government has a major role to play in removing these constraints. In the case of commercial infrastructure (telecommunications, water, electricity) there is an emerging trend in several countries of government-owned private sector managed operations.[78] Uganda should seriously consider this new approach. The Government will also have to embark upon a major program of production-oriented skills training, with the active participation of industry.

Savings, Investment, and the Balance of Payments

5.45   *Savings and Investment.* Projections of GDP by expenditure, in constant prices, are presented in Table 5.12. Rapid economic growth requires a rapid increase in savings and investment. Consequently, in order to achieve a GDP growth rate of 8 percent, gross domestic investment as a share of GDP is projected to more than double, from 11 percent to 23 percent, between now and the year 2005. The share of public investment, which is presently largely donor-financed, is expected to increase from its current level of 5 percent of GDP to about 8 percent by the end of the projection period, as domestic revenues pick up. However, the private sector is projected to account for most of the increase in the share of investment in GDP. That means gross domestic savings must rise correspondingly, if Uganda is to reduce its reliance on foreign savings. Domestic savings are now very low; under 6 percent of GDP. Given the exceptionally low domestic revenue effort, the Government remains a dissaver. The prospect of the Government becoming a major saver during the next 10-15 years is not bright. The private sector would therefore have to carry the burden of generating large increases in domestic savings. While Uganda will remain a poor country for a very long time to come, it is capable of saving a much larger proportion of GDP. This is confirmed by the experience of poor countries like China, India, and Kenya with saving rates of 20 percent or more. This places a premium on the development of the financial sector because the key to higher rates of saving is an efficient financial system capable of mobilizing small savings from a large number of the population. In Uganda a rising saving rate means a steady decline in the share of private consumption in GDP, from around 90 percent at present to about 74 percent by the year 2005.

5.46   *The Balance of Payments.* A viable balance of payments is another essential element in any strategy to achieve rapid growth. Table 5.13 shows the balance of payments scenario underlying the GDP growth targets presented in Table 5.11. At present Uganda's external position is very fragile, mainly on account of its weak export base. Despite severe import compression, it had a large negative current account balance in 1991/92 (over US$340 million) which was financed largely by official

---

[78]   The Botswana Telecommunications Corporation has operated under such an arrangement for many years.

Table 5.9: Key Macroeconomic Indicators

	1987	1991	1993	1995	2000	2005
Growth rates:						
GDP at factor cost	6.7	4.1	6.0	6.2	7.3	8.0
Gross domestic income	3.1	4.2	5.8	6.4	7.1	7.5
GDY per capita	0.6	1.7	3.3	3.9	4.6	5.0
Private consumption per capita	2.9	-1.6	1.8	0.1	2.9	3.2
Debt Service:						
Debt service, US$ million	195	215	185	197	189	195
o/w Interest, US$ million	52	74	83	93	75	91
Debt service/XGS [1]	41.0	71.4	49.5	42.0	22.0	11.7
Debt service/GDP	3.9	7.2	5.2	4.5	2.6	1.5
Ratios to GDP, constant prices:						
Domestic savings	3.7	5.8	7.1	10.8	15.5	21.3
National savings	4.9	5.8	7.1	10.8	15.7	21.5
Public savings	-0.7	-2.9	0.2	3.0	5.5	7.0
Private savings	5.6	8.6	6.9	7.8	10.2	14.5
Gross Domestic Investment[2]	9.2	10.7	13.0	16.2	18.9	23.4
Ratios to GDP, current prices:						
Government revenues	6.4	7.2	8.4	12.5	15.0	16.5
Government expenditures	12.4	19.0	17.8	19.5	18.6	18.6
Overall deficit [3]	-6.1	-11.8	-9.4	-7.0	-3.6	-2.0
Miscellaneous:						
Inflation	199.8	28.1	23.5	9.0	5.0	5.0
Export growth rate	21.3	-8.3	10.9	11.4	13.2	15.3
Exports/GDP [4]	7.3	5.0	5.2	5.7	7.0	9.8
Import growth rate	11.6	-13.2	15.6	5.0	5.0	7.3
Imports/GDP [4]	12.9	8.2	8.6	8.3	7.1	6.8
Terms of Trade Adjustment	0.0	-2.2	-2.5	-2.7	-3.2	-5.2
Current account, US$ million [3]	-218.0	-393.5	-507.5	-568.0	-573.5	-601.0
Current account/GDP [3][4]	-4.4	-3.2	-3.4	-2.6	0.0	3.2

[1] *Exports of goods and services, including private transfers.*
[2] *Since the data are presented in constant prices, the terms of trade adjustment must be taken into account for the national income identities to hold.*
[3] *Excludes grants.*
[4] *Expressed in constant prices to remove the impact of exchange rate adjustments. While the balance of payments current account remains negative over the projection period in current prices, it is projected to turn positive, in constant 1987 prices after the year 2000.*

Source: Staff estimates based on data provided by Government authorities.

assistance from the multilateral lending institutions and bilateral donors. Uganda cannot rely entirely upon these sources indefinitely. At any rate, competing demands for such resources have emerged from the former Soviet Union and Eastern Europe. Improving the balance of payments must therefore focus on two aspects namely, export expansion and foreign investment promotion.

5.47   Exports are projected to increase their share in GDP from their present levels of about 5 percent of GDP to slightly under 10 percent by the year 2005, implying an annual average rate of growth in excess of 10 percent from a severely depressed base. While the international price of coffee is projected to recover from the present depressed levels, the growth in export earnings is expected to materialize from the re-emergence of traditional export crops like cotton and tea, and nontraditional exports such as simsim, beans, vanilla, and cashewnuts. The level of imports has declined significantly over the past few years, partly as a result of the tight foreign exchange situation until 1991. As economic growth picks up, the import compression is expected to reverse itself. However, import growth will be moderated by the dominant share of agriculture in GDP, a sector which is neither capital-intensive nor foreign exchange-intensive. Consequently, the projected share of imports in GDP, while increasing in the initial years, declines marginally to about 7 percent in 2005.

5.48   Foreign investment will also play a major role in the transformation of Uganda. The Uganda Investment Authority is reporting growing foreign investor interest in the country. However, the actual amount of foreign investment coming into the country remains a trickle. That has begun to change in the aftermath of the return of large numbers of expropriated properties to the owners. Although the investment climate has improved a great deal, it will take some time to rebuild investor confidence. Significant amounts of foreign investment are therefore not expected during the rest of this decade. It is projected that by the turn of the century, Uganda could see annual investment inflows of about US$30-40 million, growing thereafter to over US$100 million by the year 2005. However, for this to happen, Uganda will need to ensure that the foreign investor is not looked upon in suspicion, as has been the case in the past, is made to feel welcome and is treated as a partner in development.

UGANDA

TABLE 5.10

GDP BY SECTOR IN CONSTANT PRICES
Percentage of GDP at FC

	1987	1988	1989	1990	Prelim 1991	1992	1993	1994	1995	Projected 1998	2000	2003	2005
Agriculture	62.2	61.4	60.9	60.2	59.3	67.2	67.7	67.6	67.3	65.5	63.9	61.2	59.0
Cash crops	2.6	2.3	2.3	2.2	2.6	2.5	2.5	2.4	2.3	2.1	2.0	1.7	1.5
Food crops	45.6	45.2	45.3	44.6	43.3	43.3	43.8	43.5	43.1	41.0	39.2	36.5	34.7
o/w Horticulture/spices	8.3	7.8	7.6	7.8	7.8	8.1	8.4	8.7	9.1	10.3	11.2	12.6	13.4
Livestock	9.8	9.8	9.5	9.5	9.4	9.4	9.2	9.2	9.2	8.8	8.4	7.6	6.9
Forestry	1.7	1.6	1.5	1.5	1.5	1.5	1.5	1.4	1.4	1.3	1.1	1.0	0.9
Fishing	2.5	2.4	2.2	2.4	2.4	2.4	2.4	2.3	2.3	2.1	2.0	1.8	1.6
Industry	7.8	8.4	8.8	9.1	9.6	9.8	9.9	10.0	10.3	11.5	12.7	15.2	17.1
Mining & quarrying	0.1	0.1	0.1	0.2	0.3	0.3	0.3	0.3	0.3	0.3	0.3	0.2	0.2
Manufacturing	3.6	4.1	4.6	4.7	5.2	5.4	5.5	5.6	5.8	6.8	7.7	9.6	11.1
Coffee, cotton, sugar	0.2	0.3	0.4	0.5	0.7	0.7	0.7	0.7	0.8	0.9	1.0	1.2	1.4
Food products	0.3	0.4	0.4	0.4	0.5	0.5	0.5	0.5	0.5	0.6	0.7	0.8	1.0
Miscellaneous	3.0	3.4	3.8	3.8	4.1	4.2	4.3	4.4	4.5	5.3	6.1	7.5	8.7
Public utilities	0.4	0.4	0.4	0.4	0.4	0.4	0.4	0.5	0.5	0.5	0.6	0.7	0.8
Construction	3.7	3.7	3.7	3.7	3.7	3.7	3.6	3.6	3.7	3.9	4.1	4.6	5.0
Services	30.0	30.2	30.3	30.7	31.1	31.1	30.8	31.1	31.5	33.2	34.5	36.2	37.2
Trade	13.5	14.1	14.5	14.7	14.9	14.9	14.8	15.0	15.3	16.5	17.4	18.6	19.3
Transport & communication	3.9	3.8	3.7	3.7	3.7	3.7	3.7	3.7	3.7	3.8	3.7	3.7	3.6
Community services	10.2	10.1	9.9	10.2	10.4	10.4	10.4	10.5	10.6	11.2	11.8	12.6	13.1
Owner-occupied dwellings	2.4	2.2	2.2	2.1	2.1	2.0	2.0	1.9	1.9	1.7	1.5	1.4	1.2
GDP at factor cost	100.0	100.0	100.0	100.0	100.0	108.1	108.4	108.7	109.1	110.3	111.2	112.6	113.4
Net indirect taxes	5.2	4.5	5.1	6.4	6.3	6.3	6.3	7.4	7.8	8.0	8.0	8.0	8.0
GDP at market prices	105.2	104.5	105.1	106.4	106.3	114.4	114.7	116.1	116.9	118.3	119.2	120.6	121.4

Source: Statistics Department and staff estimates.

UGANDA

TABLE 5.11

GDP BY SECTOR IN CONSTANT PRICES

Annual growth rates

	1987	1988	1989	1990	Prelim 1991	Projected 1992	1993	1994	1995	1998	2000	2003	2005
Agriculture	5.2	6.2	6.4	2.9	2.5	4.6	6.3	5.3	5.2	4.7	4.7	4.9	4.6
Cash crops	4.0	-4.4	7.3	-4.2	25.0	2.4	3.3	3.4	3.4	3.2	3.2	2.9	2.9
Food crops	5.5	6.7	7.6	2.5	1.0	5.0	7.2	5.4	5.1	4.8	4.9	5.3	5.1
o/w Horticulture/spices	0.0	0.0	5.0	7.5	3.0	10.0	10.0	10.0	10.0	12.0	12.0	12.0	10.5
Livestock	4.3	7.7	3.5	4.0	4.0	4.0	4.0	6.0	6.0	5.0	5.0	4.0	3.0
Forestry	6.7	6.2	1.1	3.9	3.8	3.5	3.5	3.5	3.5	2.5	2.5	2.5	2.5
Fishing	4.1	2.5	-0.4	14.8	4.0	4.0	4.0	5.0	5.0	4.0	3.5	3.5	3.5
Industry	23.0	15.0	12.7	7.5	10.3	6.6	6.7	8.1	8.8	12.0	13.0	14.4	14.7
Mining & quarrying	-17.3	-5.3	15.4	88.5	21.4	10.1	9.0	8.0	5.0	4.5	4.0	4.0	4.0
Manufacturing	16.8	22.7	19.1	7.5	14.1	7.9	8.0	9.2	9.9	13.6	15.0	15.9	16.2
Coffee, cotton, sugar	7.7	36.0	44.7	21.2	44.7	8.1	8.1	9.2	9.6	13.2	15.2	15.4	15.5
Food products	34.5	27.8	1.9	10.7	14.4	7.9	8.2	8.8	9.0	13.5	14.8	16.1	16.3
Miscellaneous	15.9	21.0	18.8	5.6	10.2	7.9	8.0	9.3	10.1	13.7	15.0	16.0	16.3
Public utilities	6.2	2.9	6.7	7.9	8.1	8.0	8.0	9.0	10.0	12.0	14.0	15.0	15.0
Construction	35.1	9.7	6.0	4.4	5.0	4.4	4.4	6.2	7.1	9.9	9.9	11.8	11.8
Services	6.2	8.5	7.6	5.3	5.4	5.1	5.1	7.2	7.2	9.3	9.3	9.4	9.5
Trade	9.2	12.1	10.2	5.4	5.5	5.1	5.1	8.0	8.0	10.0	10.0	10.0	10.0
Transport & communication	6.1	6.6	5.0	3.7	4.2	4.7	4.7	7.0	7.0	7.0	7.0	7.0	7.0
Community services	3.2	5.8	6.1	6.3	6.3	5.6	5.6	7.0	7.0	10.0	10.0	10.0	10.0
Owner-occupied dwellings	2.7	2.7	2.7	2.7	2.7	2.7	2.7	3.0	3.0	3.0	3.0	3.0	3.0
GDP at factor cost	6.7	7.6	7.3	4.0	4.1	5.0	6.0	6.2	6.2	7.0	7.3	7.9	8.0

Source: Statistics Department and staff estimates.

UGANDA

TABLE 5.12

GDP BY EXPENDITURE AT CONSTANT PRICES

Percentage share of GDP at MP

	1987	1988	1989	1990	Prelim 1991	1992	1993	1994	1995	1998	2000	2003	2005
						Projected ---------->							
Consumption	96.3	96.7	95.3	93.0	92.0	92.0	90.4	88.4	86.4	83.6	81.3	76.6	73.5
Private	89.8	91.2	89.4	87.1	84.5	83.5	82.2	80.1	76.9	74.1	71.8	67.1	64.0
Public	6.5	5.5	5.9	5.9	7.5	8.6	8.2	8.2	9.5	9.5	9.5	9.5	9.5
Gross domestic investment	9.2	8.9	9.7	10.4	10.7	10.9	13.0	14.6	16.2	17.6	18.9	21.7	23.4
Fixed investment	9.2	8.9	9.7	10.4	10.7	10.9	13.0	14.6	16.2	17.6	18.9	21.7	23.4
Private	3.3	3.6	3.8	3.9	5.2	5.8	7.5	9.0	10.4	10.8	11.5	13.6	15.0
Public	5.9	5.3	5.9	6.5	5.5	5.1	5.5	5.6	5.8	6.8	7.4	8.1	8.4
Exports, G+NFS	7.3	6.6	6.2	5.6	5.0	5.0	5.2	5.5	5.7	6.3	7.0	8.6	9.8
Imports, G+NFS	12.9	12.2	11.3	9.8	8.2	7.9	8.6	8.4	8.3	7.5	7.1	6.9	6.8
Terms of trade adjustment	0.0	-1.1	-1.7	-2.4	-2.2	-2.3	-2.5	-2.6	-2.7	-2.9	-3.2	-4.3	-5.2
Import capacity	7.3	5.5	4.5	3.3	2.7	2.6	2.7	2.9	3.0	3.4	3.7	4.3	4.7
Resource balance	-5.5	-5.6	-5.2	-4.2	-3.2	-2.9	-3.4	-3.0	-2.6	-1.2	-0.2	1.7	3.0
Net factor service income	-1.0	-1.1	-1.2	-1.1	-1.4	-1.8	-1.7	-1.6	-1.5	-1.1	-0.9	-0.6	-0.5
Net current transfers	2.2	2.0	1.6	1.2	1.4	1.7	1.6	1.6	1.5	1.2	1.1	0.8	0.7
Current account balance	-4.4	-4.7	-4.8	-4.1	-3.2	-3.0	-3.4	-3.0	-2.6	-1.1	0.0	1.9	3.2
GDP at market prices	100.0	100.0	100.0	100.0	100.0	100.0	100.0	100.0	100.0	100.0	100.0	100.0	100.0
GNP	99.0	98.9	98.8	98.9	98.6	98.2	98.3	98.4	98.5	98.9	99.1	99.4	99.5
Gross domestic savings	3.7	2.2	3.0	4.7	5.8	5.6	7.1	9.0	10.8	13.4	15.5	19.1	21.3
Gross national savings	4.9	3.2	3.4	4.8	5.8	5.5	7.1	9.0	10.8	13.6	15.7	19.3	21.5
Gross domestic income	100.0	98.9	98.3	97.6	97.8	97.7	97.5	97.4	97.3	97.1	96.8	95.7	94.8
Gross national income	99.0	97.8	97.2	96.6	96.3	95.9	95.9	95.8	95.8	96.0	95.9	95.1	94.4

Source: Bank of Uganda, IMF and staff estimates.

UGANDA

TABLE 5.13

BALANCE OF PAYMENTS
In millions of US dollars

	1986/87	1987/88	1988/89	1989/90	1990/91	Prelim 1991/92	1992/93	1993/94	1994/95	Projected 1997/98	1999/00	2002/03	2004/05
Exports (g+nfs)	406	324	304	246	200	195	215	253	295	450	613	986	1355
Merchandise (fob)	384	298	282	210	177	172	190	227	268	409	558	901	1241
o/w Coffee	365	286	276	159	126	117	103	119	139	206	243	294	334
Non-factor services	22	26	22	36	23	23	25	26	27	41	55	85	114
Imports (g+nfs)	600	682	712	676	658	523	707	771	842	1050	1221	1623	2010
Merchandise (cif)	514	545	562	584	550	425	591	647	709	893	1046	1417	1779
o/w Petrol	63	69	76	78	87	57	81	89	98	131	159	202	237
Non-factor services	86	137	150	92	108	98	116	124	133	156	175	207	232
Resource balance	-194	-358	-408	-430	-458	-328	-492	-518	-547	-600	-608	-638	-655
Net factor income	-47	-57	-67	-77	-66	-142	-136	-150	-159	-156	-154	-151	-149
o/w Net interest	-47	-57	-66	-77	-62	-87	-79	-87	-90	-78	-74	-83	-89
Current private transfers	100	120	114	78	80	127	133	147	150	174	191	202	211
C/A Balance (excl grants)	-141	-295	-361	-429	-444	-343	-494	-521	-556	-582	-570	-586	-593
C/A Balance (incl grants)	-101	-203	-230	-276	-239	-126	-234	-236	-269	-321	-335	-384	-410
Official transfers	40	92	131	153	205	217	261	284	287	261	235	202	182
o/w Import support	0	33	49	29	87	77	117	128	139	119	108	92	83
Net M&LT loans	45	101	125	215	131	21	133	132	166	223	230	248	264
Disbursements	135	186	211	292	217	146	212	231	238	295	309	337	359
Project loans	135	141	143	125	118	77	134	146	150	216	238	275	304
Import support loans	0	45	68	167	99	69	78	85	88	79	72	61	55
Repayments	90	85	86	77	86	125	79	99	72	72	78	88	95
Foreign investment	28	10	13	6	77	2	3	4	5	15	30	81	136
Short-term, net	-31	37	-17	12	2	-4	0	0	0	0	0	0	0
Errors/value adjustment	-20	-10	-7	0	0	-11	0	0	0	0	0	0	0
Overall balance	-79	-65	-103	-44	-105	-118	-98	-101	-97	-83	-75	-55	-11
Financing:	79	65	103	44	105	118	98	101	97	83	75	55	11
Monetary authorities	22	-14	18	10	41	-2	-4	4	-40	-73	-55	-50	-40
Gross reserve changes	33	-4	12	11	-11	-23	-15	-15	-15	-17	-19	-30	-30
IMF, net	-3	-17	7	-1	52	21	10	19	-25	-56	-36	-20	-10
SAF/ESAF and purchases	57	34	94	42	89	55	28	28	0	0	0	0	0
Other, net	-8	7	0	0	-2	-4	-1	0	0	0	0	0	0
Short term/commercial	10	-10	6	12	65	124	0	0	0	0	0	0	0
External arrears	-45	47	18	-19	1	-0	0	0	0	0	0	0	0
Exceptional financing	92	41	61	41	0	0	103	97	137	156	130	105	51
Rescheduling	92	40	57	40	1	0	50	16	0	0	0	0	0
Debt cancellation	0	0	3	2	0	0	53	82	137	156	130	105	0
Residual finance gap	0	0	0	0	0	0	0	0	0	0	0	0	51
Memo item:													
Gross reserves (EOP)	37	41	30	19	30	53	67	82	97	146	183	258	318
in months of imports	0.9	0.9	0.6	0.4	0.6	1.5	1.4	1.5	1.6	2.0	2.1	2.2	2.1

Source: Bank of Uganda, IMF, and staff estimates.

Annex to Chapter 5: Agricultural Growth Prospects

A5.1   This Annex examines briefly the status and prospects of each of the major crops as well as livestock. The most striking thing to emerge from this analysis is that in crop after crop Uganda has a vast scope for raising yields. This requires painstaking and sustained effort over the long term. In the long term, area expansion is not a substitute for such an effort.

Traditional Export Crops

A5.2   The traditional export crops are coffee, cotton, tea, tobacco and cocoa. Of these only coffee has survived as a major export crop. The production of the rest declined to the point where Uganda was no longer a serious supplier in foreign markets. For cotton and tea things have begun to change in that production has started to pick up and Uganda is slowly regaining some of its lost markets.

A5.3   *Coffee* is the number one export crop. It occupies about 240,000 hectares of land. The entire crop is produced by smallholders and it is estimated that 1.2 million farm households are engaged in coffee production. In two thirds of the country's 38 districts, coffee is a major source of cash income. At the beginning of the ERP, coffee accounted for nearly 95 percent of total export earnings. That share has now fallen to about 75 percent partly as a result of the difficulties facing the industry (principally the collapse of international coffee prices since July 1989 and domestic supply problems) and partly in reflection of the rising trend of nontraditional exports. Coffee was also, until recently, the mainstay of government revenue, contributing, in the form of an export tax, to over a third of total domestic revenue. Again because of the problems plaguing the industry the export tax on coffee was eliminated in 1992/93.

A5.4   Uganda's coffee is predominantly of the Robusta variety, accounting for 90-95 percent of total production. Robusta is in oversupply on world markets. However, that does not mean that Uganda should not increase production so as to regain its position in the world market. The balance of production is Arabica coffee whose international market prospects are more favorable. It is grown in the high altitude (1,500-2,000 meter) areas, mainly in Mbale. While there is some scope for increasing the area under Arabica cultivation (presently 30,000 ha), suggestions of doubling and even tripling the area have so far not yielded much results.

A5.5   The present coffee yields are very low; about 0.6 tons/ha and 0.5 tons/ha of clean coffee for Robusta and Arabica, respectively. Yet six clones of Robusta coffee capable of giving yields in the range of 2-3.5 tons/ha of clean coffee, with some application of fertilizer, have been available from the research program since the mid-1970s. Only small quantities of these clones have been forthcoming from the 28 existing nurseries. Partly as a result, the yields obtained from the research trials have yet to be fully validated at the farm level. A major replanting program is needed since the coffee trees are not only very old (30-60 years) but have been neglected. Aside from introducing new high-yielding varieties, Uganda must tackle the problems posed by disease and pest, low soil productivity and poor management practices.

A5.6   *Cotton* was once a major export earner for Uganda, second to coffee. The industry was at its best around 1970 when the area planted reached 900,000 ha and production peaked at 469,730 bales (86,900 tons) of lint.[79] From this strong position the industry went into a long period of decline. By 1988 the farmers had practically ceased growing cotton: only 1.8 tons were produced in that year. A steady recovery has been evident since then and, in 1992, some 60,000 tons of cotton were produced.

A5.7   Although cotton is cultivated in many parts of Uganda, the main growing areas are Teso, Busoga, Lango and Bukedi districts as well as parts of the western and northern regions. It is a smallholder crop grown at altitudes of less than 1,500 meters, requiring annual rainfall of over 800 millimeters. The medium-long staple cotton produced in Uganda is of high quality but the yields are very low. Average yields are estimated at 0.25 tons/ha of lint cotton. An important reason for the low yields is the lack of improved varieties. The present standard varieties (SATU and BPA) are no longer pure. They have become susceptible to a host of pests and diseases. Institutional weaknesses in the industry, as exemplified by the lack of competition among ginneries and exporters, also constitute a major constraint on production. In the absence of these constraints and with good management, it is possible to achieve yields of 0.75-1 tons/ha; yields of 1 ton/ha and above have already been achieved in some field trials.

A5.8   The other major traditional export crop is *tea*. Production peaked in 1972 at 23,000 tons, of which 21,000 tons was exported. Production then dropped off dramatically during the years of political and military upheaval; in 1979 only 1,500 tons were exported. Being a tree crop, the tea bushes more or less survived and thus are only in need of rehabilitation. Approximately 22,000 ha of land are presently under tea, of which about half has already been rehabilitated. The gestation period for rehabilitation investments in tea is very short—about three months. This means that production from existing tea gardens can be increased very quickly; output of tea is already nearing 10,000 tons.

A5.9   Tea requires good soils, altitudes of over 1,200 meters and rainfall of more than 1,200 millimeters per annum. The best growing conditions can be found in the districts of Bushenyi, Rukungiri, Kabarole, Hoima and Masindi as well as the northern shores of Lake Victoria, especially near Lugazi. Tea is produced on smallholder farms (accounting for 9,400 ha) and small-to-large estates which account for the rest of the area planted. In the past Uganda achieved high yields in tea; average yields in 1972 were 12 tons/ha and 5 tons/ha for the estates and smallholders, respectively. Yields dropped precipitously over the years and are now in the range of 1.4-1.6 tons/ha. With improved management of the plantations and the introduction of improved clones over the long term, Uganda should be able to regain the previous yield levels and even surpass them. Full rehabilitation of the remaining tea plantations would enable Uganda to attain the previous peak production.

A5.10   The other traditional export crops are cocoa and tobacco. *Cocoa* has always been a minor crop in Uganda. Presently only 300 tons are exported in a year. Given the oversupply from the traditional producers, cocoa is not destined to become a major export crop in Uganda. *Tobacco*, on the other hand, is a major import-substitution crop which is grown by smallholders. The crop has been revived, thanks to BAT, the cigarette manufacturer. Aside from procurement, BAT provides a full range of research and extension services to the farmer. Production is now around 5000 tons per annum. About half of this production goes to meet domestic requirements and the rest is

---

[79]   A bale weighs 185 kg.

exported. Exports are, however, not expected to increase much beyond this level primarily because of the worldwide health concerns about smoking.

Matoke (Banana)

A5.11 Matoke is the major staple food crop in the high rainfall areas of the country. It occupies the single largest cultivated area, estimated at 1.5 million hectares in 1992. The yield, presently about 5.5 tons/ha is low, because of declining soil fertility and problems caused by disease and pests. Given the favorable climatic and soil conditions, the yield could be increased to 10-20 tons/ha with the use of disease-free improved clones, better management practices and fertilizer application. There is no prospect of matoke exports on any significant scale, even to markets within the subregion. Domestic (human) consumption therefore sets the upper limit to production.[80] Accordingly, growth of matoke output can be expected to equal the population growth rate. The first priority is to stabilize yields at current levels. This in turn would suggest that research and extension activities should be focused on making present varieties pest resistant and capable of giving sustained yields under variable conditions. The expansion of the cultivated area would thus continue to account for much of the growth of matoke output. The next stage is to initiate programs aimed at raising yields. This is necessary in order to free some of the land occupied by matoke for other crops.

Cereals

A5.12 The main cereals produced in Uganda are millet, maize, sorghum and rice.[81] *Finger millet* is extensively cultivated in the drier and less fertile areas in the east and north. Bulrush millet is grown mainly in the semi-arid areas of Karamoja. Millet is an important part of the diet in the areas where they are grown, have a high nutritive value, have high tolerance for drought, and they can be easily stored. They also form the basis of an important local beer brewing and food processing industry. The production of finger millet declined sharply between 1970 and 1982, from 783,000 tons to 401,000 tons, although production has since picked up to just under 600,000 tons in 1992. Yields have always been very low. On average farmers obtain 0.8 tons/ha while research stations have achieved yields of 3 tons/ha with improved varieties and better management practices. The main constraints to increased output are low-yielding varieties, poor husbandry practices, degraded soils, low adoption of improved varieties, competition with other crops and disease and pests, including birds. Given its place as a staple food in mainly the low-rainfall areas of the country, millet deserves high priority in Uganda's agricultural development strategy.

A5.13 In terms of overall output of cereals, *maize* ranks second to millet. Although historically maize has not been part of the Uganda diet, the cultivation of this crop has expanded rapidly over the past ten years. The area under maize increased from 260,000 ha in 1981 to about 440,000 ha in 1992. The cultivated area and output actually peaked at 527,000 ha and 674,000 tons, respectively in 1976. Except for a sudden burst of output expansion in 1989 to 624,000 tons, maize production declined or stagnated during much of the 1980s. Maize yields have remained very low, fluctuating between 1.2 and 1.5 tons/ha. Although climatic conditions in Uganda are very favorable for high maize yields, production is constrained by a number of factors. One of the most important constraints is the lack of suitable improved varieties. The present cultivated variety, a Kawanda composite, was

---

[80]   This does not, of course, rule out the emergence of industrial uses for matoke.

[81]   Wheat is also grown in Uganda but on a very small scale (around 10 MT per annum).

released in 1971. It is a tall late-maturing variety which is susceptible to maize streak virus. Other constraints include inefficient farming practices, nonapplication of fertilizer, poor harvesting, drying and storage. The production potential for maize is very good as shown by the fact that new selections from the ongoing maize research program at Kawanda have given yields of 3-4 tons/ha, based on trials in farmers' fields. Moreover, maize varieties with a higher yield potential (5-7 tons/ha) can be obtained from some of the International Agricultural Research Centers (IARC).

A5.14 Another important cereal is *sorghum*. It is a staple food as well a raw material for beer brewing. It is grown mainly in the drier areas of Karamoja, Teso and the highlands of Kabale. The area planted under sorghum has remained more or less stagnant for a long time while production has been on the decline. In 1975, 467,000 tons were produced; by 1992 production was down to 375,000 tons. Present yields are very low (0.8 tons/ha) for the familiar reasons of low-yielding varieties, poor production practices, poor soils and pests and disease. Improved varieties which mature faster and are resistant to drought are available from the IARCs. Under improved management practices these varieties can give yields as high as 3 tons/ha.

A5.15 The other cereal worthy of mention is *rice*, which is gaining in importance in the urban diet. Domestic demand used to be met largely from imports but the situation is now quite different. Production has expanded to about 60,000 tons per annum to meet domestic requirements. Aside from increasing domestic demand, there is export potential in regional markets. The climate and soils in many parts of Uganda (particularly the swamps) are very favorable for rice cultivation. The present low yields of 1-1.5 tons/ha can be increased to 3-4 tons/ha with the aid of high-yielding varieties and improved production practices.

Roots and Tubers

A5.16 The main crops in this category are cassava and sweet potatoes. In terms of output the former ranks second and the latter third among the food crops grown in Uganda. *Cassava* is a staple food in the eastern, northern and northeastern parts of the country while sweet potatoes are grown mainly in the south and west. Between them cassava and sweet potatoes take up nearly one million hectares of cultivated land; this is another measure of the importance of these crops in Ugandan agriculture. There has been a steady improvement in cassava yields, from under 5 tons/ha in 1970 to around 9 tons/ha in recent years but Ugandan yields still fall far below those prevailing in many other countries. Uganda should at least stabilize yields at current levels and possibly seek to achieve higher yields by tackling the main production constraints which are: nonavailability of high-yielding, disease resistant varieties, the prevalence of pests and poor agronomic practices. The diseases that pose the greatest threat to cassava are the African cassava mosaic virus and cassava bacterial blight.

A5.17 There is also big potential for the cultivation of *sweet potatoes*. Compared to those of other developing countries, the present sweet potato yields are exceptionally low. Yields are generally around 5 tons/ha when it has been demonstrated in the east and north that yields of 35 tons/ha can be achieved by planting currently available high-yielding, disease resistant varieties and introducing improved cultivation methods.

A5.18 A recent addition to the list of roots and tubers grown in Uganda are *Irish potatoes*. The crop now occupies 40,000 ha of land which produce about 300,000 tons a year. Kigezi and Ankole account for the bulk of the production. While soil and climatic conditions are favorable for potato growing, present yields are very low: only 8.5 tons/ha. Other countries achieve yields which are several times higher than this. Moreover, using new selections, the Kalegyere Research Station has demonstrated that yields of 25-30 tons/ha (four times current levels) are possible. The production constraints that need to be addressed are lack of improved varieties and plant diseases.

Pulses

A5.19 Of the pulses, the only one grown on a large scale in Uganda are beans.[82] The area planted under *beans* now stands at over 500,000 ha and the annual harvest is around 400,000 tons. Production is concentrated in the western parts of the country but significant quantities are also grown in Buganda, the east and the north. Beans provide a cheap source of vegetable protein in the Ugandan diet. Beans also have export potential. In spite of its attractions, bean production has either been stagnant or has declined during the past two decades. The main constraint on production is the lack of improved varieties together with the associated improved farming practices. The present variety grown in Uganda (K20) was released as far back as 1968 and now gives very low yields of 0.6-0.8 tons/ha. Uganda is considered capable of achieving a yield of 1.5 tons/ha. Still higher yields may be possible since research stations have been able to achieve yields of over 2 tons/ha. With improved varieties two and possibly three crops can be grown each year. To realize this potential Uganda must tackle the other constraints on production; that is, eradicate viral, bacterial and fungal diseases as well as the bean fly pest.

Oilseeds

A5.20 The most important oilseeds grown in Uganda are groundnut (peanut) and simsim. *Groundnut* is both a food crop and a cash crop and is a source of protein and vegetable oil. It is grown all over the country but more so in the north than elsewhere. In the 1960s significant quantities of groundnut were exported. However, there was a sharp decline in area planted between 1979 and 1985, with a corresponding drop in annual output to as low as 70,000 tons. Since then steady increases in area and output have been recorded. Production has almost returned to the 200,000 tons level that had been achieved in the mid-1970s. However, output remains constrained by the lack of high-yielding varieties, the ravages of disease and pests, poor husbandry practices, nonapplication of fertilizer and unreliable rainfall in some areas in the north. The present yield is estimated at 0.8 tons/ha of dried pods. This could be raised to 2.5 tons/ha, a result that has already been achieved on experimental plots in some parts of the country.

A5.21 *Simsim (sesame)*, the other important oilseed, is grown mainly in northern and eastern Uganda. Production was adversely affected by insecurity in these areas but it has been boosted in recent years by the return of peace and security and growing export demand. The area under cultivation is approaching 150,000 ha and annual output is in the 60,000-70,000 tons range. At about 0.4 tons/ha the yield is very low. Aside from the absence of high-yielding varieties, production is plagued by the shattering of mature pods, leaf disease, insect pests and poor agronomic practices. Given improved varieties and farming practices, yields can be raised significantly. Research trials have already shown that yields can be doubled.

A5.22 Among the oilseeds, *soya beans* and *sunflower* are also grown in Uganda. During the past three years the area planted under soya bean has expanded rapidly to about 60,000 ha at present, with

---

[82]   The other pulses are field peas, cow peas and pigeon peas which are produced in comparatively small quantities. The combined area occupied by the these three crops is less than 150,000 ha.

a corresponding rise in output to a little over 50,000 tons. With regard to sunflower, only insignificant quantities are being produced at present.

Industrial Crops

A5.23 Aside from cotton, the only industrial crop of significance is *sugarcane*. Favorable climatic conditions for cultivation exist on the northern shores of Lake Victoria and there are three sugar factories (Kakira, Lugazi and Kinyala) which process the raw cane. Production of processed sugar peaked at a little over 154,000 tons in 1970. However, with the expulsion of the Asians in 1972 and the general chaos prevailing in the country, the sugar industry suffered such a sharp decline that in 1985 only 1,000 tons of sugar were produced. The cane is produced on large estates owned by the sugar companies as well as on small outgrower plots.[83]

A5.24 The cane yields and sugar yields are low. In 1991 Kakira and Lugazi achieved cane yields of 70 and 83 tons/ha, respectively. The respective sugar yields were 8.6 percent and 6.9 percent. These cane yields could be raised substantially with the help of improved varieties, better crop and soil management practices and adequate pest and disease control measures. A major rehabilitation of the sugar plantations and the factories at Kakira and Lugazi has been underway since 1986. As a result the annual output of processed sugar has climbed up to a little over 30,000 tons, enough to meet about one fifth of the domestic demand which is estimated to be in the range of 150,000-200,000 tons. Domestic consumption is expected to increase to 250,000 tons by the mid-1990s, implying thereby that even when production capacity is fully restored (to around 170,000 tons per annum) it would still not be adequate to meet domestic requirements.

Horticultural Crops

A5.25 A large variety of horticultural crops are grown in Uganda. These include fruits, vegetables, spices, flowers and ornamentals. There exists a wide range of soil and climatic conditions which are ideal for the cultivation of these crops. The main vegetable-growing areas are Kabale, Kasese, Mbale, Masaka, Jinja, Mpigi and Kampala. Fruits are grown in small lots in most parts of the country. There are no reliable figures on horticultural crops, on either area planted, total annual production or marketed production. However, it can be said that horticultural crops make only a minor contribution to agricultural GDP. Encouragingly, small but increasing quantities of pineapple, green beans, chilies, passion fruit, ginger and citrus are now being exported to Europe and the Middle East.

A5.26 The potential for increased production of horticultural crops, especially for export, does exist but there are formidable obstacles. To start with, being a landlocked country, Uganda faces high transport costs. Then there are problems of poor produce quality, poor post-harvest handling, weak distribution and marketing infrastructure and inadequate or nonexistent refrigeration facilities. In addition to fresh produce, Uganda could at a later stage enter the market for processed products such as juices, concentrates and canned products.

---

[83]   It is estimated that there are 130,000 outgrowers each with 2-3 hectares of sugarcane.

Livestock and Dairy

A5.27 Poultry, sheep and goats are sources of cash income for large numbers of farmers. They are also a source of protein in the Ugandan diet. However, in numbers and value the livestock subsector is dominated by *cattle*. The zebu, an indigenous animal, accounts for 70 percent of the cattle, the sanga (Ankole), another indigenous animal, 15 percent, the cross-bred animals, 13 percent and the exotic breeds, 2 percent. The indigenous animals are adept at surviving in the local environment but they are also susceptible to epidemics of rinderpest, contagious bovine pleuropneumonia (CBPP) and trypanosomiasis. The exotic and cross-breeds are prone to catch tick-borne diseases and must therefore be kept in fenced farms or some other enclosure. Livestock depend almost entirely on natural grass-dominated pastures. The productivity of indigenous animals is low. Cows mature in 3-4 years, calve every second year and produce about 350 liters per lactation. The mortality rates are high; for example, for calves it is 25-30 percent annually.

A5.28 Annual domestic meat consumption is estimated at 55,000 tons which is equivalent to about 3 kg per capita. Domestic demand is expected to increase in line with the growth of population and per capita income. Based on the 1989-90 Household Budget Survey, the income elasticity of demand for livestock products is put at 1.5. This would imply a strong growth of domestic demand for meat products in the future. Regional markets also offer opportunities for increased livestock production and offtake. Moreover, Uganda should in principle have access to overseas markets too, particularly the lucrative EEC market governed by quotas. Access to foreign markets outside of the region will require the attainment of rigorous quality and health standards in the livestock industry, from production and processing to marketing.

A5.29 Milk is the only dairy item of any importance that Uganda produces. About 350-400 million liters of milk are produced each year. The bulk of this production is consumed on-farm and in the rural areas. About 10 million liters are collected, processed and marketed by the Uganda Dairy Corporation (UDC). UDC's output falls far short of the demand for milk in the urban centers. This means that additional capacity for collection and processing is needed. This is turn should stimulate milk production at the farm level.

6

Labor Market Policies for Poverty Reduction

"The countries that have succeeded in reducing poverty over the long term have encouraged broadly based rural development and urban employment, thereby increasing the returns to small farm production and wage labor." (World Development Report, 1990, World Bank, p. 56.)

6.1   The purpose of this chapter is to identify policies and programs for the improved functioning of factor markets from the standpoint of facilitating economic growth and reducing the incidence of poverty in Uganda, particularly with respect to the functioning of the labor market, although access to land and capital are also discussed. The first section puts together a picture of the actual pattern of the distribution of employment and labor use in Uganda today. The second section analyzes some of the distinctive features of Uganda's labor market. The final section outlines policies that would help improve the productive use of labor resources in Uganda within the framework of a pattern of distribution of benefits of increased productivity that would help reduce the incidence of poverty in Uganda.

The Distribution of Labor Force

6.2   Uganda does not have a recent labor force survey. However, the HBS provides some basic information about the distribution of labor force by gender, location and sector of occupation which is summarized in Table 6.1. Combining this information with the estimates of population by gender and location, Table 6.2 provides the bare outlines of the allocation of Uganda's labor force, along with its gender distribution, into three broad sectors—agriculture, industries and services—in each of the urban and rural economies.[84] Table 6.3 attempts to further disaggregate the urban labor force into employment in the public sector, the formal private sector and the informal sector by pooling the information from the Census of Civil Service (1987), the National Manpower Survey (implemented in 1988 and published in 1989) and government payroll statistics.[85] Together these three tables provide a picture of employment in Uganda, whose broad features are discussed below.

6.3   *Sectoral Composition of Employment.* Most Ugandans work in the rural economy and are predominantly employed in agriculture. Eighty nine percent of the members of the Ugandan labor force are employed in the rural economy, a slightly higher share than that of the rural sector in total population, reflecting a higher activity rate in the rural sector than in the urban sector.[86] Nearly 80 percent of all workers and more than 87 percent of the rural workers are employed in agriculture. Even in the urban economy, agriculture employs 18 percent of all workers, a third more than are employed in all industrial sectors, broadly defined. Most of the agricultural employment is in household-farming based on a very high degree of labor intensity. On average, a member of the agricultural labor force works on 0.9 ha of land. It is estimated that the amount of land per agricultural worker could be raised to 3 ha if labor and/or complementary resources to bring land

---

[84]   As is the case with similar information from labor force surveys elsewhere, these are distributions of individuals by "principal occupation", not distributions of actual labor time.

[85]   See Annex to this chapter for details.

[86]   The term "activity rate" is used to mean the ratio of labor force to population.

Table 6.1: Distribution of Population by Primary Activity
(Percent of Population in Each Category)

Activity	Urban		Rural	
	Male	Female	Male	Female
Members not in labor force	56.6	69.4	58.6	64.9
o/w "Homemakers"	1.3	19.8	1.3	13.2
Members in labor force	43.4	30.6	41.4	35.1
o/w employed in:				
Agriculture	5.6	7.5	33.7	33.0
Industries	8.7	1.3	1.3	0.2
Services	27.6	20.4	6.3	1.8
Unemployed	1.4	1.5	0.1	0.1

Note: *Members not in the labor force include those who are too young or old to work, students, those attending to household work ("homemakers"), pensioners, renters and a small (0.2 percent of total) undefined residual category of "others". Agriculture includes farming, fishery, animal husbandry and forestry. Industries include both modern and traditional (cottage) manufacturing as well as construction, electricity, gas and water. Services consist of all the rest. As noted in the text, these are contributions of individuals by "principal occupation", not distribution of labor time.*

Source: *The Household Budget Survey for 1989-90.*

under cultivation were available.[87] Relative to land, labor is in this sense a scarce factor of production. Only a tiny proportion of the agricultural labor force is employed in large-scale commercial farming for which no reliable recent estimate is available.

6.4   Services rank next to agriculture in terms of the share of the total labor force, employing 16 percent of all workers. Their incidence is however vastly different between the urban and the rural economies: 65 percent of all urban workers and only 10 percent of the rural workers are employed in services. Services include a wide variety of activities, ranging from the relatively highly productive, but numerically tiny, tertiary services (e.g., modern finance, transport and trade) to rudimentary trading in the urban informal and rural subsistence sectors. Employment in urban services is dominated by public sector workers (see below).

6.5   Industries—broadly defined to include both modern and traditional manufacturing as well as construction, electricity, gas and water—employ only 3 percent of all workers; 13 percent of the urban workers and 2 percent of the rural workers. Formal manufacturing enterprises—those employing five or more workers—together account for a mere 53,500 workers, 0.8 percent of the labor force.[88] Thus a very large proportion of those employed in industries are actually engaged in informal and rudimentary activities providing low output and income.

---

[87]   An estimated 4.6 million ha were under cultivation in 1990 which is believed to be only 30 percent of total cultivable area. See *Uganda: Agricultural Sector Memorandum*, ibid.

[88]   This information is based on the National Manpower Survey and refers to the year 1988.

Table 6.2: Estimated Mid-Year Distribution of Labor Force, 1992
(Thousand Persons)

Category	Urban Uganda			Rural Uganda		
	Male	Female	Total	Male	Female	Total
Employed in:						
Agriculture	53.6	75.8	129.4	2530.0	2573.1	5103.1
Industries	83.3	13.4	96.7	98.4	17.9	116.3
Services	264.2	206.7	470.9	473.3	139.7	613.0
Unemployed	14.1	14.7	28.8	9.8	6.2	16.0
Total	415.2	310.6	725.8	3111.5	2736.9	5848.4

Category	Total Uganda		
	Male	Female	Total
Employed in:			
Agriculture	2583.6	2648.9	5232.5
Industries	181.7	31.3	213.0
Services	737.5	346.4	1083.9
Unemployed	23.9	20.9	44.8
Total	3526.7	3047.5	6574.2

Note 1: *The January 1991 census population of 16.6m is assumed to have grown to 17.3m by July 1992 (i.e., an annual growth rate of about 2.8 percent). A variation of growth rate within the above range will not have a significant effect on the numbers. The growth in urban population between January 1991 and July 1992 is assumed to have been higher (5 percent over 18 months) than the growth in Uganda's population. The overall gender distribution is assumed to be the same as in the 1991 census. The gender distribution of urban population is assumed to be the same (48.6 percent male) as in municipalities and town councils shown in Table 35 of the Background to the Budget, 1992-93. The gender distribution in rural Uganda is residually obtained. The population for July 1992 by gender and location are thus: urban: 1.970m (0.956m male and 1.014m female) and rural: 15.314m (7.512m male and 7.802m female). Ratios in Table 6.1 have been applied to these population estimates.*

Note 2: *Overall activity rates (excluding the "homemakers" from the labor force) are: 38 percent (41.7 percent for the male and 34.6 percent for the female). If the "homemakers" are included as members of the labor force the activity rates turn out to be 42.9 percent for the male and 48.6 percent for the female.*

6.6   *Gender Distribution of Employment.* If labor force is conventionally defined to exclude those who are predominantly occupied with "household activities" then the male activity rate in Uganda would be higher than the female activity rate. On this basis 42 percent of the males and 35 percent of the females are members of the labor force (Table 6.4). The gender gap in activity rates thus defined is greater in urban areas than in rural areas.

6.7   There is however little justification for adhering to the above conventional definition of labor force. Those who are predominantly engaged in household activities should be included in the labor force because: (i) "household activities" by and large represent worthwhile labor that produces welfare, though conventional national accounting does not capture it; and (ii) women "predominantly"

Table 6.3: Some Facts About Urban and Public Sector Employment

A Further Classification of Urban Employment, Mid-1992

	Thousand Persons	Percent of Total
Public Sector	314.7	43.4
of which:		
Traditional civil service	97.9	13.5
Other government/parastatals	216.8	29.9
Formal Private/Cooperative Sector	80.4	11.1
Informal Sector	330.7	45.6
Total Urban Employment	725.8	100.0

Growth of Government/Public Sector Employment
(Persons)

July 1987	Civil Service Employment	239,528
January 1988	Government Employment	244,195
	Parastatal Employment	53,593
	Total Public Sector Employment	297,788
July 1990	Public Sector Payroll	320,669

Growth of Traditional Civil Service
(Persons)

July 1987	89,750
July 1992	98,873
August 1992	97,854

Note: See Annex to this chapter for sources and explanation.

engaged in household activities also engage in more conventional kinds of productive work. In an economy like Uganda—without an overt abundance in the supply of labor—both these phenomena are stronger than elsewhere in a typical labor abundant economy. For a Ugandan woman being "predominantly engaged in household activities" almost always means having two sets of occupations: domestic work and work in the normal economic enterprise of the household. The fact that the former is the dominant activity does not mean a lower overall intensity of work, but its exact opposite (see discussion in Chapter 3). Although no systematic documentation can be presented to justify this claim there is little doubt about its general validity.

6.8   If those "predominantly" engaged in household activity are included, the female activity rate substantially exceeds the male activity rate: 49 percent of the women and 43 percent of the men are engaged in productive labor (Table 6.4). There is little doubt that women contribute much more to social labor than men. A higher proportion of women than men are members of the labor force when the latter is appropriately defined. Secondly, it is virtually certain that, on average, a female member of the labor force works more hours than does a male member, especially if domestic work is included.

6.9   Discrimination against women as members of the labor force does not simply consist of extracting more labor out of them. They are also relegated to less productive sectors and activities and more often kept out of directly remunerative activities than men are. For each man principally engaged in household work—which is not directly remunerative, nor conducive to control over household income—there are more than eleven women. In industries and services—sectors with higher than average productivity—for each female worker there are respectively 5.8 and 2.3 male workers.[89] Women account for only 20 percent of employment in the formal sector and 26 percent of employment in the skilled categories.[90]

6.10   *Dominance of Public Employment in the Formal Sector.* The public sector accounts for less than 5 percent of aggregate employment in Uganda, but a staggering 80 percent of the urban formal sector employment.[91] The public sector also accounts for 43 percent of all categories of urban labor force.

Table 6.4: Percent of Male and Female in the Work Force

Excluding those in "Principally Employed in Household Work"

	Male	Female
Urban	43.4	30.6
Rural	41.4	35.1
Overall	41.7	34.6

Including those "Principally Employed in Household Work"

	Male	Female
Urban	44.7	50.4
Rural	42.7	48.3
Overall	42.9	48.6

Source: Tables 6.1 and 6.2.

6.11   It is difficult to determine, *a priori*, if a certain level of public sector employment is too high or too low. The appropriate level of public employment would depend on numerous factors, e.g., the structure of the economy, the need for public services and the composition of public services (especially between directly productive and "unproductive" services). Considering the extremely undiversified structure of the economy and the low level of public services (especially in directly productive and production-promoting activities) in Uganda, even the five percent share of aggregate employment would appear to be too high a share for the public sector.

---

[89]   None of these broad sectors is homogeneous in terms of productivity and/or earnings. There is no information about the gender distribution of employment in homogeneous activities within each broad sector.

[90]   Manpower Planning Department, Ministry of Planning and Economic Development, *Manpower and Employment in Uganda, Report of the National Manpower Survey*, 1989, Kampala, xi.

[91]   Is there a non-urban formal sector? In principle, the very large commercial farms may be considered to form that category. The National Manpower Survey included some government, parastatal and private agricultural enterprises (together employing 30,578 persons) as a part of the formal sector. To the extent that these are located in the rural area, the urban formal (informal) sector employment in Table 6.3 is overstated (understated). The extent of modern large-scale enterprises in the rural economy that have not been captured by the National Manpower Survey is not known, but it is likely to be small.

6.12   Of far greater concern however is the overwhelming dominance of public employment in the formal sector of the economy. Modern economic activities under non-government enterprise together employ only 1.2 percent of the nation's labor force!

6.13   The Annex to this chapter discusses how difficult it is to estimate the growth in public employment in Uganda in recent years. In the five years since 1987 public employment in Uganda has increased by something between a tenth and a third, not a very helpful range of estimate. The point, however, is that even the lower limit of this range would appear unwarranted in the context of the rudimentary levels of public services and their failure to achieve a meaningful expansion.

6.14   *The Low Incidence of Unemployment.* The HBS data indicate that unemployed workers represent 1.5 percent of the urban labor force and an incredible tenth of one percent of the rural labor force.[92] By and large, these estimates are consistent with the phenomenon of relative shortage of labor in the economy. The shortage of labor is relative to the comparative abundance of land and the virtual absence of complementary inputs to cultivate land. The result is a great deal of unassisted labor required to eke out a modest living under almost primeval conditions. There is little opportunity for labor to remain idle although the return to it is modest.

Features of the Labor Market

6.15   *Nearly Universal Access to Land.* In agriculture, which employs most Ugandans, there is nearly universal access to land and a negligible incidence of landlessness. The HBS reports that there are 2.9 million households (2.5 million rural households) and that 2.4 million households have farm land. Approximately 2 percent of agricultural labor force is located in urban areas. If one assumes that landownership is uniformly distributed among the rural households and those of the urban households that supply agricultural workers, then approximately 95 percent of the rural households have land. If one assumes that only rural households have *farm land* (i.e., urban agricultural laborers work on others' land or on nonfarm land) then 97 percent of the rural households have land.

6.16   The HBS also shows that most households have small farms, i.e., 62.2 percent farm households have 1 hectare or less land; 85.1 percent farm households have 2 hectares or less land; and 95.5 percent farm households have 4 hectares or less land. These refer to the distribution of operational landholding units. Ownership distribution of land is much more skewed, although no quantitative measurement of it is available. Large-scale commercial farms—including plantations—command very small proportions of both agricultural land and labor.

6.17   The inequality of the distribution of land ownership by itself is not a major source of income inequality. This is because land rent is negligible. Kibanja tenants of mailo land do not pay any rent. Even informal tenants of mailo land and the sub-tenants of the freeholders pay very little rent.[93]

---

[92]   The National Manpower Survey claims much higher rates of unemployment, 5 percent in urban areas and 7 percent in rural areas. Since this survey was limited to the formal sector and to a very rudimentary enumeration of the urban informal sector, it is hard to assign it as much credibility as to the HBS. As noted in the Annex to this chapter, a number of estimates made by the National Manpower Survey appear implausible and/or inconsistent with usual expectation. Its claim of a higher rate of unemployment in rural areas than in urban areas is yet another example of such implausibility.

[93]   There is no information available on these rental rates. A field trip to some villages in Luwero in August 1992, yielded evidence of annual rent per ha being as little as U Sh 200.

6.18   *The Low Incidence of Wage Labor in Agriculture.* Universal access to land means that most members of the rural labor force are predominantly engaged in agricultural work on their own farms. There is no significant rural proletariat, i.e., the landless workers, who are perennially available for wage employment. This means that wage labor is limited and that a very small proportion of agricultural wage labor consists of permanent workers.

6.19   There are three types of wage employment in agriculture: (i) casual laborers hired and paid on a daily basis; (ii) permanent workers paid on a monthly basis and hired for even longer durations; and (iii) contract workers who are paid at piece rate specified for given tasks per ha. Most of the wage labor takes the form of casual labor or contract labor. In the past, permanent workers, employed by large commercial farms, were mainly drawn from immigrant workers from adjacent countries. At present, however, this source of labor supply is insignificant.

6.20   There is little quantitative information available on the incidence of wage labor in rural Uganda. A recent study states that 32 percent of farmers (28 percent in the western region, 37 percent in the central region and 28 percent in the eastern and northern regions) use hired labor at some time to meet their labor requirement.[94] The critical question is what, on the average, is the proportion of hired labor to total labor used by the labor hiring farms. Given the extraordinary fact that 68.3 percent of farms use no hired labor at all and the implausibility of a clear dichotomy between farms using hired labor and farms using family labor, it appears that the average share of hired labor in the labor hiring farms can not be very high. It may be reasonable to consider one third as the upper limit. Indeed it may be much lower. Thus hired labor would at most account for only about ten percent of all labor used in agriculture.

6.21   Another source of information is the recent UNDP survey of 334 rural households in western, southwestern and eastern regions.[95] These are the relatively land scarce and labor abundant regions of Uganda. Ninety two of these households, about 27.5 percent, reported wage labor of all kinds (i.e., including wage labor in nonfarm activities) as their primary economic activity. Once again, the questions are: what proportion of the labor of these households is used as agricultural wage labor and what proportion of labor of the remaining households (for which wage labor is not the primary economic activity) is used as the same. Assuming, quite arbitrarily, that the former is two fifths and the latter is one fifth, the incidence of wage labor in these regions turns out to be about a quarter of total labor used in agriculture [0.4(27.5) + 0.2(72.5) = 25.5 percent]. Since these regions are relatively labor abundant, the average for rural Uganda will be lower, let us say less than (perhaps far less than) 20 percent.

6.22   Where within the above range the figure actually lies is impossible to ascertain. On the basis of the available records of visual reports of observers however one would tend to tilt in favor of the lower limit of the range.

[94]   Alison Evans, *A Review of the Rural Labour Market in Uganda*, School of African and Asian Studies, University of Sussex, May 1992, Table 5. The author does not cite the source of the data, nor the time period to which they refer.

[95]   UNDP, *Preparatory Study on Poverty Alleviation and Rural Development in Uganda*, Draft Report, Kampala, July 12, 1992 (prepared by Management Systems & Economic Consultants Ltd.).

6.23   The two conclusions that are suggested by the above may be summarized as follows:

(i)   In agriculture, where most Ugandans work, the incidence of wage labor is low, perhaps not much more than a tenth of total labor used.

(ii)   Of the total wage labor employed in agriculture, casual and short-term contract workers account for a very high proportion. The incidence of permanent workers is very low. This is because most members of the rural labor force are predominantly occupied with work on their own farms. Very few are available for employment on a long-term basis.

6.24   The labor market is constrained by the fact that the supply of wage labor comes from farmers who are tied to their own farms. Thus differences in the regional balance between the demand for and the supply of labor does lead to substantial differences in wages, often between adjacent regions.[96] This has probably been exacerbated by civil unrest, the lack of information and the absence of infrastructure necessary to promote greater labor mobility. The critical constraint however is the institution of small scale farming that permits nearly universal access to land.

6.25   *Labor Allocation and Returns to Labor.* Small-scale farming still appears to be about the most profitable economic activity for Uganda so that it has not been possible for other parts of the economy to offer high enough wages to pull labor out of it. The vast rural household farming sector is the primary pool of labor supply in the economy. Any movement of labor between this sector and the rest of the economy would depend on the relative remuneration of labor in this sector and in competing activities. Labor could be pushed out by low return to work in household farms or pulled out by high earnings offered by alternative activities that are profitable enough to be able to do so.

6.26   Alternative activities to household farming exist in both rural and urban economies. Within the rural economy these consist of: (i) working for other household farms on a casual basis as a source of income supplement; (ii) working for large-scale commercial farms as an alternative to household farming; and (iii) finding alternative work in other, often "informal", activities within the rural economy either as the principal occupation or as a source of supplementary income.

6.27   The alternative to remaining within the rural economy is to migrate to urban areas where three kinds of employment opportunities might be distinguished: (iv) entry-level unskilled employment in the formal sector of the economy; (v) government employment; and (vi) employment in the informal sector either as a transitional stage before finding more permanent formal/government employment or as a sufficiently remunerative permanent activity.

6.28   The return to labor in household farming is perhaps the standard in relation to which the remuneration in all the alternative activities are determined. This is because the household farms can potentially compete for the labor of the small pool of permanently available workers and the casual workers are principally employed on household farms. The relationship between the return to labor in household farms and wages in alternative activities can however be very complex. Permanently available workers may accept permanent employment in large-scale commercial farms at a lower daily wage equivalent than the wage rate for casual workers in order to have the assurance of continued employment. The wage rate for casual labor can fluctuate quite a bit around the return to *average* household labor depending on the return to labor of the particular groups of peasant households that

[96]   See Alison Evans, *Op. Cit.*

Table 6.5: Relative Earnings of Labor in Different Activities
(Ugandan Shillings)

1. Return to family labor in household farming per day	1991 season	606
2. Wage of casual agricultural labor per day	February 1992	700
3. Wage of permanent agricultural labor per month	February 1992	10,000
4. Wage of agricultural contract labor per ha	February 1992	30,000
5. Urban formal sector wage for unskilled labor per month	July 1992	6,000 - 15,000
6. Average wage of group workers in government per month	August 1992	10,263

Sources:

1.   *Agricultural Secretariat (Bank of Uganda),* **Report on Export Crops and Producer Prices 1992.** *The conversion of the figure at February 1992 prices has been made by using the price index for Kampala between July 1992 and February 1992 (27 percent increase).*

2,3,4. *Agricultural Secretariat, Bank of Uganda.*

5.   *Data gathered by mission in the field.*

6.   *Office of the Commissioner of Data Processing, Ministry of Finance.*

supply casual labor, the pattern of seasonality and the extent of distress supply of labor in order to meet cash needs. To induce labor to move to urban areas, urban wages must be significantly higher than the return to labor for the relevant groups of household farms with potential migrants to compensate for the increased cost of urban living.

6.29   Table 6.5 summarizes some information on the relative earnings of labor in different activities and sectors. Even after allowance is made for significant error in the measurement of these indicators, it is quite clear that work in household farms is, on the average, the most remunerative occupation for an unskilled person. If an average worker ventures out of the household farm for cash earnings as a casual worker in agriculture, he/she has to settle for a lower daily earning at the margin than the average return to a day's work on the household farm. This means that casual labor is supplied by peasant households with less than average return to labor and/or that casual labor is supplied by households that would encounter sharply diminishing returns by trying to use available additional labor on household farms.

6.30   More intriguing is the fact that, on a daily basis, the wage rate for permanent agricultural employment is lower than the wage rate for casual labor. At this wage rate it is still possible to attract the small pool of permanently available workers (the landless, including the "surplus" members of households endowed with large supply of labor relative to the supply of land). But this wage rate is lower than what would be necessary to induce workers on any but the very marginal of household farms to move out. It is not surprising that the estate sector has been finding it hard to attract as much labor as it needs.

6.31   The entry-level wage in the urban formal sector has a rather wide range. Even at the top end, the earnings are only modestly above that in household farming.[97] Unskilled wages in the public sector are significantly below the average return to labor in household farming on the assumption of a reasonable intensity of work.[98] Thus, it would appear that, none of the activities in the formal sector has the dynamism and productivity high enough to enable them to offer labor an earning higher than what labor on the average receives in household farms. The silver lining to this gloomy scenario is that, despite the overwhelming dominance of the public sector, the formal sector of the economy has avoided foisting an artificially inflated structure of wages. As a result the incentive to migrate to urban areas has remained low and the urban informal sector has remained modest in size.[99] Another implication of this is that the suffering of the civil servants retrenched by the civil service reform program, which the Government has recently embarked upon, will be mitigated by the fact that household farming and/or the urban informal sector can offer them returns on their labor which are comparable to what they were receiving from the Government.

Which Employment Categories are Poor?

6.32   A direct ranking of the employment groups in terms of the incidence of poverty is not possible. It is, however, quite obvious that the greatest concentration of poverty is in the group of smaller household farmers, among those 62 percent of farms that have a hectare or less land. This statement may appear to be in apparent conflict with the preceding argument that return to labor is about the highest in household farming. But that comparison was with the average return to labor in the entire household farming sector, a finding that need not have any conflict with the proposition that the per capita income of the very small household farms would be much lower than average.

6.33   Virtually nothing is known about the incomes of the nonfarm households in the rural economy. They account for about 13 percent of rural households. In view of the relatively widespread access to land in rural Uganda it does not appear that nonfarm occupations generally consist of residual activities providing very low incomes to which the landless are driven. It is nevertheless possible that these groups have a high incidence of poverty. Even so, the poor among them must be a small proportion of all the rural poor simply because these groups represent a small proportion of the rural population.

---

[97]   Assume that an average laborer on a household farm has 200 days of work per year. At the average estimated daily return of U Sh 770 this works out at U Sh 154,000 per year or U Sh 12,833 per month. The upper end of the range of wages for unskilled categories, according to data made available to the mission (see annex to this chapter), was U Sh 15,000 in July 1992, perhaps barely enough to compensate for the difference in cost of living.

[98]   How has it been possible for the Government and the formal sector to get workers for employment? One can even observe moderate queues for such employment which need to be explained. Tentatively, the following explanations might be advanced. First, to a degree this is due to "market segmentation". School leavers in urban areas rule themselves out of the rural labor market and offer themselves for employment only in the urban formal sector, especially for public sector jobs. Secondly, as suggested by the Ministry of Labor, it is possible to recruit at the bottom end of the range of unskilled wage in the formal sector if the enterprises making recruitment are located near depressed rural areas from which labor is drawn. Thirdly, a further flexibility is available in the public sector in the form of the opportunity for moonlighting and effectively reducing the contribution of labor (i.e., increasing the earning per hour of *actual* work done).

[99]   In the recent past urban crowding was further relieved by civil strife that encouraged migration out of urban areas.

6.34   Those employed in the urban formal sector are probably protected from extreme poverty. There are of course several instances of very low wages for the unskilled categories in some of these enterprises, but these probably represent cases of low supply price of labor (due to the proximity of the location of employment to the workers' homes in rural areas) or the failure of the inspectors of the Ministry of Labor to account for all the benefits. It is nevertheless possible that a certain proportion of these workers would belong to poverty groups although it is hard to imagine that their number would be large.

6.35   Earnings in the urban informal sector were estimated by the National Manpower Survey to be only about 13 percent below the average earnings in the formal sector.[100] It is therefore reasonable to conclude that the incidence of poverty in the urban informal sector is only moderately higher than the incidence of poverty in the formal sector.

6.36   To conclude, there probably are pockets of poverty among the rural nonfarm households, households of the low paid workers in the urban formal sector and the families employed in the informal sector. But the greatest concentration of poverty in Uganda is among the smallest half or so of the peasant households in terms of the size of land holding. Focussing attention on this group is also critical in view of the earlier conclusion that a rise in the earnings in the peasant sector is likely to push up earnings throughout the economy.

The Objective of Employment and Labor Market Policies

6.37   The above analysis suggests that the central objective of employment and labor market policies for the reduction of poverty in Uganda should be to increase the earnings of labor in agriculture. This will directly reduce poverty because most of the poor in Uganda are employed in agriculture. This will also help alleviate whatever poverty exists elsewhere in the economy because a rise in the earnings of the agricultural workers will filter down to the rest of the economy and raise the earnings of the workers in the other productive sectors.

6.38   The overall context of the strategy of development within the framework of which the objective of increasing the earnings of agricultural labor is to be pursued needs to be spelled out clearly to make it possible to determine the elements of employment and labor market policies in a consistent and coherent manner. In principle, there is no unique path along which to pursue the objective. One might illustrate alternative paths by citing the following polar cases.

(i)   One possible strategy is to promote a system of peasant agriculture by further consolidating the de facto universal access to land. In this case the proposed land reform legislation must find ways of guaranteeing tenancy rights to *all* the existing users of land and by improving the land endowment of the very small farms. This must be supplemented by the institution of a system of supply of technology, extension services and credit that is appropriate for the small peasants and adequate in enabling them to overcome the absence of economies of scale.

(ii)   The polar opposite strategy is to create a framework for the exploitation of economies of scale by promoting as much of large-scale commercial farming as possible. In this case the

---

[100]   Manpower Planning Department, Ministry of Planning and Economic Development, *Manpower and Employment in Uganda, Report of the National Manpower Survey*, 1989, Kampala, p. 181.

proposed land reform must perform a very different function. It should limit tenancy right only to those cases in which the right has already been granted de facto (e.g., the kibanja tenants on mailo land). Elsewhere the landowners might be encouraged to resume their ownership by evicting the informal tenants and converting them into rural proletariat. Incentives for large-scale agricultural entrepreneurship might be strengthened. Employment and labor market policies might be backed by technological policies for an appropriate expansion of demand for labor. Conceivably real wages in agriculture would rise as fast as agricultural productivity to help reduce poverty.

6.39   While in principle both of the above strategies can lead to poverty reducing growth of the rural economy, their practical feasibility needs to be carefully analyzed. Also the choice among these strategies is not simply a matter of economic calculations. There are important social and political issues to be considered. The point however is that the overall strategy needs to be clearly outlined and agreed upon to provide a consistent framework for the determination of employment and labor market policies.

6.40   It does appear from the objectives of the proposed land reform legislation that Uganda wants to take the first route to rural development. This paper cannot possibly outline the components of such a strategy in any detail,[101] but it is useful to highlight the following three main sets of its elements.

6.41   First, the proposed land reform should clearly determine the institutional framework for rural development. Freehold rights must be guaranteed to all cultivators, not merely those who have formal tenancy contracts.[102] Thus, for example, in the mailo areas, it appears that in addition to the kibanja holders there exists a large category of tenants who rent and borrow land without any written acknowledgement of arrangements from landlords. On such land often the landlords determine the crops to be planted. This category of virtual squatters must also be given freehold rights if the strategy of peasant farming is to be successfully implemented. It is not clear from the documents related to the proposed legislation if adequate provision is being made for this. Land endowment of the smaller size groups should also be improved both by investment in land augmentation and by changes in the system of incentives to make it unprofitable for the large land owners to leave land unused, a practice that seems to be widespread.[103]

6.42   Secondly, to enable the small peasants to overcome the absence of the advantage of economies of scale steps should be taken to facilitate their access to an appropriate technological package. At present Ugandan agriculture operates under almost primeval conditions: the limited spread of tractors and ox ploughs that took place in the past has been wiped out, fertilizer use has dropped to virtually nothing, there is an acute absence of basic implements, and the knowledge of farming system and crop husbandry practice is rudimentary. Basic equipments supply (weeder, planter, thresher for grain

---

[101]   For further details of the land tenure system and the proposed land reform, see *Uganda: Agriculture Sector Memorandum*, ibid.

[102]   The purpose of this paper is not to provide a blueprint for land reform, which involves complex issues, but merely to emphasize that universal access to land should be institutionalized. In the mailo area this can clearly be done best by granting freehold rights to the tenants. The question of guaranteeing access to land in the areas of traditional land tenure—where communal control over land prevails—is obviously more complex and needs careful analysis.

[103]   A system of progressive land tax, if feasible, would help ensure this.

crop areas, harvesting tools, and a reintroduction of ox ploughs and selective access to tractor service where essential) needs improvement. Selection and multiplication of appropriate seed varieties for the use of the peasants is of high priority. Soil fertility measures and the introduction of fertilizer deserve attention. All these need to be backed by the dissemination of knowledge about farming systems and crop husbandry practices. The emphasis should be on the provision of these services through the market, backed by an access to credit. The role of the public sector should be to help augment the supply of the technological ingredients by providing appropriate incentives to private producers/suppliers and build a network of extension services.

6.43   The third major element of the strategy is to ensure an appropriate composition of peasant output that would help avoid the constraint on demand. If agricultural growth takes place without any change in the composition of output, soon the production of most subsistence crops and many traditional cash crops would face some kind of demand constraint that would lead to reduced prices and profit. For the earnings of the peasants to continue to grow, it would be essential to bring about a change in the composition of output in favor of products for which demand is not a constraint. In the case of Uganda it would mean looking for agricultural products that would end up as exports, with or without processing. An agriculture consisting of small peasants would need outside help in anticipating the appropriate pattern of demand and in obtaining the infrastructure necessary to get access to new markets.

6.44   While the emphasis of the development strategy in Uganda should be on agriculture with a focus on the small peasants, the process of gradual lowering of the share of the labor force employed in agriculture must begin to take place. The necessary condition on the supply side would be created by the improved productivity of the agricultural laborers. On the demand side, nonfarm activities in which Uganda has comparative advantage must be identified and developed. Several categories stand out as potential candidates. First, agricultural development should create demand for a variety of both producer and consumer goods. This should create a basis for the growth of rural nonfarm employment. Secondly, a part of this demand should spill over in the form of demand for the output of industries and services in the formal sector. Existing industries, reported to be operating at a fraction of capacity, should be able to productively absorb more labor. There should also be a basis for the creation of production capacities in new activities, i.e., to supply producer and consumer goods to the rural economy and to process the agricultural products both for export and for absorption in the domestic market.

Annex to Chapter 6: Urban Employment

A Further Disaggregation

A6.1   The purpose of this Annex is to disaggregate urban employment shown in Table 6.2 into employment in public sector, the formal private sector and the informal sector. There are several estimates of public sector employment for recent years although it is not always easy to reconcile them.

A6.2   First, there is the Census of Civil Service for July 1987 which shows a total *government* employment of 239,528. Second, there is the National Manpower Survey of January 1988 which shows a total formal sector (enterprises employing five persons or more) employment of 378,227 divided into the following categories:

Government employment	244,195
Parastatal employment	53,593
Formal private sector employment	80,439
(including cooperative and "other")	

A6.3   The same survey also implemented a rather limited enquiry of informal sector employment in four cities. It arrived at an estimate of total urban informal sector employment of 7.136m which must be rejected as too high.[104] Clearly, there was an illegitimate extrapolation of the incidence of informal activities in four major cities in which there is a concentration of such activities. Finally, there is an estimate of government/public sector employment of 320,669 for July 1990 based on the payroll statistics.[105]

A6.4   The problem is that it is not altogether clear if government employment according to the three sources are quite comparable. For example, does the payroll estimate for July 1990 include employment in parastatals? If it does, employment in the *public sector* in two and a half years since the Manpower Survey in January 1988 went up by only 8 percent. If it is assumed that the July 1990 estimate excludes the parastatals then *government* employment over the same two and half years went up by nearly a third! It is impossible to know which is the right assumption and what happened to employment in parastatals if the July 1990 estimates exclude them. This paper makes the assumption

---

[104]   Manpower Planning Department, Ministry of Planning and Economic Department, *Manpower and Employment in Uganda, Report of the National Manpower Survey*, 1989, Kampala, October 1989, says that "the informal sector ... is estimated to be providing work opportunities to about 13.7 percent of the labour force" as compared to a formal sector employment of 5.3 percent of the labor force (pp.ix-x). The implied estimate of the labor force is 7.136m which itself is too high for 1988. There was no nationwide survey of labor force at the time and hence one must conclude that this estimate was based on a presumed set of activity rates which are too high. Moreover, the estimate of informal sector employment is far greater than aggregate urban employment based on the ratios of HBS, the only source of labor force participation rates for recent years. Thus this estimate of informal sector employment must be rejected as being too high.

[105]   Quoted in an unpublished paper by the ILO consultant Q.U. Khan, *Employment Situation in Government Sector*, in the Manpower Planning Department (undated typescript).

that the 1990 payroll statistics actually include the parastatals which are excluded from the 1987 Census of Civil Service.[106]

A6.5   To arrive at 1992 midyear estimates the following additional assumptions are made:

(i)   Formal private-cooperative sector employment remained unchanged between 1988 and 1992.[107]

(ii)   For mid 1992 the only part of public sector employment for which a direct estimate is available refers to traditional civil service, employing 97,854.[108] No estimate is available of total employment in government and parastatals. We make the plausible, but unconfirmed, assumption that this is 314,669, i.e., 6,000 fewer than the level in July 1990. It is well known that there has been a reduction in public employment in recent period and the figure that is often mentioned is 6,000 although it is not at all clear to what time period and/or categories this number refers to.

(iii)   All formal sector employment is located in urban Uganda, an assumption that seems to be implied by the National Manpower Survey.

A6.6   These assumptions, together with the estimate of total urban employment in Table 6.2, provide the following distribution of urban employment in mid 1992 (in thousand persons):

Public sector	314.7
o/w Traditional civil service	97.9
Other government/parastatals	216.8
Formal private (& miscellaneous) sector	80.4
Informal sector	330.7
Total urban employment	725.8

---

[106]   Besides reiterating that great uncertainty surrounds all these data, we would like to argue that this interpretation is additionally justified by the widespread belief that the 1990 public employment estimates suffer from a serious upward bias due to the high incidence of "ghost" workers. We want to avoid a possible further overestimation of public sector employment even at the risk of understating it somewhat.

[107]   A survey of 26 enterprises—employing a total of 15,511 persons in 1991—based on the inspection reports of the Ministry of Labor leads us to conclude that there is no way to judge what happened to employment in private formal sector during the period under review. No change seems to be as good an assumption as any other.

[108]   This estimate is provided by the office the Commissioner of Data Processing, Uganda Computer Services, Ministry of Finance and Planning. Excluded categories are teaching services, so-called group employment (temporary workers), and parastatals.

Growth in Public Sector Employment

A6.7   The above sources of data shed a limited amount of light on the trend of public sector employment. Indeed the only part of public sector employment about which the change in recent years can be established is traditional civil service in which employment changed as follows:[109]

July 1987	89,750
July 1992	98,873
August 1992	97,854

A6.8   There was a 9 percent increase over the five years since 1987. As a result of the recent government effort to reduce public employment the number of traditional civil servants declined by just over one percent.[110]

A6.9   Precise changes in total public employment are much harder to determine. It is quite clear that there was a substantial increase between 1987 and 1990 although the precise measurement of the change is obviated by the problem of comparability of data over time. If the 1987 census of civil service accounted for the parastatals then public employment during the next five years increased by more than a third. If the 1987 census excluded the parastatals and our assumption that the 1992 payroll data include the parastatals is correct then the increase was of the order of 12 percent.

A6.10   The comparison over time is made even more difficult by the problem of ghost workers. It appears that there is a widespread practice of inflating the payroll by including nonexistent workers. No one knows how their incidence has changed over time. There is an ongoing government program to weed these ghosts out. It seems highly likely that the recent decline in employment in traditional civil service was largely the result of the elimination of some of these ghosts. Currently an attempt is being made to eliminate them from teaching and other services in which their incidence is believed to be greater.

---

[109]   The sources are as follows: July 1987: Census of Civil Service; the other dates: The Office of the Commissioner of Data Processing.

[110]   The office of the Commissioner of Data Processing gave the impression that the decline in the number in the traditional civil service payroll between July and August 1992 actually took place over a longer period. Those retrenched in recent times were not taken out of the payroll until the month of August.

Providing Key Services and Safety Nets

"Growth is vital to reducing all aspects of absolute poverty.... But growth unaccompanied by other measures may neither boost the incomes of the poor much, nor lead to much progress on the non-income aspects of poverty. On both counts, human development programs have a part to play".
(Poverty and Human Development, World Bank, 1980, p. 63.)

Introduction

7.1   As the World Development Report 1990 stressed, economic growth is a necessary but not a sufficient condition for the reduction of poverty. It is imperative to ensure that the poorest segments of society are able to participate productively in such growth. Consequently, public expenditures, specially on social sectors, have an important role to play in tackling poverty and reinforcing a growth-oriented poverty reduction strategy.

7.2   The most important goal of economic development is the improvement in the standard of living of the population. In a poor and resource-constrained country such as Uganda, where socio-economic indicators reveal extremely low levels of welfare (Table 1.4), such improvement in the standard of living requires substantial investment in human capital (education and health care) and in rural infrastructure (rural feeder roads and clean water supply). It is also important to insure that the growth in population is not so rapid as to undermine the growth in income and the generation of investable surpluses. The development of human resources is both a means and an end of the development process. It is a means to an end in that investment in human resources and economic infrastructure is a prerequisite for increasing productivity and expanding income-earning opportunities both at the individual and national level. It is an end because those with a well-developed human capital base can insure a better quality of life for themselves and their children. Investments in human capital and rural infrastructure, however, have long gestation periods and therefore require active and sustained government involvement in these sectors for long periods of time.

7.3   While public expenditures have an important role to play, the Government's role must necessarily be guided by cost-effective criteria. It is essential that the Government allocate its limited resources to those activities which provide the maximum social and economic rates of return. For example, it has been shown that the average social rates of return to primary education for Sub-Saharan Africa, Asia, and Latin America and the Caribbean, are 26 percent, 27 percent and 26 percent, respectively; these are roughly twice the social rates of returns from higher education. Furthermore, experience from several countries has demonstrated that it is the poor in general, and girls in particular, who benefit most from expenditures on primary education whereas it is the nonpoor who benefit disproportionately from higher education. The nonpoor also generally have sufficient financial resources to bear the cost of such higher education. Consequently, where the beneficiaries can afford to pay for services rendered, it is advisable that cost recovery measures be instituted. The Government of Uganda, therefore, faces a number of challenges in allocating its limited domestic and foreign resources efficiently and in implementing cost-recovery schemes successfully so that economic growth is facilitated, poverty is alleviated, social equity is enhanced and the welfare of its people is maximized.

7.4   The following sections briefly review the level and composition of government expenditure in key economic and social sectors, particularly primary education, primary health, and rural

Table 7.1: Sectoral Expenditure Performance of the Central Government
(Locally Funded Expenditures)

| | As a % of GDPMP | | | | As a % of Total Expenditures | | | |
	1989/90	1990/91	Prelim. 1991/92	Budget 1992/93	1989/90	1990/91	Prelim. 1991/92	Budget 1992/93
Social Services	1.6	1.8	2.5	2.4	20.0	23.2	29.7	33.4
Education	0.9	0.9	1.3	1.1	10.5	12.0	16.0	15.6
Health	0.4	0.4	0.5	0.6	4.7	4.9	6.3	8.5
Local Gov't	0.2	0.4	0.5	0.6	2.5	5.0	6.3	8.5
Other	0.2	0.1	0.1	0.1	2.2	1.3	1.0	0.9
Economic Services	1.3	1.4	1.1	0.9	15.7	17.3	13.5	12.5
Agriculture	0.2	0.3	0.3	0.2	2.9	3.3	3.7	3.5
Infrastructure	0.7	0.8	0.6	0.5	8.5	10.7	7.2	6.4
Other	0.3	0.3	0.2	0.2	4.3	3.3	2.6	2.5
Defense	3.1	2.8	2.3	1.5	38.7	36.3	27.8	21.7
Public Administration	2.1	1.8	2.4	2.3	25.6	23.2	29.0	32.4
TOTAL	8.1	7.9	8.4	7.0	100.0	100.0	100.0	100.0

Sources: Ministry of Finance and Economic Planning, Background to the Budget (July 1992) and staff estimates.

infrastructure.[111]

Government Expenditure on the Social Sectors

7.5   A review of the structure of public expenditures in Uganda indicates that the expenditure pattern is characterized by a low level of aggregate public expenditure even by Sub-Saharan Africa's standards. Constrained by an extremely low domestic revenue effort, public expenditure as percent of GDP was only about 10.5 percent in 1987/88 rising to 20.6 percent in 1991/92,[112] as compared to an average for Sub-Saharan African countries of 30 percent (the average for developing countries in general is about 21 percent). Between 1987/88 and 1991/92, revenues collected as percent of GDP increased slightly from about 5 percent of GDP to 7 percent, as compared to an average revenue effort of about 20 percent for Sub-Saharan African countries. Consequently, the weak revenue effort and the serious internal security problems until the late eighties, which required high expenditures on defense, have prevented the Government from allocating sufficient funds to priority sectors such as education, health and rural infrastructure. It has also forced the Government to rely on foreign aid to finance a significant proportion of its expenditures; in 1991/92, foreign aid financed nearly 60 percent of government expenditures. The Government's locally funded sectoral expenditure

---

[111]   For a detailed assessment of the policies, priorities and expenditures in the areas of health, education, and population, the interested reader is referred to *Uganda: Social Sector Strategy*, 1993, Report No. 10765-UG, World Bank.

[112]   There is general agreement that data prior to 1987/88 are not very reliable. Therefore, the base year used here for the purpose of evaluating changes in public expenditures is 1987/88.

Table 7.2: Poverty Focus of Government Current Expenditures
(As a Percent of Total Current Expenditures)

	1989/90 Actuals	1990/91 Actuals	1991/92 Prelim.	1992/93 Budget
Human Resource Development	20.4	24.6	32.5	35.1
Education	13.9	16.2	20.8	19.5
Health	4.6	5.4	6.3	8.3
Local Government	1.9	3.0	5.4	7.3
Economic Services	5.9	5.7	6.8	7.7
Agriculture	2.5	2.7	2.9	2.8
Infrastructure	3.4	3.0	3.9	4.8
TOTAL	26.3	30.3	39.3	42.8

Note: *Actuals for 1991/92 are preliminary. In addition to the Ministries of Health and Education, the Ministry of Local Government also provides health and education services.*

Source: Ministry of Finance and Economic Planning.

performance is summarized in Table 7.1. As the table shows, the share of expenditures allocated for defense purposes has traditionally been several times higher than those for the social sectors, reflecting the security concerns of the Government. However, expenditures for 1991/92 indicate a noticeable reduction in defense expenditures as percent of GDP (from 3.1 percent in 1989/90 to 2.3 percent in 1991/92), a real decline of 14.5 percent, reflecting the improved security situation throughout the country. Defense expenditures are projected to further decline to about 1.5 percent of GDP in the 1992/93 budget.

Incidence of Government Expenditures

7.6   It is possible to evaluate the effectiveness of poverty-reducing government expenditure programs by determining what fraction of government expenditure in any given sector actually reaches the poor. Such analysis, however, requires reasonably precise information of who the poor are, what proportion of the total population they represent, where they live, their sources of income (agriculture, informal sector activity, wage labor, etc.), the level of their education (primary, secondary, secondary, tertiary) and the types of diseases (preventable, curable) that they are afflicted with. Detailed household budget survey data, which contain the relevant questions to enable a full-fledged incidence analysis, can usually be used to determine such information. Unfortunately, such data do not exist for Uganda and the analysis will have to await the results of the Integrated Survey which is presently underway. Although data limitations make it extremely difficult to analyze who the actual beneficiaries of these expenditures were, the following sections try to infer this from the existing bits of information and from the evidence in other countries.

7.7   Table 7.2 examines the relative share of broad categories of poverty-oriented programs in current expenditures. The table shows that while the share of expenditures with the *potential* of reducing poverty in Uganda remains low, recent years have seen a significant improvement in the right direction, reflecting a recognition on the part of the Government of the importance of economic

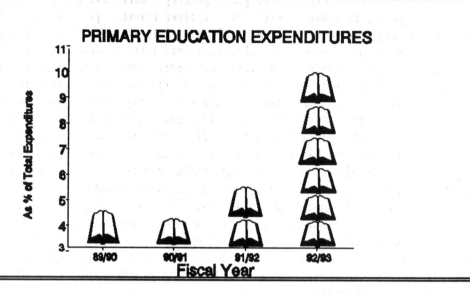

Figure 7.1: Primary Education Expenditures

and social sectors. The table shows that in 1991/92, approximately 33 percent of total locally funded expenditures were allocated for the purpose of enhancing human resource development, while about 7 percent went towards critical economic services.

Education

7.8   The role of education in increasing economic productivity and improving the quality of peoples's lives through better health and nutrition has been well documented.[113] As mentioned earlier, it has been demonstrated that the economic and social returns to primary education are significantly higher than the rates of return for secondary and tertiary education. Policies that expand access to good quality primary education contribute significantly to poverty reduction. Furthermore, even if they never enter the labor force, the returns for expenditures on educating women are substantially higher than those for men. Studies in Bangladesh, Brazil, Kenya, and Columbia have shown that families tend to be better fed and the children less likely to die, the more educated the mother. Countries are justified in giving priority to primary education both on equity and efficiency grounds.[114] The Government of Uganda appreciates the importance of education and its expenditures on education as percent of GDP increased from 0.9 percent in 1989/90 to 1.3 percent in 1991/92, implying an average real growth rate of over 20 percent.

---

[113]   For examples, see *Primary Education: A World Bank Policy Paper*, World Bank, 1990; for the socio-economic benefits of educating women, see *Investing in All the People: Educating Women in Developing Countries*, Lawrence Summers, 1992 (summarized in Box 3.9).

[114]   The economic and social returns of primary education are well known. According to the World Bank's policy paper on primary education, four years of education increased small-farm productivity by 7 percent across 13 developing countries and by 10 percent in countries where new agricultural techniques were being introduced. Primary education is also observed to have positive social effects. For instance, women with more than four years of education have 30 percent fewer children than women with no education and their children have mortality rates only half as high.

7.9   The Government also clearly recognizes primary education as a priority area in its poverty reduction strategy and its stated objective is to achieve universal primary education by the year 2001/02. The strategy, as set out in the White Paper on Education Policy, is to shift the distribution of expenditure away from secondary and tertiary institutions towards the primary levels.[115] At present, secondary and tertiary education continue to receive financial resources which are in excess of what can be justified, given the resource constraint and the Government's priorities. While the share for secondary education has remained stable at an average of 0.2 percent of GDP during the period under review, the share of expenditure on tertiary education, as percent of GDP, has grown from 0.3 percent in 1988/89 to 0.8 percent of GDP in 1991/92. This represents an increase of 170 percent as compared with the 131 percent increase in primary education. In addition, on a per pupil basis, government expenditure on secondary and tertiary education is quite high relative to primary education. Expenditures on university education and secondary education were 157 times and 3 times that of primary education respectively in 1991/92. Generally, post-primary students come from relatively better-off families, who can afford to pay for the advanced education of their children. Given that the rich benefit more than the poor from expenditures on higher education and that the returns to higher education are less than those for primary education, prompt action to increase cost recovery at the tertiary level, as recommended by the White Paper and the Report of the Makerere University Visitation Committee, is justified.

Health

7.10   It is common knowledge that poor health reduces the capacity to work, constrains the ability to increase income and adversely affects the quality of life. The link between poverty and poor health, therefore, is direct. Investments in health and nutrition have a variety of socio-economic benefits, including gains in productivity, learning and life expectancy. The gains from adequate health care are particularly significant for women of child bearing age.[116] It is, therefore, encouraging that, in the Three Year Health Plan, the Government is aiming at increased expenditure on preventive and primary health care, while selectively introducing cost recovery for curative health services. It is also equally important to insure that the poor, irrespective of gender and place of residence (rural or urban), receive their share of the benefits from investments in health.

7.11   The overall resources allocated to the health sector in Uganda are low; in 1991/92, about 0.5 percent of locally funded expenditures were allocated to the health sector, and this amount represented a 28 percent real annual average increase over 1987/88. When donor funding is taken into consideration, expenditures on health increased to about 2.5 percent of GDP in 1991/92. It is generally accepted that the absolute minimum recurrent expenditure necessary for effective primary and secondary health care is equivalent to about US$3-4 per capita per annum.[117] Uganda recurrent expenditure on health is less than US$2 per capita per annum as compared with Kenya which spends US$6, Zimbabwe which spends US$14 and Botswana which spends US$29. An important feature of expenditures on health is that the share of expenditures on preventive health care is very low as

---

[115]   See also *Background to the Budget*, 1992-93, Ministry of Finance and Economic Planning, June 1992.

[116]   According to the World Bank policy paper on primary education, more than one fourth of all deaths of women of child-bearing age are closely linked to childbirth. It is possible to avoid almost all of these deaths with basic family planning, prenatal care and assistance with childbirth.

[117]   See *Public Choices for Private Initiatives: Prioritizing Public Expenditures for Sustainable and Equitable Growth in Uganda*, World Bank Report No. 9203-UG, February 12, 1991, p. 83.

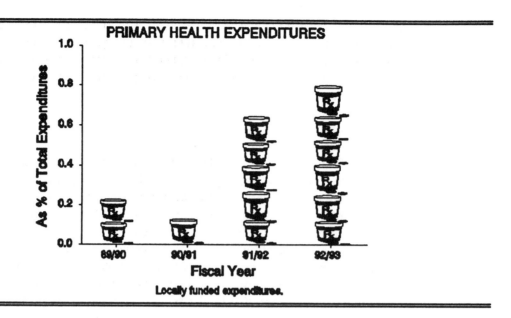

Figure 7.2: Primary Health Expenditures

compared to expenditures on curative services. In general, only about 10 percent of the expenditures on health go to preventive health care while curative care receives the remaining 90 percent.[118] During 1989/90-1991/92, the share of total expenditure on preventive health care, as percent of GDP, averaged 0.1 percent per year, while the corresponding share for curative health care during the same period averaged 1.3 percent, i.e., 10 times that for preventive health care. Since curative health care often benefits wealthier members of society in general, and those who live in urban areas in particular, the poor benefit disproportionately less from such allocation. A poverty-conscious program, therefore, should make more resources available to primary and preventive health care than curative health care. Charging wealthy members of the Ugandan society for curative medical services and using funds mobilized thus to improve access of the poor to preventive health care would be an appropriate strategy.

7.12   The Government recognizes this and its commitment is reflected in the high growth rates for the budgetary allocations to this subsector in the last few years. In 1989/90, the total actual central government expenditure on preventive health care (both recurrent and capital expenditure) amounted to U Sh 1,396 million. The corresponding amount for 1991/92 represents a real increase of 54 percent, with the budgeted amounts for 1992/93 representing a further real increase. Despite these improvements in the allocation of funds to the health sector, Uganda's per capita recurrent expenditures on primary and secondary health is very low compared to a number of African countries. The recent resurgence in preventable diseases is a clear indication of these low levels of expenditure. In 1990, preventable diseases like malaria, AIDS, diarrhea, pneumonia, anemia, and meningitis alone contributed to 53 percent of the deaths reported in 20 hospitals.[119] Nutritional levels, particularly of children, are also unacceptably low. Low nutritional levels expose a

---

[118]   According to the World Development Report 1990, on the average, an estimated 70-85 percent of the developing world's expenditure on health (both public and private) goes to curative health care. It appears that Uganda's expenditure on this sector is even higher than that for the developing world.

[119]   For details see *Uganda: Social Sector Strategy*, World Bank, 1993.

considerable proportion of the population to killer diseases. It is alarming to note that 54 percent of the deaths in hospitals are related to children under five years of age and that 55 percent of these deaths are due to malnutrition. Improvements in the quality of health conditions, therefore, have important implications not only on the welfare and productivity of individuals but also on national welfare and productivity.

Family Planning and Environment

7.13   Chapter 5 highlighted the quantitative implications of the high rate of population growth on poverty reduction in Uganda. The population growth rate, 2.5 percent according to the recent population census and higher according to the Social Sector Strategy report, is extremely high. The fertility rate of 7.3 per woman places Uganda among countries with the highest fertility rates in SSA (the other countries are Ethiopia 7.5; Cote d'Ivoire 7.3; Yemen 7.7; and Malawi 7.7). With such a high fertility rate, the average Ugandan women would spend about 22 years of her life with a child under six, as compared to only 10 years for the average Thai woman.[120] Projections made by the Population Secretariat of Ministry of Finance and Economic Planning indicate that if the fertility rate of 7.3 per women continues during the period 1988-2018, recurrent expenditures on primary education would climb from U Sh 9 billion in 1988 to U Sh 31.5 billion in 2018, in constant 1988 prices; reducing the fertility rate to 4 children per woman during the same period would cut these expenditures by more than 50 percent. Similar projections for expenditures in primary health care indicate that the Government will save about U Sh 30 billion over the same period if the fertility rate is reduced from 7.3 to 4 children per woman.

7.14   The growing population has increased the demand for charcoal and building poles and this has resulted in an increase in encroachment on the forests. In certain areas, population pressures have resulted in an intensification of farming resulting in soil erosion and stagnating yields. Population pressures, supplemented by several years of war which resulted in a breakdown of government control and abandonment of natural resource management and policies have taken a further toll on the environment.

7.15   The Government of Uganda does not have an explicit population and family planning policy and lags far behind other SSA countries in encouraging its citizens to have small, manageable families and informing them of methods of doing this. It is therefore imperative that the Government accord high priority to developing a national family planning program and closely monitor progress towards decreasing the presently high fertility rates.

Development of the Rural Areas

7.16   Uganda is a predominantly rural society, with a high dependence on agriculture for income and employment, and the poor are largely concentrated in rural areas. Consequently, emphasis on agricultural research and extension, rural roads and rural water supply should be areas of high public expenditure priority in order to impact positively on poverty reduction. As has been discussed in Chapter 5, Ugandan agriculture is characterized by extremely low productivity which can more than double if adequate provisions are made for effective and sustainable research and extension systems. Upgrading existing technology through adaptive research and supplementing this with efficient

---

[120]   *Effective Family Planning Programs*, The World Bank, 1992, p.2.

agricultural credit, marketing, input distribution, and other support services will go a long way in facilitating agricultural growth and reducing rural poverty.

7.17   Despite significant progress made over the last few years, a large proportion of the 20,000 kms of feeder roads in Uganda continue to remain in a state of acute disrepair. The rehabilitation of feeder roads should be a high priority as this will facilitate the inflow of essential farm and nonfarm inputs and the outflow of farm output and will accelerate the process of the monetization of the rural economy. Moreover, it will also encourage an expansion in the area under cultivation. While full rehabilitation of the entire feeder road network will not be possible as a result of economic and institutional constraints, even over the medium term, the rural feeder road rehabilitation program should be accorded high priority and should receive real increases in annual fiscal allocations. Where rehabilitation cannot be justified, the roads should be kept passable by making spot improvements so that smaller traffic can access the roads at all times. This is particularly important from the poverty reduction objective in that a significant amount of produce is transported via bicycle and motorcycle, particularly matoke, milk, poultry and charcoal.

7.18   At present, only about 20 percent of the entire population and about 15 percent of the rural population have access to clean, safe water. While the Government's long-term goal for the water and sanitation sector are well defined and seek to provide safe water and effective sanitation and health education for all who can be practically serviced, based on at least full cost recovery of recurrent costs, no formal strategy has been adopted to bring this about in any determinate time frame. Moreover, allocation of resources to the ministry dealing with water and sanitation have been extremely low historically. For instance, in 1990/91 and 1991/92, the share of ministerial expenditure (capital and recurrent) for water and sanitation as percent of total expenditure, was only 6.2 and 8.2 percent, respectively; these shares are extremely low when compared with other neighboring countries in SSA. Furthermore, the problems have been compounded by an extremely weak institutional structure characterized by poorly remunerated and motivated staff.

The Provision of Safety Nets

7.19   As discussed in Chapter 2, among the poor there is usually a segment of the population who need special assistance because they may not be able to take advantage of "regular" poverty alleviation measures or because these measures may not be enough. Social safety nets are intended to fill this gap. They include assistance (e.g., income transfers) to those whose poverty derives from a chronic inability to work (too old, too young, or handicapped). They also include temporary transfers to those affected by natural disasters or economic recessions. By their very nature, therefore, safety nets must be targeted. But targeting can be difficult and costly, as it requires careful monitoring to ensure that the assistance provided reaches all of those for whom it is intended and nobody else. Indeed, the administrative cost of targeting may be so high as to be unjustifiable. The following sections attempt to assess the effectiveness of existing safety nets and make suggestions for future interventions.

7.20   Generally speaking, all people falling in the category of the core poor are likely to be in need of special assistance, as they are unable to secure adequate nutrition and access to basic social services. In some cases, appropriate interventions may enable them to break the cycle of poverty within a relatively short period. For example, landless peasants may be given land and farm implements, and become self-sufficient within a couple of (good) cropping seasons; similarly, appropriate assistance to retrenched civil servants and demobilized soldiers should enable them to find new ways of earning a living. But in other instances, the assistance needed is likely to be long term, as in the case of orphans, or permanent, as in the case of the severely disabled.

Keeping Afloat

7.21   Poor and vulnerable people are constantly obliged as a matter of routine survival to devise their own coping strategies. This is particularly true of situations of increased stress and risk, such as those faced by the groups described earlier. They have no choice but to find their own solutions, because they can not afford to wait for assistance which may or may not come from outside. It should not be surprising, therefore, that in Uganda, as in many African countries, extended families have traditionally represented the main safety net. This safety net is most efficient in the rural areas, but reaches also into peri-urban and urban areas thanks to strong urban-rural linkages.

7.22   The role of the extended family in securing survival is best exemplified in the way communities have reacted to the orphan crisis. Throughout the country, orphaned children have been taken in by relatives, to the point that finding a family only caring for its own offspring is becoming a rarity. This is true in urban as well as in rural areas, and among all socio-economic strata. "In Rakai and Masaka children can be found with their paternal grandparents, uncles, aunts, and with their single parents, and maternal relatives. These established practices are now being used extensively and there are even examples of unusual and newly-emerging adaptations of this kind of child care such as divorced stepmothers and neighbors volunteering to look after children upon the death of parents."[121] The fact that in Uganda the number of street children is not particularly high for African standards (although it is growing) in spite of the large number of orphans indicates that communities are doing a commendable job in coping with the situation.

7.23   A number of factors, however, appear to threaten the continued effectiveness of such systems. First and foremost is the general impoverishment felt by people who find themselves struggling for survival and unable to offer assistance to their less fortunate relatives. In rural areas, such impoverishment appears to be caused by a combination of low agricultural productivity (because of lack of technology and labor shortage), a rise in the price of basic items, and localized land shortages. In the urban areas, households are physically separated from their larger families, and difficulties in communication and travel may be daunting. Should distance not be a problem, dependence on a (generally meager) wage has made it harder for households to afford responsibility for members outside the nuclear family. The AIDS pandemic has exacerbated all of the above. As the most productive members of society die leaving behind their children and parents, the surviving adults find themselves unable to care for an ever increasing number of dependents.

7.24   When the burden becomes too heavy, two reactions are possible. One is to literally give up, as in the case of the man in Rakai who abandoned his whole family when he realized that he had nothing to feed them. These cases are very rare. The most common reaction is to lighten the burden artificially by concentrating assistance selectively. As food and other resources become scarce, those outside the nuclear family are increasingly neglected. As a farmer put it, "if the choice is between feeding my children or my husband's mother, I will feed my children". In spite of the traditional respect accorded to older people, it appears that the elderly are the first to be left behind, but there are also reports of orphans who were refused by their indigent relatives. In the poorest areas, widows

---

[121]   Alden, John, Gerald Salole and John Williamson, *Managing Uganda's Orphans Crisis*, report prepared for USAID, July-August 1991, p. 26.

Box 7.1: The "Rwot Kweri"

"I am a member of a "rwot kweri" [=lord of the hoe]. There are twenty-six of us, all men. We work together three days a week, but there are groups that get together more often or less often. It depends on how they organize themselves. Some groups become so big that they have to split into two, because a "rwot kweri" should not be more than about thirty people. We go each time to the field of a different member. Mostly it is for digging and harvesting. Weeding is done by the women, who also have their groups—they call them "rwot awor", because awor is a nail they use as a tool to weed. We work all day together, and we eat together. We all contribute some food, depending on what we can afford; some times our host would only be able to offer us tea, so the others will provide the food. Occasionally, somebody even brings meat.

In this village the "rwot kweri" are very strong. They are what keeps us together, what helps us when things are difficult. For example, we help with widows, because we help the brother-in-law who takes them in to raise production by cultivating larger plots. The "rwot kweri" can also be like savings clubs: the harvest from a communal field would be sold to help one of the members to buy a hoe or to send a child to school. Last year we even helped an old woman who was not related to our "rwot kweri" because we felt sorry for her—her son was not helping her, and she was too weak to do the work and too poor to pay somebody. But this was an exception."

Source: Rapid Poverty Appraisal, August 1992.

---

and their children are no longer considered for assistance by relatives, because their case is not serious enough to warrant diverting scarce resources away from the nuclear family. It is not clear what is the threshold marking the onset of this selective assistance mechanism, which in any case is likely to be quite subjective. But it is clear that it is a reaction dictated by desperation, as Ugandans would generally relinquish their family obligations only in extreme cases. The point is that there is reason to believe that extreme cases are becoming more common, as witnessed by insistent reports of the destitution of many old persons.

7.25   People in the urban areas are increasingly experiencing what it means to be deprived of support from the extended family. Virtually everybody has had to resort to a variety of informal, or even illegal, activities. "Incomes earned by exacting fees for services that the public is ostensibly entitled to for free or at officially fixed prices partly supplement the wages of most civil servants. Those who are inclined to complain about the injustices of this are easily silenced by a simple, 'my friend, what shall I eat?'.... Corruption is a collective disease in Uganda that most citizens have problems passing judgement on".[122] An emerging phenomenon is that of teenage girls who resort to "sugar daddies" to pay their school fees (or even more basic needs) in exchange for "risk-free" sex; the growing incidence of AIDS among 15-19 year old girls is a sad commentary on the short-sightedness of such a coping strategy.

7.26   Fortunately, the assistance provided by the extended family is often complemented by community-based mechanisms. In most parts of Uganda, there is a tradition of community work. In Buganda, for example, rural communities would be called together by the sound of a drum to give assistance in case of death and funerals, or to achieve common objectives, such as well protection or

---

[122]   Christine Obbo, "Women, Children and a 'Living Wage'", in Holger Bernt Hansen and Michael Twaddle, eds., *Changing Uganda*, Fountain Press: Kampala (pp.99-100).

road maintenance. Communal systems of labor sharing are frequent especially in the Northern districts, and are known by different names depending on the type of labor performed and on the region—"rwot kweri", "rwot awor", "kalulu", "awak", "amuti", etc. (Box 7.1). Usually, they consist of a group of farmers (often of the same gender) who will get together on a regular basis to work on the field of each one of the members in turn.

7.27   In the absence of in-depth studies, it is difficult to quantify the contribution of these arrangements to indigenous social security systems.[123] It appears, however, that communal labor systems play a very important role, because they enable poorer families to share labor, agricultural tools and some times food (generally "superior" food rich in proteins) with more fortunate farmers. As labor shortage and lack of access to even the simplest technology are two of the main causes of poverty, it is clear that a system which gives the poor regular access to a pool of labor and tools acts as a powerful safety net. What is more, labor sharing clubs are not only an effective redistribution mechanism of key resources, but also a form of insurance against illness or other forms of incapacitation, because they guarantee continued agricultural production—and therefore survival—for their members.

7.28   Other community-based safety nets have started to operate thanks to the initiative of RCs. While the record of RCs as effective community mobilizers is mixed at best, there is no doubt that in many instances they have managed to organize youth clubs, women savings groups and other types of associations which function either as a safety net for the members themselves, as in the case of women's groups, or as a charity institution for the destitute, as in the case of youth clubs lending their labor to widows and old people (Box 2.4). There are also reports of savings associations based on occupation, e.g., among school teachers and among city prostitutes.

7.29   The positive role that RCs have the potential to play should not be underestimated. The deep emotional scars left by the horrors of the civil war and the disastrous spread of AIDS are manifesting themselves in withdrawal from communal activities, and generally speaking in lack of interest in life. Indeed, the majority of NGOs consulted felt that the biggest obstacle to poverty alleviation is people's lack of hope and the breakdown of traditional solidarity networks. In this context, the RC system, particularly at the lowest three levels, can provide a much needed catalyzing effect by forcing people to come out of their shell and search for common solutions to shared problems.

Is There Anybody to Help?

7.30   Responsibility for assistance to the most vulnerable groups falls mainly on the Ministry of Labor and Social Welfare (MLSW)[124] and the Ministry of Local Government (MLG). The former is mandated to assist vulnerable children (i.e., orphan, displaced, delinquent and abused minors), and also to handle distress cases, such as victims of natural disasters and abandoned mothers and children. The latter is in charge of community development in general and of disabled people (but disabled children are under the jurisdiction of the MLSW). Displaced families and Ugandan refugees returning from abroad are handled by the MLSW, while foreign refugees in Uganda are handled by the MLG.

---

[123]   For a quantification of "labor transfers" and a discussion of their implication in an African context see Joachin von Braun, "Social Security in Sub-Saharan Africa: Reflections on Policy Challenges", in E. Ahmad et al., *Social Security in Developing Countries*, Oxford University Press, 1991.

[124]   The Ministry of Labor and Social Welfare is the result of the union of the Ministry of Labor and the Ministry of Rehabilitation and Social Welfare. The latter was established in 1979 to cope with the impact of the civil war.

7.31   Both ministries have staff in each district, with a district officer in the district capital and field personnel (social workers, community development assistants) to cover the rural areas. In reality, many posts are vacant (either de jure or de facto), and personnel are concentrated in towns. Lack of transport makes it impossible to do field work, so only those able to report to the town office receive assistance. Even then, little assistance can be provided in the absence of a proper operating budget. District welfare officers, for example, have an imprest account of U Sh 70,000 per month for operating expenses. This sum should include an emergency fund for public assistance, but most often it has to be spent to keep the office running.

7.32   In the end, it tends to be up to the resourcefulness of individual civil servants to find ways to provide effective assistance. That is, it is a question of contacts with NGOs who can provide the needed support. Indeed, working with or through NGOs is so common for staff of MLSW and MLG that, without exception, those interviewed (both in headquarters and in the field) admitted that without NGO's help they would not be able to do their work. It must be recorded, however, that personnel in these two ministries appear to be very competent and surprisingly dedicated, given the difficult conditions under which they operate. One can not but sympathize with the frustration they expressed at their inability to carry out their mandate effectively.

7.33   A couple of examples may illustrate the degree to which the Ugandan Government depends on NGOs to provide safety nets to its people. When a displaced child comes to the attention of the social worker, there is seldom money to pay for public transport to take the child back to his/her relatives, let alone to pay for meals to be eaten while traveling. In any case, often children are not sure of where to go or public transport is not available, so they need to be accompanied with a vehicle. But usually the ministry has either no vehicles or no money for fuel. At this point, NGOs and donors are asked to step in and provide needed transport. It is estimated that about half of the operating budget of the Rehabilitation and Social Welfare Department comes from UNICEF and Save the Children.

7.34   The situation is similar for the handicapped. As it was mentioned above, disabled people (excluding children) are the responsibility of the Community Development Department. Each district, therefore, has a community development assistant in charge of such cases. But with no transport and pitifully little money, all the community development assistant can do in response to requests for help is to refer cases to NGOs, hoping to find one able to provide funding for the necessary treatment and aids. This happens in about 10 percent of the cases—90 percent of Uganda's disabled will never receive any assistance.

7.35   As a result of the inability of government finances and institutions to provide safety nets, a large number of international and local NGOs (sometimes backed by donors) have stepped in to give much needed help. While it is difficult to quantify the proportion of assistance provided by NGOs and by the Government, there seems to be wide agreement that NGOs are delivering about 90 percent of the assistance. The quality and type of safety nets offered by NGOs vary considerably, and it is beyond the scope of this document to offer an inventory. Some are very localized and specific, others cover entire counties with integrated development programs.[125] But the sheer number of NGOs (over 500 registered) and the fact that they appear to have taken responsibility for the delivery of almost all assistance should not be interpreted as an indication that help will be there for those who

---

[125]   Further discussion of the role of NGOs is presented in Chapter 8.

need it—regardless of the quality and scope of the services offered by different NGOs, only a very small proportion of those in need are reached.

7.36   In addition, NGOs have a tendency to concentrate on some vulnerable groups (generally, the most visible or the most "attractive" for sponsors) and in some areas. For example, last year there were 32 NGOs working in Rakai district,[126] but only three NGOs active in Kitgum and two in Karamoja. Similarly, there are over 70 NGOs and donors focusing on orphans, but we could not find a single organization concentrating on the elderly. Thus, it appears that whatever help is available from non-governmental sources is spread unevenly.

7.37   Asking whether it is preferable to have the bulk of public assistance delivered by the private sector rather than by the Government may be a rhetorical question. NGOs and government officials alike agree that it would be unrealistic to expect the MLSW and MLG (or any other ministry, for that matter) to be able to take primary responsibility for the delivery of assistance to the most vulnerable groups. The Government not only lacks the resources to implement direct intervention programs, but lacks the flexibility to respond rapidly to emerging local needs. NGOs are filling a need that cannot be met in any other way.

Safety Nets for the Future

7.38   What then should the role of the Government be? There seems to be wide agreement among civil servants and development workers that the MLSW and MLG (and other ministries) should focus on three responsibilities, i.e., providing policy guidance, coordinating and monitoring NGO activities, and ensuring that government bureaucracy does not get in the way.

7.39   The recently completed National Plan of Action for Children is an example of the key role the Government could play in ensuring that national policy is sensitive to the needs of the most vulnerable groups. The Plan is the result of a collaborative process which involved different government bodies and NGOs and will carry a very important message, as it will be the first case in Africa of a complete rewrite of laws for the rights of children—and inevitably, of mothers. The point here is that, while it is true that the Ugandan Government (like many other African governments) can do little to provide concrete safety nets, it can at least prevent some people from ever needing safety nets by safeguarding their rights. In this vein, a revision of inheritance and marriage property laws to strengthen the position of women and children would represent a substantial contribution, at a relatively low cost, to the welfare of orphans and widows, and of divorced women and their children.

7.40   The need for Government to coordinate and monitor NGO operations can hardly be overemphasized and will be discussed further in Chapter 8. While most NGOs are doing excellent work, the activities of some local NGOs (the so-called "briefcase NGOs") appear to be determined by political or financial ambition more than by the desire to help the needy. In other cases, intentions may be good, but a limited understanding of the situation or mere incompetence produce projects which are actually harmful. A case in point are orphanages where children have been found to live in unsanitary conditions or without proper care. Not only were these orphanages unable to provide appropriate assistance, but their very existence undermined traditional coping mechanisms, as

126   John Alden et al., op. cit., p. 36.

communities will tend to slacken their efforts for self-reliance if an institutional alternative is readily available.[127]

7.41   Given the proliferation of NGOs, and the doubtful nature of some of them, the recent establishment of some umbrella NGO organizations (UCOBAC, NUDIPU, etc.) to coordinate the activities of all NGOs operating in a specific field should be welcomed. But these umbrella organizations cannot be a substitute for government leadership. The Government must take responsibility in ensuring that the efforts of donors and NGOs produce the best possible results given the means available. This requires coordination, close monitoring, the setting of standards and, where needed, guidance.

7.42   The resources presently available to the MLSW and the MLG are not enough to allow them to carry out effectively the responsibilities described above. Notwithstanding the fiscal constraints discussed above, their budget needs to be increased to pay at least for the travel and communication necessary for effective monitoring. Coordination would be facilitated by the creation of a computerized database on projects intended to provide safety nets, including their scope, location and target group. This would avoid wasteful duplication, help spread scarce resources more evenly and identify neglected areas for future interventions. An in-depth study of how effective NGOs operate would make it possible to draw general guidelines for implementation and allow the Government to establish (and possibly enforce) standards for the operation of NGOs. For example, the MLSW and MLG are keenly aware of the importance to base outside assistance on existing coping mechanisms at the community level, so as to foster self-reliance. Identifying the key features of NGO projects which have successfully used such an approach would enable the MLSW and MLG to capitalize on the experience of these projects and to guide other NGOs in a similar direction.

7.43   Better coordination among government bodies is also essential. While the MLSW and the MLG have the major responsibility for the provision of safety nets, their work should be facilitated and complemented by the concerted efforts of a number of other ministries. The computerized database on NGOs mentioned above, for instance, could only be created with the assistance of the NGO Board in the Ministry of Internal Affairs. Similarly, a revision of existing laws to strengthen the position of women and children necessitates close collaboration with the Ministry of Justice, especially for its enforcement. The provision of basic social services which are presently beyond the reach of the most vulnerable groups is primarily the responsibility of the Ministries of Health and Education, while the Ministry of Information and Broadcasting could play a critical role in changing societal attitudes and behaviors which contribute to, or even cause, the misery of the neediest (e.g., shunning of the handicapped).

7.44   Regardless of the efforts of Government and NGOs, the bulk of the work will still have to be done by the communities themselves. Community mobilization is therefore imperative.[128] The question is how to bring it about, especially because the capacity to mobilize people tends to be determined more by personal qualities than training or position. Some NGOs have employed village development workers with good results, while others have relied on community development

---

[127]   For examples and further discussion, see John Alden et al., op. cit., and Abby Nalwanga-Sebina and James Sengendo, *Orphaned and Disabled Children in Luwero and Kabale Districts*, and in *Uganda Child Care Institutions*, mimeograph, December 1987.

[128]   Too often mobilizing the community turns out to mean mobilizing women. Given the already very heavy demands on women time, any effort to mobilize the community should be mindful of women's tight schedule.

assistants (whose work is facilitated by providing transport or other perks). Indeed, experience from other poor African countries suggests that one of the best ways of mobilizing communities to improve their own welfare, *and to do so in a sustainable fashion*, is to work through local people reputed for their honesty and their leadership skills.[129] Teachers, traditional chiefs and RC1 members are likely candidates to play such role, provided there are mechanisms to prevent them from taking advantage of the increased power they will inevitably acquire. Biannual popular elections of RCs are one such mechanism, as demonstrated by the considerable turnover observed in the second round of elections.

7.45   Self-help initiatives at the community level can go a long way, but where absolute poverty is widespread, little can be achieved without extra resources. In extreme cases, it is a question of handouts such as resettlement kits. But in most cases, the challenge will be to find a way of reinforcing the capacity of communities and families to care for their less fortunate members while at the same time providing outside help for those who are likely to fall through the local safety nets. Integrated projects run by a number of NGOs have chosen an approach whereby communities are mobilized and their efforts complemented by the provision of in-kind inputs, either material (agricultural tools, blankets, iron sheets) or technical (training, preventive care). But NGOs can only reach a small minority, so an alternative mechanism for giving communities access to extra resources must be found.

7.46   Because hardship cases are generally well known in the village, the community itself is in the best position to identify those who most need help. Thought should be given to the establishment of a village development fund to be used in projects that would increase the effectiveness or coverage of safety nets at the community level, either by assisting the disadvantaged people directly (e.g., giving hoes and fertilizers to widows) or by enabling the community members to provide assistance (e.g., giving hoes and fertilizers to those who take responsibility for abandoned old people). The fund should be made available directly to the communities and accountability at the local and national level should be firmly established. The proposed Community Action Trust appears to be conceived along these lines and deserves closer consideration (Chapter 8).

---

[129]   A word of caution is needed here. Although community efforts are recommended, they should not be pursued at the expense of people's work for their own sustenance. We heard complaints of peasants who had to contribute time to community projects in spite of the fact that their fields needed immediate attention. But the RCs had promised to the NGOs, and refusing to participate in the communal work would have meant having to pay a fine.

Institutional Framework for Delivering Essential Services

"Institutional development concerns the creation of organizational competencies and values that are functional to development. And if development is to be accompanied by poverty reduction, those organizational competencies and values must also be attuned to the needs of the poor." (Lawrence Salmen, "Institutional Dimensions of Poverty Reduction", PRE Working Paper 411, May 1990, p. 16.)

Background

8.1   The current situation in Uganda offers unique opportunities as well as challenges. The aftermath of decades of war, continuing security problems in some areas, AIDS, and drought magnify the general problems of poverty. Despite the advances made by the Government to improve the security situation, the rural poor (indeed, the rural population in general) receive few, and in many cases, no services from the government administration. While the RC system is bringing rural Uganda back into a coherent polity, there is still little government infrastructure on the ground. If the poor of Uganda are to make advances in the medium term, capacity must be strengthened or created to provide them with key social services. Building such capacity is dependent on the needs and characteristics of the ultimate clients—the citizens of Uganda, the communities in which they live, and the institutions which already serve them, or might be expected to serve them. These institutions include organizations such as government agencies, NGOs, and commercial service providers, as well as institutions not embodied in organizations, such as customary law, and shared labor and revolving credit associations. These inter-related institutions form networks which can help or impede communities in reducing poverty.

8.2   Given the urgency and magnitude of the problems faced by the poor of Uganda, the Government has recently shown interest in a model of development oriented toward government support for community initiative. Supported by the Government's stated objective of decentralization, the emerging model is one where communities will be given increasing responsibility to formulate their own development activities, which will then be supported by the district administrations with the help of NGOs and other community based organizations. The objective of this chapter is to lay out some of the issues which need to be addressed to make this model work, and to suggest some initial steps.

Governmental Institutions

8.3   The Ugandan administration can currently do little more than it has been doing: pay minuscule salaries (often late), provide equipment and supplies occasionally, and in far smaller quantities than needed, and pay allowances for meeting attendance to Kampala and Entebbe based civil servants. There are staff on the ground, but the Government is without the means to pay them a living wage or to provide fuel and vehicles for them to visit their "clients."[130] When they do reach the communities they are meant to serve, it is almost always through donor projects—with donors in

---

[130]   "Clients" will be used here instead of "beneficiaries," which has a connotation of passive receiver of goods and services.

Uganda consisting of both official bilateral and multilateral aid agencies and of non-governmental organizations.

8.4   Many civil servants at all levels have been able to survive only by supplementing income from government jobs. Often they do this through outside business activities, or through having salaries supplemented by donor and NGO projects. The "tipping" system also seems extremely widespread. In effect, these tips represent user fees. Now, in addition to the civil service, there are reports that some RC members also must be "tipped" for various functions.

8.5   The net result is that many staff are unable to perform their duties on a regular basis. This system will not end among civil servants at least until they are paid a living wage. Despite the resulting low morale, NGOs and donors who have worked with Ugandan staff in the field indicate that most are eager to do their jobs, if only they can be assured of a reasonable salary in return. When field staff are drawn into adequately funded projects, they have proven, in most cases, to be competent and dedicated.

8.6   While no reliable information is available on how many communities are being served in this way, observers agree that most of rural Uganda is not systematically receiving basic services that contribute to poverty reduction. In recent policy documents, the Government has emphasized refocusing the institutions of Government on basic poverty-reducing or -alleviating services such as community-based primary health care, clean water and basic sanitation, primary education, feeder roads, and integrated agricultural extension services, but Government presently and for the foreseeable future lacks resources for staff and equipment to implement this policy change. Considerable emphasis must be put, for the short and medium term, on projects and programs of official donors and NGOs.

8.7   Outside agencies, both official and NGOs, have been implementing service delivery projects directly through parallel systems, such as project implementation units, often using their own personnel and equipment. These are managed outside the mainstream of government ministries so that donors have more control over the outcome. Often these agencies are motivated by their need to account, in turn, to critical stakeholders: their own financiers. However, with such a system in place, government agencies and staff are shut out from the learning experience they could be getting in planning, managing or producing the services. Individual Ugandans may acquire experience and skills while working for these projects, but institutional problems cannot be solved simply by improving the skills of individuals; instead, the patterns of relationships and behavior (including accountability) at the organizational level must change. This is what is missing when quasi-independent implementation units are set up.

8.8   Another problem has been the fragmentation of government ministries: donors (again, including some NGOs) fund vertical interventions which ultimately work against focusing ministries on integrated efforts to relieve poverty. The result has been a series of unconnected services offered to communities by different individuals in an uncoordinated way; the total may be less than the sum of the parts, rather than more, as some of the interventions may work against each other. Rather narrow objectives may be achieved, but at the expense of even more basic concerns.[131]

---

[131]   For example, the French fund a French Teachers Program and French Teacher Training. While this might be an important initiative, it does not necessarily reflect the priorities of a country where there are no texts in rural schools, and where teachers' salaries have to be paid by communities.

8.9   An unintended effect of projects like the Program for the Alleviation of Poverty and the Social Costs of Adjustment (PAPSCA) may have been to increase the perception of poverty alleviation as something which is not done through the core functions of line ministries. Originally meant to be a focal point within Government for the coordination and monitoring of poverty reduction work, PAPSCA has come to be widely regarded not as part of the Ministry of Finance and Economic Planning but as an autonomous World Bank project (even though other funders are also involved). Its physical location in a suburb of Kampala accompanied by a general lack of information about it (among other government bodies as well as NGOs) reinforces its isolation.

8.10   While PAPSCA was set up with the intention of facilitating anti-poverty efforts, the long, slow procedures and detailed reporting required have made it difficult for NGOs to work with PAPSCA. As implemented, it has underscored the fact that, at present, providing essential social services e.g., in the areas of primary health and education, is not the core function of Ugandan ministries, but rather the province of a few scattered projects. The design team, including the NGOs on it, each put in a piece in their area of action; the few donors who contribute to the project have completed the "Christmas tree" effect by funding projects in their area of interest. The result is certainly not a national program; rather, it is a marginal collection of projects of varying quality spread far too thinly to have a broad impact on poverty.

8.11   The overall result of the "projectization" of ministries has been that staff are getting paid and doing work, but the senior ministry officials are little involved in prioritizing, deciding the mix of projects, or in realistic strategic planning, and they have no responsibility for seeing that the complex system moves overall in the desired direction. They also get very little experience in managing the budget, whereas the project directors have much more control of resources. In this context, there is little incentive for government planning to be anything more than devising a "wish list." While the arguments for donors keeping control of the money can be compelling for the donors, and for the sake of the desired programs, the problem of government incapacity will never be solved if this state of affairs continues.

8.12   There are signs that this trend is being reversed both within Government and among donors. The Government has recently embarked upon a comprehensive civil service reform program aimed at "professionalizing" the civil service and the beginning of movement toward strengthening government ministries to carry out core poverty alleviation functions has been perceptible. Among the donors, UNICEF, for example, has consolidated diverse projects into one project called "Capacity Building for Sustainable Primary Health Care," to support the Government's desire to put primary health care at the core of the ministry's functions. Ultimately, Government and donors will have to agree together on the priority actions for investment in the productive sectors and in human resources, as well as on how to fund safety nets in the interim. Better coordination of aid to Government (including aid from the large NGOs) is a prerequisite to long-term poverty reduction.

Self-Help Groups

8.13   At the same time, Government recognizes that self-help groups have often organized to meet their own most pressing needs; for example, communities have kept schools running through parent - teacher associations (PTAs) which have supplemented and paid teachers' salaries and overhauled facilities, and families have expanded to take in AIDS orphans. Policy documents emphasize the Government's desire to design a system which will support these community initiatives. A major step in this direction is the decision to decentralize many government decisions to the district level, and to redeploy much of the administration to district and local field offices. Certain policy documents have also referred to Government's intention to establish policy and mobilize resources for the provision of services, but to arrange with other bodies to actually deliver the services. The Government can contract with either voluntary or commercial sector organizations[132] to actually run the services. Indeed, the Government increasingly recognizes the important role played by the voluntary sector,[133] whether organized into community-based groups or non-governmental organizations. The next sections will discuss features of community self-help groups and NGOs which affect the degree to which their capacity to serve the poor can be increased in the short and medium term.[134]

8.14   Community organization has been responsible for keeping some services—most notably primary education—running in Uganda. The developmental resources represented by communities have always been underutilized because development was conceived of as coming from the outside, "modern" sector. The Government now recognizes that it should support the efforts of the ordinary people of Uganda, rather than expecting them to wait for government-initiated development activities, which may be long in coming and unsuitable for prevailing conditions.

8.15   Those communities that have received support services from Government and donors have often received them through vertical projects, with one agent prepared to offer only a narrow, if essential, service—vaccinations *or* drugs *or* nutrition, advice on livestock *or* on crops. Both Government and donors have stated their intent to move toward integrated service delivery, where the same person could be a resource for all basic health services or for all of a farming system. This would ensure that separate interventions do not work against each other, and that clients can have "one-stop shopping."

8.16   The Government's new position of supporting community action would ensure a more demand-driven system, with communities empowered to say what they need. The resulting projects would be better adapted to their micro-environments. At the same time, community-managed development projects, whether providing community services or upgrading returns from economic activities, are labor-intensive and require time. Community health management committees, for example, have a benefit (over the long term, better health means less time spent caring for the sick and more people engaged in economically productive activities which improve family quality of life) and a cost (members have to attend meetings, work out arrangements with health care providers, and manage the production of health services).

Non-Governmental Organizations

8.17   Government is increasingly stating its commitment to support community self-help, but NGOs have long experience in doing so. The state of knowledge about NGOs in Uganda is typical for

---

[132]   Together, these are often referred to as the "private" sector, but since that term sometimes includes and sometimes excludes the voluntary sector, they will be referred to by the more specific "voluntary" and "commercial" sectors here. The voluntary sector is also sometimes referred to as "non-governmental".

[133]   See for example the Health Three Year Plan, cited in the Social Sector Memorandum, or the National Plan of Action for Children.

[134]   There is no legal definition of the difference between these two kinds of groups. However, informally, there seems to be agreement that, in the Ugandan context, community self-help groups are temporary and informal; if they expect to become permanent, and if they have a formal structure, they should register as NGOs.

developing countries: we do not even know how many development NGOs exist, much less how many communities they serve, what kinds of activities they engage in, how effective they are, and how much non-governmental funding they mobilize. There is not even an accepted vocabulary to help distinguish between different kinds of NGOs (some organize charitable relief; others work with communities to implement community development projects; others supply credit or other development services; some carry out advocacy or policy-advising functions; some faith-based NGOs have been operating health and education services for decades, while newer secular NGOs are developing new programs).[135] However, some general points can be made which have a bearing on what kind of partners NGOs can be in Ugandan development.

8.18   In some circles, NGOs are respected for those qualities that represent NGOs at their best. Religious NGOs run the best medical facilities in the countryside, and supply more health care of better quality than the Government. Many NGO staff work long hours for little money because of their commitment to development. They work in communities with groups that present the toughest development challenges: the disabled, AIDS orphans, war widows. Their work is based on a commitment to community participation and pluralism, rather than dependency on Government. They are closer to the clients and know more about their needs than remote officials. They can tailor services to niches, whereas Government is set up to offer a standard package which may not meet all needs; they pilot new technologies. Their costs are lower than those of Government.

8.19   In other circles, it is suspicion, based on experience of some "bad" NGOs, that dominates. Bad NGOs are fronts for private gain rather than communal benefit; they are private businesses seeking the NGO label to get tax exemptions; they are agents of external actors linked to political factionalism in Uganda; they don't have anything to contribute to policy, since they don't understand the macro aspects of development; they mobilize money from outside but are not required to account for it; they work to benefit special interest groups, whereas the Government has the responsibility to ensure services and benefits to all Ugandans. They have a reputation for low-cost service delivery, but in fact there is little information available on costs.

8.20   Both of these attitudes are based on experience; there are NGOs doing excellent work, while others calling themselves NGOs are incompetent and/or fraudulent. These are the extremes; probably most Ugandan development NGOs are somewhere in between on competence and accountability, with hundreds who are at least trying to do good development work. While NGOs can choose their own beneficiaries, those they choose are sometimes the most vulnerable.

8.21   It is incontestable, however, that NGOs will be an important element of the poverty-reducing institutional framework. The challenge is to develop a framework for partnership among Government (both administration and RCs), NGOs and community groups to enhance competence, transparency and accountability in NGOs and community groups as well as Government. The recently established District (or National) Community Action Trust could be one such instrument (see below).

Coordination between Government and NGOs

8.22   The Government of Uganda has set up registration and coordination systems to weed out fraudulent NGOs and strengthen legitimate NGOs. The intention has been admirable, but there are

---

[135]   The Ministry of Finance and Planning, with World Bank support, is undertaking a study to answer some of these questions.

now many government bodies involved in NGO coordination, with no one having sufficient resources and staff to offer real assistance to NGOs. The result is that rather than assisting NGOs, the system confuses them, with different actors each having their own requirements.

8.23   Ugandan NGOs are required to register with the National Board for NGOs, housed in the Ministry of Internal Affairs. International NGOs first have to work out an agreement with the most relevant line ministry. To register, Ugandan NGOs explain their objectives and plans to their local RCs. If they can get endorsements from the RCs 1-3 in the area in which they intend to work, the applications then go to the National Board through the district administrator. NGOs report that recently an extra step, not specified in the legislation, has been required. The district administrator, instead of forwarding applications with endorsements from the RCs to Kampala, gives them to the Internal Security Organization, which goes back to the RCs 1-3. If no problems are found, the application is sent to the National Board.

8.24   The Board consists of a two members of the public and one representative from each of 12 ministries/government agencies.[136] Each NGO is required to present its organization chart, work plan, and constitution to the Ministry of Finance and Economic Planning (MFEP), which has to certify that the NGO's program is in line with national priorities. It is recommended that NGOs take this material in person to the MFEP; those which are sent from the National Board may languish in someone's in-box. In practice, then, the system works best if someone from the NGO can come to Kampala to hold the necessary discussions with officials in MFEP, and often with the relevant line ministry or ministries as well.

8.25   After registering with the National Board, NGOs may be able to obtain tax exemptions for imported goods and work permits for foreign staff. There are long delays in processing these, and they are not always granted. As a result of the system of "tipping" officials who provide service (such as signatures), NGOs may also need to make payments at any point in this process. When such payments are large—reportedly 10-15 percent of foreign currency expected—NGOs inflate items such as staff salary in their accounts for donors, since donors will not supply money for "tips," and NGOs cannot afford them from their own resources.

8.26   Records on NGOs are kept in different locations in Government. The National Board keeps the applications, but work plans, constitutions and organization charts, as mentioned above, are sent to the MFEP. The Aid Coordination Secretariat (ACS) in the Prime Minister's Office has been designated as the lead government agency for NGO coordination, and it has periodic progress reports which some NGOs send. Many NGOs are never heard from again at the national level until it is time to re-register. They should, however, make annual reports to their District Development Committee.

8.27   Both the ACS and the National Board try to monitor NGOs activities, the ACS through requesting regular reports and the Board through occasional field visits. Fuel, vehicles and allowance are necessary for the latter, and they are rarely available. The District Administration (DA) may also have progress reports or otherwise be well informed about what NGOs are doing in the district. Some DAs have held coordination meetings including NGOs; others have sought to control NGO activities too closely, and have lost the cooperation of NGOs for these meetings.

---

[136]   See Non-Governmental Organizations Registration Statute, 1989; Statutory Instruments 1990 No. 9, The Non-Governmental Organizations Regulations, 1990; Report of the Vice President's Select Committee on Non-Governmental Organization, April 1992.

8.28   With formal authority for NGO coordination, the ACS holds monthly discussion fora. The ACS has also tried to mediate in NGO-financier disputes. The ACS seems to be generally considered by the NGOs as trying to offer assistance, even if this is limited by resource constraints. Officials of other ministries also have an interest in coordination: Ministry of Local Government in the coordination of NGO activities on the ground; MFEP in advising on how foreign currency should be used; the Ministry of Foreign Affairs in the programs of international NGOs and local chapters of international NGOs (such as the YMCA). The Ministry of Labor and Social Welfare may try to revive the National Council of Voluntary Social Services, a body which used to have some of the functions carried out by the ACS. In addition to all these agencies, NGOs may need multiple contacts in the line ministries as well.

8.29   As of July 1992, 506 NGOs were registered, of which 104 were listed as foreign NGOs. Estimates of the total number of NGOs in Uganda range from 800 to 1,000; some may be registered at the district level without being registered at the national level.

Creating a Framework for Collaboration

8.30   The institutional challenge facing Uganda is to create a framework in which Government, NGOs, self-help groups, and donors all make a contribution to poverty reduction. Uganda, like many countries, is a conglomeration of micro-environments which makes it difficult to apply blanket solutions to the whole country. Activities in one sector may be organized quite differently from those in another, e.g., a system for providing rural credit can be quite different from one providing primary health care or education. The system that is ultimately needed is a "learning system", in which numerous small activities develop effectiveness and then efficiency before expanding.[137] These grassroots-level activities should be closely adapted to local needs and preferences, and supported by government policies creating favorable conditions for increasing productive activities and investment in human resources at the local level.

8.31   *Assisting Community Projects.* In the short term, there is little question that with Government and NGO capacity for delivering services able to satisfy only a portion of need, community self-help will be the vehicle for many community improvements. In line with the intention to support self-help efforts of Ugandan communities, the 1992/93 budget speech introduced the idea of a District Community Action Trust (DCAT), a fund which would finance community projects throughout Uganda. Development efforts would not have to go through the long, complex donor project cycle, and money could be released quickly for small projects. Community groups would be the primary users of such funds, but they could call on NGOs for technical assistance if needed. The funds would be administered at District level, and not necessarily by Government.

8.32   There is experience in Uganda with this sort of assistance to small, local NGOs and community-initiated projects. The experience of the Small Funders' Network and some NGOs is particularly relevant, since many already provide this kind of support. The Community Action Program in the Northern Uganda Reconstruction Project will generate further lessons about setting

---

[137]   See, among others, David Korten, "*Community Organization and Rural Development: A Learning Process Approach,*" Public Administration Review, Sept.-Oct. 1980: 480-511, and Larry Salmen, "*Reducing Poverty: An Institutional Perspective*", Poverty and Social Policy Series, Paper No. 1, Program Design and Implementation, Washington, World Bank, 1992; Sharon Holt, "*The Role of Institutions in Poverty Reduction: A Focus on the Productive Sectors,*" PRE Working Paper No. 627, Washington, World Bank, 1991.

up a national program. The rest of the development community needs to listen carefully to and learn from these funds as these are the groups who have the experience of funding community projects.

8.33   Typically, the fund is meant to respond to community demand. Communities articulate their needs; the funder investigates the feasibility of the project, and then provides materials and/or small amounts of money. However, as one of the officials running a fund for small projects said, "We have concluded that pure *responsiveness* is not *responsible*." Communities often present the kernel of a good idea, but need much assistance in making it into a workable activity. Even before getting viable project proposals, there is also a need to help communities analyze their situation and prioritize actions. Getting involved in this kind of community preparation is labor-intensive, both for members of the community and for the outside facilitators who are needed to help the process (supplying information as well as process facilitation). The small funders' limits are set less by the amount of money they can mobilize than by the small number of projects to which staff can give the necessary attention. A recent workshop on community-based women's income-generating activities showed that much of the women's profits were invested in community services, but the women's own longer-term needs were neglected.

8.34   While the DCAT would make funding available, the problem of technical assistance to communities in deciding what to do remains. Many NGOs and small funders in Uganda are convinced that it is a mistake to begin development activities without prior preparation of communities, in particular to identify strategic actions. In their experience, this preparatory phase—which might once have been called consciousness raising—can itself be slow. This stage requires outside facilitation, meaning that there must be considerable staff on the ground. These efforts should be supported by information sharing so that communities can learn from successful activities in other places.

8.35   *The Role of Information Systems.* Community experiments can fail if the policy environment does not support them. Policymakers need to know what is happening at the grassroots. But development cannot be only bottom-up, just as it cannot be only top-down; a mutual learning process is necessary. Policymakers need to know how innumerable small farmers make decisions about what to grow, and what the effects of policy changes are likely to be; communities need information about prices, markets, improved health and nutrition behaviors, etc. One dimension of learning systems, therefore, concerns two-way (or multiple-way) information channels.

8.36   Policymakers therefore have to learn: (i) what information they need; (ii) who has it; and (iii) what incentives need to be offered to the people who have the information to share it. NGOs often have useful information which is underutilized. Two typical obstacles to information sharing arise. Sometimes administrators do not recognize that they could use such information, and that the NGOs have it. At other times, the Government and NGOs cannot agree on terms under which they could share information; the Government may want the information NGOs have, without offering anything in return. The institutional chain has to get information back to the communities that need it, in ways that make sense to them. The RC system has been designed to be such a two-way system. While they have made much progress, more could be done using mass media, especially radio, as well as face-to-face communications.

8.37   In addition to developing channels for sharing information, a learning system has content requirements. Given the gravity of Uganda's problems, and the sense of urgency, there is a tendency for those trying to alleviate poverty to carry out as many activities as possible at full speed; unfortunately, often without learning much in the process about the impact of these activities on individuals and on sets of people. Success tends to be measured in terms such as numbers of people trained or crops planted, rather than enquiring what behavioral changes have occurred as a result of the intervention.

8.38   Without knowing much about impact of particular activities, it is impossible to cumulate learning through a system. Thus, while there are apparently numerous coordination meetings and mechanisms in Uganda, there is apparently too little learning as a result. In some cases, waves of fads sweep through the development community and are adopted with little examination; in others, a multiplicity of conflicting approaches leads to divisiveness. The result is the same in both cases: little learning about what works.

8.39   The activity frenzy has also led to a willingness to fund projects involving community-based organizations or NGOs with little investigation of the legitimacy of such organizations. Accountability, to either funders or client groups, is not very advanced, with the exception again of the RC system (three-year terms, with community recall possible).

8.40   The result has been too little cumulative learning about what works. The information that is available quantifies activities and inputs, but not usually outcomes. The entire system—donors, Government, and NGOs—must begin to ask more questions about, and require more evidence of, impact. Monitoring and evaluation systems should be devised to help individual organizations (whether community-based, NGO, government office, or donor) learn whether they are making progress. Recent participatory evaluation designs developed by several Ugandan NGOs are an encouraging sign, and should be discussed in the NGO forum and among the issue-based networks.

8.41   As important as the content of the information is the form in which it is presented. The monthly and quarterly reports from field offices (Government or NGO) are rarely converted into a form which is interesting to read. Central ministries may collate these into reports for the Prime Minister's office, but they still need to be transformed in a way that highlights innovations and lessons learned. A number of NGO consortia have started sectoral newsletters which are readable and offer useful information. At the level of the development community in Uganda, there is also much more potential for organizations to learn from each other, if information-sharing systems can be constructed. These do require the investment of resources in staff who can write readable articles geared to particular audiences and the communications equipment to support publication and dissemination.

8.42   The development of a learning culture would mean that Government, donors, communities, and NGOs would have to build a sense of shared purpose. None of these actors can control the others; they have to work from mutual appreciation and influence. Each set of actors has its own interests and constraints; nevertheless they also share a core commitment to building a socio-economic climate of development and poverty reduction. At present, there is little (positive) appreciation among some of the actors, and a lot of name-calling. Yet no one set of actors—Government, NGOs, donors, or communities—can achieve development on its own. The institutional framework has to build trust and interdependence.

8.43   *Expanding NGO Capacity.* In the current donor climate, there has been relatively abundant funding for NGO projects. Financial resources do not translate directly into good programs, however. In some instances, abundant funds have tempted NGOs to expand beyond their capacity to manage and program control quality. Sometimes they branch into new areas in which they have little experience, which also makes demands on management capacity. At one of the large international NGOs, a staff member declared that they have reached their current limit and will need a period of consolidation before taking on new activities or more clients. Thus, even with abundant financing, NGOs may not be able to expand capacity quickly.

8.44   While official donors have sought to fund NGO projects, they have been less eager to fund institutional development for local NGOs. There are two basic reasons for this:

(i)   NGOs are valued because they are seen as cheap service providers, and supporting better management systems and staff training raises costs;

(ii)   donors want their money to be used for the poor, not to support overhead.

However, investment in institutional development is necessary to help improve the quality of NGO programs as well as being a prerequisite to expansion. Monitoring and evaluation systems are scarce in NGOs (as they are in government programs). They take time and some specialized knowledge to set up. Receiving donor funding notoriously requires NGOs to set up special accounting and financial management systems. And NGO staff, no less than staff of official development agencies, need occasional training to keep up with the innovations in their fields.

8.45   Abundance of donor funding carries another danger for NGOs. In addition to mobilizing voluntary contributions, by definition NGOs are supposed to represent independent citizen initiatives. Donors (NGOs as well as official) have their own interests and priorities. NGOs seeking funding from such sources quickly learn to cast their proposals in terms of these donor priorities if they seriously expect to be funded. The result is strikingly parallel to government-to-government assistance: the donors, not the Government or the Ugandan NGOs, make the decisions about which programs are implemented and which are not. Nationals are shut out of one of the basic institutional development functions: setting priorities and strategies, unless they are prepared to risk losing donor funding.

8.46   Improving NGO competence is another complex process. In Uganda, many people have the most respect for the work of small, localized NGOs which mobilize committed local people to work for community benefit. Typically, such people can only spend part of their time on NGO work, because NGOs do not have the resources to pay a living salary. While their commitment and local understanding give them one set of competencies, such NGOs often plunge into activity to relieve a problem without a very broad analysis of the context and therefore without a strategy. They may end up intervening in the wrong time or place—for example, getting street children to return to their families rather than working with vulnerable families to prevent run-aways. Often such NGOs do not have monitoring and evaluation systems in place that would allow them to learn systematically from their experience. Their management systems are weak, limiting their scope to a very restricted scale.

8.47   Improving quality is often seen as professionalizing NGOs—hiring staff who have skills at project analysis, feasibility studies, proposal writing, monitoring and evaluation, accounting and management. Hiring professionals, however, is expensive, and often demotivates the volunteer staff who were the organizations' strength. It also tends to move the organizations toward a Kampala base, which adds further expense and distance between decisionmakers in the NGO and the clients. Opening a Kampala office to mobilize donor resources also opens the NGO to the temptation to tailor what it does to donor interests of the moment.

8.48   Another solution which is practiced in the NGO community is training. Typically, this training is offered to local NGOs by international ones, or by Ugandan professional intermediary

NGOs that specialize in services to the more localized ones. Staff can be trained through courses in accounting, proposal writing, analytic techniques, and so on. Staff can also be developed through working with larger (often international) NGOs on their projects. A small number of Ugandan NGOs are in a position to train other NGOs. Unlike other developing countries, in Uganda the international NGOs appear to be more oriented toward implementing their own projects than to strengthening capacity of Ugandan NGOs, though there are a few exceptions such as OXFAM (which acts in Uganda purely as a funder).

8.49   A third option would be to develop a corps of consultants or consultant NGOs who work with these small, local NGOs as needed. Such consultants would perform the tasks for which individual NGOs do not need full-time, long-term staff. They could help NGOs turn their project ideas into proposals which will stand up to funder analysis; set up new management systems to meet funder requirements; develop indicators for monitoring and evaluation. The use of these consultants need not be expensive: many NGO-oriented consultants offer their services at concessional rates to NGOs.

8.50   Networks or consortia of NGOs, or which include NGOs with other actors, can also help improve quality. The ones which have the most impact appear to be those organized on a subsector or issue basis.[138] At their best, networks and consortia structure the exchange of experience (informing members of innovations and lessons of experience) and information (about policies, research findings, etc.). Uganda also has an NGO-specific network, DENIVA, which attempts to raise quality by offering training, issue discussion sessions with donors and Government, and a code of conduct (adopted by the General Assembly but so far un-implementable because of lack of sanctions).

8.51   Discussions such as these also help NGOs, Government and donors become more familiar with each other. They identify possible allies and sources of interesting new approaches. These discussions can also help organizations judge each others' quality, although field visit must also be part of a system of choosing reliable partners.

8.52   *Building Government Capacity.* The Government has begun to articulate a vision of poverty alleviation through institutional pluralism (combining government initiatives with those of the voluntary sector in areas where market mechanisms will not suffice). The model is an attractive one built on recent understandings of limitations of the state and the value of independent citizen development action. The model is one of facilitation rather than control, and conforms closely to lessons learned from 30 years' experience of development interventions: where there is an economic base of millions of small farmers, Government can influence but not control socioeconomic activities. The same is true of the relationship between Government and NGOs: Government can seek to influence NGOs; it can control some areas of behavior regarding taxes and legal standing; but it risks losing their support altogether if it tries to turn them into mere instruments of Government.

8.53   As a consequence of its newness, this model is not yet widely understood or shared within Government. With much outside funding already going through NGOs, due in part to lack of accountability in Government, Government will not, in the short term, even be responsible for paying

---

[138]   In Uganda, there are existing networks and consortia in the fields of: community-based health care (UCBHCA), community-based child welfare (UCOBAC), disabled (NUDIPU), women (ACFODE), and natural resources (Natural Resource Management Project run out of Experiment in International Living, EIL). There are also coordination meetings on AIDS.

for all public services.[139] This gives the Government some time to develop a common understanding with the public of the role of the public sector, and to begin reorienting civil servants toward the new development model which emerges from the dialogue.

8.54   If the agreed upon system is one in which Government retains control of identifying, designing and producing services, the government needs to prepare one set of staff to plan and manage projects and to strengthen technical skills of extension staff in health and agriculture so that they can act competently as service producers, in addition to strengthening policy analysis and formulation skills. If an objective is to encourage community participation, staff will need some kind of training or reorientation. Supporting incentives will have to be designed to reward staff for working collaboratively with communities rather than executing directives from their superiors within government.

8.55   Certain government documents have recently proposed that Government will provide for services, but not produce them directly. There are two alternatives possible that conform to this model, and there is a crucial difference between the alternatives as far as both management of government staff and working with NGOs are concerned.

8.56   One alternative is for Government to hire contractors to carry out government-designed programs. In this case the Government will need personnel to identify, design and set standards. They will still need staff who are technically competent in community health, agriculture, and water and sanitation, but they will use these skills in judging how competently services are being provided by contractors, and they will need skills to write criteria, judge responses, and manage contracts. Many NGOs may decline to work with the Government on these terms, which would make them little different from contractors in the commercial sector. NGOs and many outside observers value the independent solutions and perspectives which NGOs bring to the development process, which would be in jeopardy under this system.

8.57   The other alternative is that Government and NGOs would jointly work out the nature of the programs to be implemented, possibly in consultation with the affected communities. For this option, government officials will need yet another set of skills, in negotiating, listening, and facilitating, as well as some familiarity with the technical fields.

8.58   Whichever option is chosen, Government will need to allow lead time for the development of training and personnel management systems congruent with the option they choose. Many of these skills, such as decentralized financial management, are discussed in more detail in the District Management Study.[140] Training and management systems can be tested in the pilot decentralization districts. Others are implied by the Government's decision to move toward integrated service delivery in health and agriculture; the Ministry of Health in particular needs to design incentives to reorient senior staff away from hospital-based health care to community health.

---

[139]   It is not, in the long run, desirable to have basic services funded through contributions of the voluntary sector. When services are tax-funded, citizens have more leverage and can be assured that services will be extended to the whole country.

[140]   See *Uganda: District Management Study*, Infrastructure Operations Division, Eastern Africa Department, World Bank, 1992, for further details.

Decentralization

8.59   The decentralization process offers an opportunity to simplify procedures for project preparation and financial management (including procurement). A simpler system will support community and NGO initiative, while complex regulations raise transaction cost, providing disincentives to collaborate with Government. Public information may be more helpful than complex procedures in bringing transparency to use of financial resources.[141]

8.60   For projects designed outside the communities they are intended to benefit, client assessment (preferably carried out in a participatory way) should become a regular part of identification and design. Uganda does not have money to waste on projects that do not meet client needs.

8.61   Donor as well as government discipline is necessary in this process. Ideally, Government, donors and NGOs can agree on the priority programs. Public expenditure reviews can be used as tools to hold both Government and donors to these agreements, which would include recentering government ministries around poverty-reducing programs and reducing the number of project implementation units. At the district level, NGOs could also be included in these reviews, permitting a more comprehensive picture of development interventions.

8.62   Donors should provide modest support for information sharing at central and district levels. District Development Committees should convene quarterly sectoral meetings including NGO and government staff. At these meetings, special attention should be given to NGO projects which are developing monitoring and evaluation systems and/or who have promising new approaches to share.

8.63   Making districts the primary level for registration of Ugandan NGOs is a logical extension of the decentralization policy and should be tested in the pilot districts for the decentralized management. District officials can forward information to the designated office in Kampala. With increasing security in the country, it may be time to reconsider the institutional location of the NGO Registration Board; its placement in the Ministry of Internal Affairs sends a powerful message of suspicion. More of the burden of coordination should fall on Government rather than NGOs (i.e., getting information to the necessary officials in different central ministries).

The District Community Action Trust (DCAT)

8.64   To address poverty on a broad scale, the DCAT should be designed as a social investment fund which disburses funds quickly for projects generated by self-help groups, with technical assistance being provided from NGOs or possibly local private firms as needed (and funded by the DCAT). The staff of the DCAT would be relatively small and based at district level; the main function would be publicizing the existence of the Trust, project appraisal and monitoring/evaluation. The district-level project approval committee should also be small and should include at least one representative of local NGOs, preferably chosen by NGOs within the district. Government or NGO technical people would not be permanent members, but would be invited to have a say on proposals in their sector. Some local resources should be mobilized for the projects in addition to outside financing.

---

[141]   Donors and NGOs alike recognized that it is easy to get around "paperwork accountability," whereas they could cite instances in which publicizing misuse of resources and corrupt practices by radio led to rapid improvement.

8.65   The process of designing the DCAT will be critical to its success. Few people in Uganda (whether Government, donor, or NGO) now understand what is meant by a social investment fund (SIF). However, the Government needs to establish a design process which will have the greatest possible chance of gaining commitment from donors, staff of the Government itself, and NGOs. In this process, focus group discussions (a well-understood methodology in Uganda) will be useful in generating ideas and concerns about the DCAT. Action-planning workshops could be used at a later stage to involve different groups of Government/donor/NGO stakeholders.

8.66   The Government might start by forming a small task force of no more than 6-8 people, including one Ugandan NGO, one international NGO, and one representative of the small funders network in Uganda to design the process for designing the DCAT. This group would draw out lessons from experience of the small funders and the NURP with such mechanisms, and would visit other countries (such as Guinea, Sao Tome and Principe, and Ethiopia) which either have or are farther ahead in designing SIFs. Part of their terms of reference would be to share their knowledge with others. This Task Force would not be charged with actually designing the DCAT (although they might ultimately do so); they would be in charge of seeking out information and ensuring that critical stakeholders participate in the DCAT design process, so that maximum ownership is generated.

Conclusion

8.67   The Government of Uganda presently lacks the capacity to deliver key social services to the poor, thereby adversely affecting their capacity to participate in the economic growth process. The decentralization program adopted by the Government, together with the interest that Government has shown in supporting community initiative, offers a unique opportunity to put in place an institutional framework capable of reaching and delivering these services to the poor. However, this new model is not widely understood or shared within Government. To take maximum advantage of this opportunity, the Government should devote some time and effort to develop a common understanding of what the new system will entail and to begin reorienting civil servants towards this new development model.

8.68   In order to effectively involve community based organizations and NGOs into the new process, government officials will need to learn to listen to their problems and to play a facilitating role. The excessively stringent procedures that presently exist for NGO registration, e.g., the verification by the Internal Security Organization, are not warranted and only serve to confuse and isolate these organizations. The Government should establish a simplified procedure for NGO registration, preferably at the district level, and there should only be one government body vested with the authority to coordinate NGO activity. As has been discussed above, such coordination should only involve the dissemination of valuable information and should not be interpreted as permission to regulate. The information system that is developed for the purpose should be a two-way system which provides policymakers with data of what is happening at the grassroots level and also feeds information back to the NGOs and the communities. With the right design, the DCAT can be used effectively as a tool to develop a framework of partnership among the Government and the NGOs and community groups. Learning from the experience that other countries have had with social funds, the Government should give high priority to designing a system which will gain the maximum commitment from the donor community, the NGOs and the cadre of civil servants who will ultimately be responsible for the day-to-day functioning of the system.

A Strategy for Reducing Poverty

"With appropriate policies, the poor can participate in growth and contribute to it, and when they do, rapid declines in poverty are consistent with sustained growth."(World Development Report, World Bank, 1990, pp. 51-52.)

9.1   As has been discussed earlier in this report, the decade and a half of civil strife which plagued Uganda during the 1970s and the early 1980s shattered its economic base, depleted its stock of human capital and, despite its rich soil and fertile climate, reduced it to one of the poorest countries in the world. While peace and security have now returned to most parts of the country and the economy has started to pick up again, the quality of life in Uganda today is much lower than it was when the country attained independence in 1962. As if this historical legacy were not enough, the AIDS pandemic has now gripped the nation in a vise and threatens to rob it of its most productive segments of society, i.e., those falling between 15 and 45 years of age. Against this backdrop, and the seemingly overwhelming problems facing them, the NRM Government must be complimented for their tenacity and determination to improve the lot of Uganda's citizens. During the past five years, the Government has implemented a far-reaching economic reform agenda which has today transformed Uganda into one of the most liberal economies in Sub-Saharan Africa. With the liberalization of the exchange and trade regime, the abolition of the Industrial Licensing Act, the promulgation of a new investment code, and the gradual liberalization of agricultural pricing and marketing, the Government has succeeded in establishing some of the fundamental pre-conditions that are essential for sustainable growth. However, the unfinished agenda is large and there is little cause for complacency. If the Government's overarching objective is to make a serious dent in poverty over the next decade, it will have to focus its attention on two sets of policies: (i) policies which will accelerate economic growth; and (ii) policies which will deliver key services to the poor and, by investing in human capital, ensure that the poor are able to participate equitably in that growth. Both legs of this strategy are consistent with, and serve to reinforce, the recommendations of the 1990 World Development Report. While there is broad ownership of these policies within Government, the principal challenge ahead lies in building the capacity to ensure that policy changes can be implemented efficiently. Furthermore, there is an urgent need to strengthen the database and develop a poverty monitoring system which can provide policymakers with regular information on the impact of economic and social policies on the lives of the poor.

A. Policies for Accelerating Growth

9.2   As pointed out in Chapter 5, experience from other countries has shown that macroeconomic stability, a high rate of investment backed by domestic savings, and high rates of literacy and numeracy are vital for rapid economic growth. Uganda continues to do poorly in each of these three areas. Inflation continues to be high and savings and investment continue to be low as do rates of literacy and numeracy. The key to achieving macroeconomic stability is to get firm control over the government budget. Despite the rationalization of the tax and tariff regime and the establishment of the Uganda Revenue Authority, the Government's revenue effort remains one of the lowest in the world. In the coming years, it will be imperative to further tighten tax administration and to broaden the tax base. The Government has made remarkable progress in keeping expenditures in line with the budgeted amounts and such discipline has to be maintained. However, given the low revenues, the Government will probably continue to be a dissaver for several years to come thereby necessitating that the private sector generate the large increases in savings that will be necessary to finance the investment needed for rapid economic growth. Experience of countries like China, India, and Kenya has shown that poor countries are capable of saving 20 percent of GDP or more. This places a premium on the development of the financial sector because the key to higher rates of saving is an efficient financial system capable of mobilizing small savings from a large proportion of the population. Uganda, at present, is saddled with an extremely underdeveloped and thin financial sector where the ratio of broad money to GDP has been of the order of 7 percent compared to 38 percent in Kenya. Uganda had, in fact, achieved a ratio of 30 percent in 1974.

Policies for Accelerating Agricultural Growth

9.3   At the heart of its growth strategy will have to be the transformation of agriculture. The agricultural sector has the potential to feed the country, to supply food to the regional market, to export horticultural products in addition to the traditional export crops, to produce industrial raw materials (sugarcane, cotton, etc.) and generally to act as the engine of growth. The key to realizing this potential is increasing yields by raising the productivity of the farmer. That means security of land tenure, investment in research and extension, control of plant and animal diseases and rural feeder roads. For some crops high-yielding varieties are available from local research stations or foreign stations. What remains is to adapt them as necessary, and propagate and disseminate them. An effective extension service is needed to ensure rapid adoption of improved varieties by the farmers. Many countries in Asia have shown that rapid and sustained improvements in yields are possible. The key question is one of timing, i.e., how quickly can Uganda put in place the infrastructure needed to raise yields. The answer partly lies in targeting incremental national and donor resources towards agriculture, particularly research and extension and rural feeder roads. Raising agricultural productivity, along with increased access to basic health and education, must take priority in the Government's spending program. Markets, with the associated infrastructure of storage and refrigeration, also matter a great deal. This is a matter for private investors rather than Government except with regard to government support for the collection and dissemination of market intelligence.

9.4   In addition to raising yields, Uganda must pay more attention to the working of the domestic markets in agricultural products. This is not an invitation to Government to intervene in the affairs of producers, processors and traders. Rather, it is to draw attention to the need to use public policy and public expenditure to facilitate the proper functioning of markets in agricultural products. Poor rural roads, for example, can place producers of certain crops, or producers in a particular region, at a disadvantage vis-a-vis producers in other regions or producers of the same or other crops. Or the way truck operators are licensed or regulated may have adverse effects on the markets for agricultural commodities. In Uganda there is anecdotal evidence of very low farmgate prices for some crops relative to final consumer prices. It is the legitimate responsibility of Government to find out whether the gap between farmgate and final prices is broadly reflective of costs or whether it is indicative of a malfunctioning market.

9.5   Rural feeder roads constitute an essential element of Uganda's strategy for accelerated agricultural growth. Roads are needed to bring in agricultural inputs and implements, facilitate the work of extension staff, bring access to manufactured goods, create access to basic social services such as education and health and, most important of all, provide access to markets for farm goods. During the early phase of the ERP the Government placed emphasis on the rehabilitation of the major trunk roads and much progress has been achieved in this area. The Government has recently shifted attention to rural roads and the donors have responded enthusiastically with funds, equipment and technical assistance. However, progress with the rehabilitation of rural roads has been slow. The main reason for this is the weak implementation capacity of the Ministry of Local Government and the district authorities upon which falls the responsibility for the construction, repair and maintenance of rural roads. This is a task which will be gradually shifted to the districts, in parallel with the necessary financial and trained manpower resources. The decentralization of responsibilities will probably start with feeder roads maintenance.

9.6   In the drive towards greater reliance on market forces and on the private sector, Uganda has moved quickly to dismantle the monopolies in the agricultural sector. These monopolies were the Coffee Marketing Board for coffee exports, the Uganda Tea Authority for tea exports, and the Produce Marketing Board for the export of food crops. In all three areas the emergence of competition is acting as a spur to further market development. In food crops, for example, private traders have been the driving force behind the penetration of the European and Middle East markets in simsim. Unfortunately, Uganda is not entirely rid of monopolies. The Lint Marketing Board still has the right to purchase all cotton for export. Ginneries are free to sell lint to the domestic cotton-processing mills. However traders in cotton lint and seed must be licensed by the Lint Marketing Board. The Cotton Act, last revised in 1964, provides for the zoning of cotton production, the setting of fixed seed and cotton lint prices, restrictions on the importation of, or trade in cotton and for the licensing of ginneries and restrictions on the siting of the same. As a result the cooperative unions have a de facto monopoly of cotton ginning. There has been much talk of amending the Cotton Act and the Lint Marketing Board Act with a view to introducing more competition into the cotton industry but little action so far. Given the potential for fast growth of a once-thriving industry, Government must set itself monitorable targets for removing the institutional factors constraining the revival of cotton.

9.7   Ineffective and inefficient financial intermediation hurts all sectors of the economy, including agriculture. At present agriculture does not depend much on purchased inputs and implements, whether locally made or imported; nor is the bigger proportion of agricultural output marketed or processed. The heaviest demand for credit in the agricultural sector has come from the agencies responsible for the procurement, processing and marketing of the traditional export crops, particularly coffee. Apart from the Rural Farmers Scheme that has been operated by the Uganda Commercial Bank, institutional credit has generally not been available to the smallholder. As a result not enough is known about the capacity of the smallholder to absorb and repay loans. The usual presumption is that credit is a constraint on production. This may well be true in Uganda but it does not follow that rushing credit to the farmer would translate into increased production. The first priority should rather be to get a better understanding of the different factors limiting the smallholder's ability to expand output.

Policies for Accelerating Industrial Growth

9.8   Although import substitution, certainly the old-fashioned, state-directed kind, is out of favor, it must be said that Uganda has substantial scope for replacing imports, provided this is done efficiently. A wide range of basic products are still imported, including cement, paints, biscuits, processed milk, garments, blankets, tomato paste, and tinned fruit juices. Import substitution is more likely to succeed if it is part of an outward-oriented development strategy than one focused entirely on the domestic market. The Republic of Korea, China, and other fast-growing countries have demonstrated the superiority of outward orientation. Thus, Uganda must exploit, to the full, the opportunities for entering export markets. As far as manufactured exports are concerned, there are no obvious winners on the horizon but these cannot be ruled out. It is private investors, not governments, who pick winners (or losers). The Government's role is to ensure that the investment climate is conducive to attracting investors who can produce a wide range of manufactured goods for the local and export market. In this regard, the great success achieved by Mauritius in identifying and exploiting an export market niche (in this case, wearing apparel) provides an indication of the opportunities that Uganda can seize.

9.9   Given the dearth of long-term finance, modern technology, knowledge of foreign markets and management skills in Uganda, foreign investment has a crucial role to play as the catalyst for the transformation of the economy. In some countries minorities from a particular foreign country or region have performed this role. In Uganda the Asians fit the bill. A significant number of the Asians expelled by Amin in 1972 have become successful entrepreneurs in Britain, Canada and other countries. The courageous decision of the NRM Government to return the expropriated properties to the owners opens the way for these entrepreneurs to invest in Uganda. Having been dispossessed once, they will most likely exercise maximum caution in committing resources to Uganda. Nevertheless, the early signs are encouraging and a number of Asians have embarked upon a major rehabilitation of their properties once they got the properties back. Uganda needs to be forthright about the catalytic role that investors can play in the economy and it should mount investment promotion exercises directed at Asian and other foreign investors.

Employment and Labor Market Policies

9.10   As has been pointed out in Chapter 6, the central objective of employment and labor market policies for the reduction of poverty in Uganda should be to increase the earnings of labor in agriculture. From the objectives of the land reform legislation proposed by the Agriculture Policy Committee, it appears that the Government rightly wishes to pursue a strategy of rural development which promotes a system of smallholder agriculture by further consolidating the de facto universal access to land. For this strategy to work, the proposed land reform legislation must find ways of guaranteeing tenancy rights to all the existing users of land and by improving the land endowment of the very small farmers. To encourage the small farmers to overcome the absence of the advantage of economies of scale, steps should be taken to facilitate their access to an appropriate technological package. As has been stated throughout the report, Ugandan agriculture operates under primitive conditions and the knowledge of farming systems and crop husbandry practices is rudimentary.

9.11   *Labor Mobility.* The operation of the rural labor market will continue to be constrained due to the absence of a large and mobile rural labor force. This is not by itself a problem as long as the concentration of labor in smallholder agriculture is not artificially promoted by inappropriate incentives. Improved systems of information and infrastructural facilities, along with the steady improvement of productivity in smallholder agriculture, is likely to make as much labor available to the rest of the economy as it can efficiently employ.

9.12   *Government Role in the Formal Sector.* Regulation of employment and wages in the formal sector has traditionally been kept low in Uganda and the Government has rightly resisted pressures to regulate formal sector wages, through such measures as the legislation of minimum wages. As long as there is a healthy growth of earnings in the primary sector of the economy, the market might be trusted to ensure that the formal sector of the economy pays a price for labor that is adequate for living above the poverty threshold. Creating too great a differential between earnings in the primary sector and the earnings in the formal sector often leads to a lower than optimal rate of industrialization, an unwarranted influx to urban areas leading to an overcrowded informal sector, and a rising differential in the earnings between the formal and informal sectors.

9.13   *Education and Training.* Education and training facilities must adjust to make the allocation of labor more efficient. Improved productivity of agricultural labor hinges critically on the expansion of primary education. Urban educational services would be better advised to reduce the focus on general higher education and instead increase the emphasis on technical training. Clearly the entire system of pricing of educational services is in need of a basic reappraisal. As has been discussed in Chapter 7, at present a primary school student in Uganda is charged a tuition which is often a significant proportion of the cash income of an average rural household whereas university education continues to be free of tuition, often with access to additional subsidies.

9.14   *AIDS.* The effects of the AIDS pandemic on employment and the labor market in Uganda cannot be determined with any precision. It is however clear that AIDS, which disproportionately strikes people in their prime, will increase the dependency ratio and make the task of poverty reduction more difficult. The pessimistic prognosis is heightened by the fact that measures to prevent the spread of HIV infection—critically important though they are—will have little effect on the incidence of AIDS during the next decade. The Government of Uganda deserves credit for dealing with the AIDS issue in an open manner. Besides concentrating efforts on containing the further spread of the HIV infection, e.g., by promoting the use of condoms, the Government, working with the NGO community, should explore the need to make targeted interventions in order to reduce the extreme effects on households whose labor endowments have been depleted by AIDS.

9.15   *Public Sector Employment.* Expansion of public sector employment is not an effective method of poverty reduction. Indeed an expansion in public employment almost certainly hurts the cause of poverty reduction by appropriating resources that might be used to expand employment more productively elsewhere in the economy. The number of persons employed in the public sector has grown too rapidly over the years from the standpoint of the actual expansion of public services and the capacity of the Government to protect real wages of public employees from serious erosion. The result is widespread resort to corrupt and fraudulent practices (e.g., bribery, keeping "ghost" workers on the payroll) and moonlighting and second informal jobs. On the whole, the effective labor time spent in public employment may have declined at the same time that there has been a steady rise in the number of persons on payroll. Recently the Government has succeeded in reversing the trend and reducing the number of persons on payroll. The task is incomplete and should continue. To the extent that the reduction in government employment comes through the elimination of ghost workers and attrition (i.e., not replacing the low priority retirees) the process does not impose any burden on the current budget. A further opportunity may become available if the increase in capacity utilization in formal sector enterprises provides a leeway for productive expansion of employment. In that event positions in these enterprises might be filled by the redundant government workers. However, a reduction in public employment is by itself a rather minimal measure. A central objective of the presently underway civil service reform program must be to introduce a culture of improved job performance, matched by higher real earnings commensurate with skill levels. This in turn means that a way must be found to prevent employment in public sector to be determined by the supply of high school and university graduates in a system of highly irrational relative costs of different forms of education.

Policies for Gender-Responsive Growth

9.16   As argued in Chapter 3, the strategies adopted by the Ugandan Government to reduce poverty and to foster sustainable economic growth need to take explicit account of the gender dimension. In this respect, they must recognize and seek to address the asymmetries in the respective rights and obligations of men and women, and pay particular attention to the gender division of labor, and differential incentives and opportunities facing men and women, as the country embarks on monetization, diversification, and productivity enhancement in the critically important agricultural sector. It is, in particular, necessary that gender-responsive actions be undertaken as an interconnected package of measures which are mutually reinforcing. The priority areas requiring attention if Uganda is to enable both men and women to break out of poverty, and to contribute more fully to economic and social development, are:

(i)   to promote, through literacy and education, and in conjunction with the vigorous pursuit of the gender-responsive legal (and customary) reform efforts underway, the legal rights and *protections* enabling women to benefit from their own labor and to have greater access to and control of economically productive resources, including capital and land, thereby raising the status of women to enable more equal participation in household-level, community, and national decisionmaking;

(ii)   to raise the productivity of women's *economic* (paid) labor through investment in education aimed at overcoming social, financial, and cultural barriers to female participation, including at the post-primary level; through investment in basic, accessible, and affordable health care responsive to the wide range of women's health needs; and through targeted actions aimed at raising women's access to information, technology, inputs, credit, and extension services;

(iii)   to alleviate the *domestic* labor constraint through substantially increased attention to and investment in labor-saving technologies, in infrastructure (especially transport, feeder roads, and markets), and in water supply and woodlots, that take explicit account of female users' needs in design and implementation;

(iv)   to provide maximum political and financial support to the efforts, spearheaded by UNICEF, to *reduce AIDS risk among young girls*; and to protect the rights of children, including through institutional measures in the RC system to ensure appropriate representation and articulation of children's needs.

B. Policies for the Delivery of Social Services

The Public Expenditure Agenda

9.17   The Government recognizes that, since the single most important asset owned by the poor is their labor, the central element of its poverty reducing public expenditure strategy should be to accord highest priority to developing their human capital. Human capital, more than any other factor, increases the income earning opportunities of the poor and contributes both to individual and national productivity. Accordingly, during the past two years, the Government has been attempting to foster such development in human capital by restructuring government expenditures in favor of the social sectors and rural infrastructure. Notwithstanding the severe resource constraints, the Government must continue to ensure that these priority programs remain protected. Not only should more resources be channelled towards primary education and primary health care, but the efficiency of these expenditures should also be improved by ensuring that money is spent on high impact programs and that the combination of expenditures within and across sectors are optimal. The Government needs to critically review its portfolio of investment projects in order to ensure that it is responsive to the country's changing needs. In other words, Government needs to ensure that expenditures are made on a rational basis rather than the allocated on the basis of historical levels. The combination of capital and recurrent expenditure also needs to be improved.

9.18   As indicated in Chapter 7, both the quantity and quality of desired social services is adversely affected by a lack of sufficient funds. In the medium-to-long run, mobilization of domestic resources, through improved efficiency in tax collection and also through the judicious adoption of cost recovery schemes in appropriate sectors, will be essential. This will need to be augmented by shifting funds from relatively unproductive areas such as defense, state farms, teacher training colleges, universities, curative health, etc. to areas where the economic and social returns are the highest, i.e., primary health, primary education, agricultural research and extension, rural feeder roads and rural water supply.

9.19   As has been demonstrated in Chapter 5, Uganda needs to slow down population growth in order to reduce poverty within the shortest possible time. At present, the Government of Uganda does not have an explicit population and family planning policy and lags far behind other SSA countries in encouraging its citizens to have small, manageable families and informing them of methods of doing this. Whereas most women in Uganda who know about family planning have favorable attitudes towards it, contraceptive use is constrained because of lack of access and generally unfavorable male attitudes. In addition to aggravating poverty, the growing population has adversely affected the environment by increasing the encroachment on forests and by intensifying farming, resulting in soil erosion and stagnating yields. It is therefore imperative that the Government develop a national family planning program and closely monitor progress towards decreasing presently high fertility rates.

Institutional Issues and the Provision of Safety Nets

9.20   Although a strong case could be made for this in the Ugandan context, targeting the poorest and most vulnerable is far too expensive an option for the Government of Uganda to consider at present, given the extremely low revenue effort and the weak administrative capacity. Instead, the focus should be on providing fundamental services in rural areas: primary education, primary and preventive health care, rural feeder roads, safe, easily accessible water, agricultural extension, and marketing assistance. As has been discussed in Chapter 8, communities can help provide some of these themselves, with assistance from Government and NGOs. Government, donors and NGOs need to develop a tripartite system to support self-help projects, and to ensure that priority investments are undertaken. If Government wishes NGOs to follow government leadership in a scenario in which Government formulates policy and sets standards, NGOs, including Ugandan ones, should be involved in policy formulation. For the tripartite system to work, it must be "owned" by a substantial portion of the three sets of actors (Government, NGOs and donors). The policy development process in the areas of AIDS and child welfare could become a model for other sectors.

9.21   The program of decentralization being adopted by the Government offers a unique opportunity to support community and NGO initiatives, particularly in light of the fact that the Government lacks the capacity to deliver much needed services to most of its citizens. For this new model to work, it will be imperative for the Government to educate the population and to reorient and educate civil servants towards its changing role. The DCAT, which should be designed as a social investment fund which disburses funds quickly for projects generated by self-help groups, could emerge as an important instrument to address poverty on a broad scale.

Selected Bibliography

Selected Bibliography

Action Aid. 1992. *Analysis of Results of Participatory Poverty Assessment in Mityan County, Mubende District*, mimeograph.

Akiri-Kajeru, Christine. 1990. *Preliminary Assessment of Mulago Hospital Statistics*.

Alden, John, Abby Nalwanga-Sebina and James Sengendo. 1987. *Orphaned and Disabled Children in Luwero and Kabale Districts, and in Uganda Child Care Institutions*.

Alden, John, Gerald Salole and John Williamson. 1991. *Managing Uganda's Orphans Crisis*. Report Prepared for USAID.

Bwanika-Bbaale, Hon. A. Undated. *The Role of the Ugandan Government in National Strategy Formulation*. Paper presented to the Working Group on Children Orphaned by Aids in Africa.

Evans, Alison. 1992. *A Review of the Rural Labour Market in Uganda*. School of African and Asian Studies, University of Sussex, mimeograph.

Fleuret, Anne, et. al. 1992. *Girls' Persistence and Teacher Incentives in Primary Education in Uganda*. USAID, Kampala, Uganda.

Government of Uganda. 1988. *National Agricultural Research Strategy and Plan, Uganda, Vol. II: Priorities and Programs*.

Hesse, Mary Chinery. 1989. *Engineering Adjustment for the 1990s*. Report of a Commonwealth Expert Group on Women and Structural Adjustment. Commonwealth Secretariat, London.

Holt, Sharon. 1991. "The Role of Institutions in Poverty Reduction: A Focus on the Productive Sectors". *PRE Working Paper No. 627*. World Bank, Washington, D.C.

Husain, Ishrat. 1992. *Adjustment and the Impact on the Poor, The Case of Africa*. Mimeograph. World Bank, Washington, D.C.

Jarawan, Eva. 1991. *Women in Development: Current Issues and Agenda for Further Research*. Population and Human Resources Division, Working Paper, World Bank, Washington, D.C.

Kaijika, Emmanuel, Edward Kaija, Anne Cross and Edilberto Loaiza. 1989. *Uganda Demographic and Health Survey 1988/89*. Ministry of Health, Entebbe, Uganda.

Khan, Q.U. *Employment Situation in Government Sector*. Manpower Planning Department. ILO, Geneva.

Korten, David. 1980. "Community Organization and Rural Development: A Learning Process Approach". *Public Administration Review*.

148

Krueger, A.O., M. Schiff and A. Valdes. 1988. "Agricultural Incentives in Developing Countries: Measuring the Effect of Sectoral and Economywide Policies". *The World Bank Economic Review*. Vol. 2, No. 3.

Lochhead, Alison. 1991. *Gender and Development in Dodoth County, Karamoja*. OXFAM, Kampala, Uganda.

Manpower Planning Department, Ministry of Planning and Economic Department. 1989. *Manpower and Employment in Uganda, Report of the National Manpower Survey*. Kampala, Uganda.

Martin, Doris and Fatuma Hashi. *Law as an Institutional Barrier to the Economic Progress of Women*.

_____. *Sub-Saharan Africa: Gender, Evolution of Legal Institutions, and Economic Development*.

Ministry of Finance and Economic Planning. 1992. *Uganda National Plan of Action for Children, The Way Forward IV: Priorities for Social Services Sector Development in the 1990s*. Kampala, Uganda.

Moser, Caroline O.N. 1989. "Gender Planning in The Third World: Meeting Practical and Strategic Gender Needs". *World Development*, Vol. 17, No. 11.

Muyayisa, David. 1992. *Street Children in Kampala*, unpublished manuscript.

Muyinda, Herbert and Tom Barton. 1992. *Socio-Economic Influences on the Health and Rehabilitation of Physically Handicapped Rural Children: A case study in Kayunga Sub-County, Mukono District, Uganda*. Final Report. Child Health and Development Centre, Makerere University, Kampala, Uganda.

Muyinda, Herbert and Tom Barton. 1992. *Socio-Economic Influences on the Health and Rehabilitation of Physically Handicapped Rural Children*, unpublished manuscript. Child Health and Development Center, Makerere University.

Obbo, Christine. "Women, Children and a 'Living Wage'", in Holger Bernt Hansen and Michael Twaddel, eds., *Changing Uganda*. Fountain Press, Kampala, Uganda.

Palmer, Ingrid. 1991. *Gender and Population in the Adjustment of African Economies: Planning for Change*. Women, Work and Development Series No. 19. (Geneva, International Labor Office).

Saito, Katrine. 1992. *Raising the Productivity of Women Farmers in Sub-Saharan Africa*, Vol I. Overview Report, PHRWD. World Bank, Washington D.C.

Salmen, Larry. 1992. "Reducing Poverty: An Institutional Perspective". *Poverty and Social Policy Series, Paper No. 1, Program Design and Implementation*. World Bank, Washington, D.C.

Sserunjogi, Louise. 1992. *Vitamin A Intake Among Children Below Six - Kamuli District*, Child Health Development Center, Mulago Hospital, Kampala, Uganda.

Summers, Lawrence. 1992. *Investing in All the People: Educating Women in Developing Countries*. Remarks prepared for a Development Economic Seminar, World Bank, Washington, D.C.

Tadria, H.M.K. 1987. "Changes and Continuities in the Position of Women in Uganda." *Beyond Crisis: Development Issues in Uganda*, eds. Paul Wiebe and Cole Dodge, Makerere Institute Social Research, Kampala, Uganda.

Tuhaise, Charles. 1992. "Need for Foster Care in Uganda." *The Vulnerable Child*. UCOBAC Newsletter.

UNDP. 1992. *Preparatory Study on Poverty Alleviation and Rural Development in Uganda*. Draft Report (prepared by Management System and Economic Consultants Ltd.), Kampala.

UNICEF. 1989. *Children and Women in Uganda: A Situation Analysis*.

_____. 1992. *New Phase of UNICEF Support for AIDS Control in Uganda*. Summary Document. Kampala, Uganda.

UNICEF/ACFODE. 1988. *Uganda: Women's Needs Assessment Survey*.

von Braun, Joachim. 1991. "Social Security in Sub-Saharan Africa: Reflections on Policy Challenges", in E. Ahmad et al, *Social Security in Developing Countries*. Oxford University Press.

The World Bank. 1993. *Uganda: Social Sector Strategy*. Population and Human Resources Division, Eastern Africa Department, Washington, D.C.

_____. 1993. *Uganda: Agriculture Sector Memorandum*. Agriculture and Environment Operations Division, Eastern African Department, Washington, D.C.

_____. 1992. *Women in Development: The Legal Issues in Sub-Saharan Africa Today*. AFTSP Division Working Papers, Nos. 2, 3 and 4, Washington, D.C.

_____. 1990. *Primary Education: A World Bank Policy Paper*, Washington, D.C.

_____. 1991. *Public Choices for Private Initiatives: Prioritizing Public Expenditures for Sustainable and Equitable Growth in Uganda*, Eastern Africa Department, Washington, D.C.

_____. 1990. *World Development Report*. Washington, DC.

_____. 1992. *Uganda District Management Study*. Infrastructure Operations Division, Eastern Africa Department, Washington, D.C.

The Office of the Commissioner of Data Processing. 1987. *Census of Civil Service*.

1989. *Non-Governmental Organizations Registration Statute*, Government of Uganda.

1990. *Statutory Instruments*, Government of Uganda.

1990. *The Non-Governmental Organizations Regulations*, Government of Uganda.

1992. *Report of the Vice President's Select Committee on Non Governmental Organization*, Kampala, Uganda.

_____. 1992. *World Development Report*. Washington, DC.

Annex I

Statistical Appendix

Annex I

Statistical Appendix

Contents

Table I.1   Country Data Sheet 155
Table I.2   The 1991 Population and Housing Census 156
Table I.3   Population Density by Region and District 157
Table I.4   Age Structure of Population 158
Table I.5   Population by Age and Population Type by Sex 159
Table I.6   Population and Literacy by Rural-Urban Distribution 160
Table I.7   Population and Literacy by Sex Distribution 161
Table II.1   GDP by Sector at Current Factor Cost 162
Table II.2   GDP by Sector at Constant 1987 Prices 163
Table II.3   GDP by Expenditure in Constant Prices 164
Table III.1   Balance of Payments 165
Table III.2   Composition of Exports (FOB) 166
Table III.3   Composition of Recorded Imports (CIF) 167
Table III.4   Service Imports 168
Table IV.1   External Debt 169
Table V.1   Central Government Operations 172
Table V.2   Central Government Revenue 173
Table V.3   Central Government Expenditure 174
Table VI.1   Monetary Survey 175
Table VI.2   Interest Rate Structure 176
Table VI.3   Exchange Rate Movements 177
Table VI.4   Foreign Exchange Auctions 178
Table VII.1   Production of Principal Manufactured Commodities 179
Table VII.2   Index of Industrial Production (Annual Summary) 180
Table VII.3   Index of Industrial Production (Monthly Summary) 181
Table VII.4   Production and Exports of Principal Agricultural Products 182
Table VIII.1 New Consumer Price Index: Kampala 183
Table VIII.2 New Consumer Price Index: Kampala 184
Table IX.1   Orphan Census Derived from the 1991 National Census 185
Table IX.2   Pattern of Food Expenditure by Region 186
Table IX.3   Percentage Shares Spent on Selected Expenditure Categories 187

COUNTRY DATA SHEET

General

Area, land	sq km	197,096
Population (1991)		16,671,705
Growth rate	% per annum	2.5
Density (1991)	per sq km	85

Socio-Economic Indicators

Total hours worked per day, women		15–18
Total hours worked per day, men		8–10
Female ownership of land	percent	7
Share of credit to women	percent	<1

Social Indicators

Population Characteristics (1990)

Crude birth rate	per 1,000	51
Crude death rate	per 1,000	22
Life expectancy at birth, male	years	47
Total fertility rate		7.3
Contraceptive prevalence rate	percent	5
Female-headed households	percent	30

Health

Infant mortality (1990)	per 1,000 live births	117
Maternal mortality rate	per 100,000 births	500
Female morbidity rate	percent	76
Population per physician (1991)		24,700
Population per hospital bed (1991)		1,200
First birth in 12–15 age range	percent	29
First birth after age 19	percent	22

Income Distribution, (1989–90) 1/

Highest quintile of national income	% of population	8
Lowest quintile of national income	% of population	30

Access to Electricity (1989–90)

% of Urban population	percent	40.1
% of Rural population	percent	1.9

Nutrition (1991)

Calories per capita		2800

Education (1990)

Literacy rate, 1991	percent, age 10 and over	54
Female literacy, 1991	percent, age 10 and over	45
Adult literacy rate, 1991	percent, age 20 and over	52
Female adult literacy, 1991	percent, age 20 and over	39
Primary school enrollment – total	% of relevant population	72
Primary school enrollment – female	% of relevant population	63

Sources: Household Budget Survey, 1989–90; Statistics Department, MFEP;
               Uganda: Social Sector Strategy, 1993.

1/   Based on expenditure data from the Household Budget Survey.

THE 1991 POPULATION AND HOUSING CENSUS
Final Results

Region & District		Total	Male	Female	Urban	Rural	Percentage Urban
CENTRAL	Kalangala	16,371	9,929	6,442	1,376	14,995	8.4
	Kampala	774,241	377,225	397,016	774,241	0	100.0
	Kiboga	141,607	72,538	69,069	5,277	136,330	3.7
	Luwero	449,691	224,399	225,292	36,531	413,160	8.1
	Masaka	838,736	415,552	423,184	77,196	761,540	9.2
	Mpigi	913,867	455,703	458,164	137,126	776,741	15.0
	Mubende	500,976	254,081	246,895	34,541	466,435	6.9
	Mukono	824,604	413,580	411,024	98,735	725,869	12.0
	Rakai	383,501	189,082	194,419	14,869	368,632	3.9
	Totals	4,843,594	2,412,089	2,431,505	1,179,892	3,663,702	24.4
EASTERN	Iganga	945,783	461,079	484,704	44,002	901,781	4.7
	Jinja	289,476	143,336	146,140	80,893	208,583	27.9
	Kamuli	485,214	237,513	247,701	8,262	476,952	1.7
	Kapchorwa	116,702	58,577	58,125	4,604	112,098	3.9
	Kumi	236,694	112,719	123,975	11,749	224,945	5.0
	Mbale	710,980	355,803	355,177	60,298	650,682	8.5
	Pallisa	357,656	173,836	183,820	2,927	354,729	0.8
	Soroti	430,390	209,530	220,860	46,274	384,116	10.8
	Tororo	555,574	273,220	282,354	63,657	491,917	11.5
	Totals	4,128,469	2,025,613	2,102,856	322,666	3,805,803	7.8
NORTHERN	Apac	454,504	222,854	231,650	5,783	448,721	1.3
	Arua	637,941	307,679	330,262	26,712	611,229	4.2
	Gulu	338,427	166,318	172,109	38,297	300,130	11.3
	Kitgum	357,184	172,640	184,544	15,327	341,857	4.3
	Kotido	196,006	92,481	103,525	9,702	186,304	4.9
	Lira	500,965	247,607	253,358	27,568	473,397	5.5
	Moroto	174,417	80,061	94,356	12,981	161,436	7.4
	Moyo	175,645	85,054	90,591	8,787	166,858	5.0
	Nebbi	316,866	152,093	164,773	23,943	292,923	7.6
	Totals	3,151,955	1,526,787	1,625,168	169,100	2,982,855	5.4
WESTERN	Bundibugyo	116,566	57,816	58,750	9,215	107,351	7.9
	Bushenyi	736,361	354,470	381,891	14,195	722,166	1.9
	Hoima	197,851	99,547	98,304	4,616	193,235	2.3
	Kabale	417,218	197,695	219,523	29,246	387,972	7.0
	Kabarole	746,800	369,818	376,982	36,954	709,846	4.9
	Kasese	343,601	167,672	175,929	39,892	303,709	11.6
	Kibaale	220,261	109,756	110,505	2,408	217,853	1.1
	Kisoro	186,681	86,406	100,275	7,485	179,196	4.0
	Masindi	260,796	131,936	128,860	14,352	246,444	5.5
	Mbarara	930,772	458,257	472,515	46,616	884,156	5.0
	Rukungiri	390,780	187,885	202,895	12,985	377,795	3.3
	Totals	4,547,687	2,221,258	2,326,429	217,964	4,329,723	4.8
UGANDA	Totals	16,671,705	8,185,747	8,485,958	1,889,622	14,782,083	11.3

Source: Statisticts Department, MFEP.

POPULATION DENSITY BY REGION AND DISTRICT

Region & District		POPULATION '000			AREA sq km		POPULATION DENSITY per sq km, land		
		1969	1980	1991	Total	Land	1969	1980	1991
CENTRAL	Kalangala	6.8	8.6	16.4	9,340	432	16	20	38
	Kampala	330.7	458.5	774.2	181	169	1,957	2,713	4,581
	Kiboga	75.7	138.7	141.6	4,004	3,872	20	36	37
	Luwero	315.2	412.5	449.7	9,198	8,539	37	48	53
	Masaka	451.2	622.6	838.7	6,986	5,531	82	113	152
	Mpigi	513.5	661.2	913.9	6,278	4,514	114	146	202
	Mubende	255.3	371.6	501.0	6,308	5,949	43	62	84
	Mukono	541.0	634.3	824.6	14,241	4,594	118	138	179
	Rakai	182.6	274.6	383.5	4,973	3,889	47	71	99
	Totals	2,672.0	3,582.6	4,843.6	61,509	37,489	71	96	129
EASTERN	Iganga	470.2	643.9	945.8	13,114	4,823	97	134	196
	Jinja	196.3	228.5	289.5	734	677	290	338	428
	Kamuli	278.3	349.5	485.2	4,348	3,332	84	105	146
	Kapchorwa	64.5	74.0	116.7	1,738	1,738	37	43	67
	Kumi	190.7	239.5	236.7	2,861	2,457	78	97	96
	Mbale	421.4	556.9	711.0	2,546	2,504	168	222	284
	Pallisa	202.2	261.2	357.7	1,956	1,564	129	167	229
	Soroti	379.9	476.6	430.4	10,060	8,526	45	56	50
	Tororo	324.9	407.2	555.6	2,597	2,336	139	174	238
	Totals	2,528.4	3,237.3	4,128.6	39,954	27,957	90	116	148
NORTHERN	Apac	225.4	313.3	454.5	6,488	5,887	38	53	77
	Arua	369.6	472.3	637.9	7,830	7,595	49	62	84
	Gulu	223.7	270.1	338.4	11,735	11,560	19	23	29
	Kitgum	240.1	308.7	357.2	16,136	16,136	15	19	22
	Kotido	105.6	161.4	196.0	13,208	13,208	8	12	15
	Lira	278.9	370.3	501.0	7,251	6,151	45	60	81
	Moroto	164.7	188.6	174.4	14,113	14,113	12	13	12
	Moyo	90.0	106.5	175.6	5,006	4,668	19	23	38
	Nebbi	204.1	233.0	316.9	2,891	2,781	73	84	114
	Totals	1,902.1	2,424.2	3,151.9	84,658	82,099	23	30	38
WESTERN	Bundibugyo	79.4	112.2	116.6	2,338	2,097	38	54	56
	Bushenyi	410.7	524.7	736.4	5,396	4,906	84	107	150
	Hoima	112.7	142.2	197.9	5,908	3,563	32	40	56
	Kabale	288.6	328.8	417.2	1,827	1,695	170	194	246
	Kabarole	328.0	519.8	746.8	8,361	8,109	40	64	92
	Kasese	164.1	277.7	343.6	3,205	2,724	60	102	126
	Kibaale	83.7	152.1	220.3	4,302	4,208	20	36	52
	Kisoro	114.8	126.7	186.7	662	620	185	204	301
	Masindi	155.5	223.2	260.8	9,326	8,458	18	26	31
	Mbarara	450.5	688.2	930.8	10,839	10,587	43	65	88
	Rukungiri	244.6	296.6	390.8	2,753	2,584	95	115	151
	Totals	2,432.6	3,392.2	4,547.9	54,917	49,551	49	68	92
UGANDA	Totals	9,535.1	12,636.3	16,672.0	241,038	197,096	48	64	85

Source: Statisticts Department, MFEP.

157

AGE STRUCTURE OF POPULATION

Age Group	RURAL '000 Male	Female	Total	URBAN '000 Male	Female	Total	TOTAL '000 Male	Female	Total
0 - 4	1,364.5	1,382.5	2,747.0	163.6	167.2	330.8	1,528.1	1,549.7	3,077.8
5 - 9	1,102.5	1,103.2	2,205.7	111.9	125.5	237.4	1,214.4	1,228.7	2,443.1
10 - 14	1,001.9	939.4	1,941.3	96.1	121.5	217.6	1,098.0	1,060.9	2,158.9
15 - 19	747.9	781.8	1,529.7	92.7	130.0	222.7	840.6	911.8	1,752.4
20 - 24	576.5	666.6	1,243.1	114.2	127.2	241.4	690.7	793.8	1,484.5
25 - 29	488.4	552.8	1,041.2	103.6	99.1	202.7	592.0	651.9	1,243.9
30 - 34	374.5	398.0	772.5	72.4	61.0	133.4	446.9	459.0	905.9
35 - 39	274.7	298.9	573.6	46.0	37.1	83.1	320.7	336.0	656.7
40 - 44	211.5	240.9	452.4	29.5	23.4	52.9	241.0	264.3	505.3
45 - 49	185.9	204.6	390.5	20.4	16.2	36.6	206.3	220.8	427.1
50 - 54	172.9	192.1	365.0	15.3	14.3	29.6	188.2	206.4	394.6
55 - 59	118.0	115.5	233.5	8.0	6.9	14.9	126.0	122.4	248.4
60 - 64	115.2	131.0	246.2	6.5	8.4	14.9	121.7	139.4	261.1
65 - 69	77.3	77.4	154.7	3.7	4.4	8.1	81.0	81.8	162.8
70 - 74	67.7	73.1	140.8	2.8	4.4	7.2	70.5	77.5	148.0
75 - 79	38.8	35.6	74.4	1.6	2.0	3.6	40.4	37.6	78.0
80 +	58.0	54.5	112.5	2.1	3.6	5.7	60.1	58.1	118.2
Not Stated	2.0	2.6	4.6	0.6	0.6	1.2	2.6	3.2	5.8
Total	6,978.2	7,250.5	14,228.7	891.0	952.8	1,843.8	7,869.2	8,203.3	16,072.5

Source: Statistics Department, MFEP.

POPULATION BY AGE AND POPULATION TYPE BY SEX

Age Group	HOUSEHOLD POPULATION			INSTITUTIONAL & FLOATING POPULATION			TOTAL POPULATION		
	Male	Female	Total	Male	Female	Total	Male	Female	Total
0 – 4	1,556,096	1,577,815	3,133,911	9,783	9,428	19,211	1,565,879	1,587,243	3,153,122
5 – 9	1,239,759	1,254,397	2,494,156	6,806	6,029	12,835	1,246,565	1,260,426	2,506,991
10 – 14	1,122,631	1,082,973	2,205,604	7,605	7,159	14,764	1,130,236	1,090,132	2,220,368
15 – 19	853,633	924,955	1,778,588	12,147	11,525	23,672	865,780	936,480	1,802,260
20 – 24	685,664	802,034	1,487,698	24,549	13,593	38,142	710,213	815,627	1,525,840
25 – 29	589,498	664,549	1,254,047	20,725	8,535	29,260	610,223	673,084	1,283,307
30 – 34	453,478	475,085	928,563	12,194	4,830	17,024	465,672	479,915	945,587
35 – 39	332,199	350,167	682,366	7,234	2,912	10,146	339,433	353,079	692,512
40 – 44	256,403	278,091	534,494	4,422	2,132	6,554	260,825	280,223	541,048
45 – 49	221,631	231,388	453,019	3,044	1,700	4,744	224,675	233,088	457,763
50 – 54	205,447	218,939	424,386	2,264	1,522	3,786	207,711	220,461	428,172
55 – 59	136,763	128,438	265,201	1,235	799	2,034	137,998	129,237	267,235
60 – 64	133,315	148,592	281,907	1,006	781	1,787	134,321	149,373	283,694
65 – 69	88,101	86,254	174,355	696	391	1,087	88,797	86,645	175,442
70 – 74	78,774	83,546	162,320	492	341	833	79,266	83,887	163,153
75 – 79	45,005	39,941	84,946	253	150	403	45,258	40,091	85,349
80 +	69,126	62,639	131,765	328	227	555	69,454	62,866	132,320
Not Stated	3,241	3,989	7,230	200	112	312	3,441	4,101	7,542
Total	8,070,764	8,413,792	16,484,556	114,983	72,166	187,149	8,185,747	8,485,958	16,671,705

Source: Statistics Department, MFEP.

POPULATION AND LITERACY BY RURAL–URBAN DISTRIBUTION

Age 10 and Over

	RURAL			URBAN			TOTAL		
District	Literate	Total	Percent Literate	Literate	Total	Percent Literate	Literate	Total	Percent Literate
Apac	155,010	294,870	53%	2,841	3,938	72%	157,851	298,808	53%
Arua	182,108	405,732	45%	11,861	18,647	64%	193,969	424,379	46%
Bundibugyo	27,257	70,256	39%	3,367	6,346	53%	30,624	76,602	40%
Bushenyi	244,958	460,515	53%	7,541	9,806	77%	252,499	470,321	54%
Gulu	93,707	204,937	46%	19,252	27,293	71%	112,959	232,230	49%
Hoima	71,477	127,873	56%	2,518	3,174	79%	73,995	131,047	56%
Iganga	268,940	586,305	46%	20,386	28,823	71%	289,326	615,128	47%
Jinja	82,634	136,036	61%	46,979	56,281	83%	129,613	192,317	67%
Kabale	122,418	245,573	50%	14,334	20,228	71%	136,752	265,801	51%
Kabarole	218,629	457,770	48%	19,466	26,028	75%	238,095	483,798	49%
Kalangala	8,160	11,481	71%	794	964	82%	8,954	12,445	72%
Kampala	..	..	..	485,036	548,455	88%	485,036	548,455	88%
Kamuli	125,588	311,382	40%	3,814	5,546	69%	129,402	316,928	41%
Kapchorwa	38,972	72,255	54%	2,099	3,107	68%	41,071	75,362	54%
Kasese	88,899	190,123	47%	19,010	27,110	70%	107,909	217,233	50%
Kibale	69,188	137,468	50%	1,149	1,568	73%	70,337	139,036	51%
Kiboga	48,986	90,368	54%	2,756	3,503	79%	51,742	93,871	55%
Kisoro	34,625	107,558	32%	2,305	4,839	48%	36,930	112,397	33%
Kitgum	88,635	233,183	38%	7,369	11,075	67%	96,004	244,258	39%
Kotido	12,229	119,120	10%	2,962	6,325	47%	15,191	125,445	12%
Kumi	62,829	154,329	41%	5,074	7,943	64%	67,903	162,272	42%
Lira	152,636	313,908	49%	14,376	20,627	70%	167,012	334,535	50%
Luwero	157,230	272,726	58%	18,537	24,329	76%	175,767	297,055	59%
Masaka	297,260	493,519	60%	42,217	51,230	82%	339,477	544,749	62%
Masindi	81,895	163,169	50%	8,952	10,756	83%	90,847	173,925	52%
Mbale	236,032	435,239	54%	30,044	41,578	72%	266,076	476,817	56%
Mbarara	292,915	585,064	50%	27,887	34,196	82%	320,802	619,260	52%
Moroto	8,154	103,738	8%	4,701	8,760	54%	12,855	112,498	11%
Moyo	49,559	112,575	44%	4,268	6,175	69%	53,827	118,750	45%
Mpigi	358,634	506,433	71%	79,956	91,534	87%	438,590	597,967	73%
Mubende	171,420	303,855	56%	18,835	22,704	83%	190,255	326,559	58%
Mukuno	281,870	476,761	59%	49,939	64,366	78%	331,809	541,127	61%
Nebbi	88,793	194,827	46%	10,069	16,476	61%	98,862	211,303	47%
Pallisa	108,866	233,973	47%	1,185	1,899	62%	110,051	235,872	47%
Rakai	129,269	243,017	53%	8,230	10,155	81%	137,499	253,172	54%
Rukungiri	136,024	243,266	56%	6,873	9,071	76%	142,897	252,337	57%
Soroti	118,485	265,324	45%	21,031	31,210	67%	139,516	296,534	47%
Tororo	165,633	329,409	50%	30,873	43,858	70%	196,506	373,267	53%
Total:	4,879,924	9,693,937	50%	1,058,886	1,309,923	81%	5,938,810	11,003,860	54%

Source: The 1991 Population and Housing Census, Statistics Department, MFEP.

TABLE I.7

POPULATION AND LITERACY BY SEX DISTRIBUTION
Age 10 and Over

	MALE			FEMALE			TOTAL		
			Percent			Percent			Percent
District	Literate	Total	Literate	Literate	Total	Literate	Literate	Total	Literate
Apac	102,274	145,333	70%	55,577	153,475	36%	157,851	298,808	53%
Arua	131,546	201,169	65%	62,423	223,210	28%	193,969	424,379	46%
Bundibugyo	20,330	37,993	54%	10,294	38,609	27%	30,624	76,602	40%
Bushenyi	139,147	222,379	63%	113,352	247,942	46%	252,499	470,321	54%
Gulu	73,549	113,421	65%	39,410	118,809	33%	112,959	232,230	49%
Hoima	41,945	66,213	63%	32,050	64,834	49%	73,995	131,047	56%
Iganga	167,311	296,438	56%	122,015	318,690	38%	289,326	615,128	47%
Jinja	71,295	95,652	75%	58,318	96,665	60%	129,613	192,317	67%
Kabale	76,668	123,056	62%	60,084	142,745	42%	136,752	265,801	51%
Kabarole	138,649	238,208	58%	99,446	245,590	40%	238,095	483,798	49%
Kalangala	5,720	7,968	72%	3,234	4,477	72%	8,954	12,445	72%
Kampala	244,190	268,174	91%	240,846	280,281	86%	485,036	548,455	88%
Kamuli	74,721	153,886	49%	54,681	163,042	34%	129,402	316,928	41%
Kapchorwa	25,934	37,997	68%	15,137	37,365	41%	41,071	75,362	54%
Kasese	64,374	105,675	61%	43,535	111,558	39%	107,909	217,233	50%
Kibale	41,177	69,380	59%	29,160	69,656	42%	70,337	139,036	51%
Kiboga	29,144	48,784	60%	22,598	45,087	50%	51,742	93,871	55%
Kisoro	23,978	49,637	48%	12,952	62,760	21%	36,930	112,397	33%
Kitgum	68,299	116,219	59%	27,705	128,039	22%	96,004	244,258	39%
Kotido	11,425	58,007	20%	3,766	67,438	6%	15,191	125,445	12%
Kumi	41,056	75,765	54%	26,847	86,507	31%	67,903	162,272	42%
Lira	112,919	164,487	69%	54,093	170,048	32%	167,012	334,535	50%
Luwero	94,225	147,950	64%	81,542	149,105	55%	175,767	297,055	59%
Masaka	176,201	268,745	66%	163,276	276,004	59%	339,477	544,749	62%
Masindi	56,412	88,851	63%	34,435	85,074	40%	90,847	173,925	52%
Mbale	150,876	239,572	63%	115,200	237,245	49%	266,076	476,817	56%
Mbarara	184,527	304,178	61%	136,275	315,082	43%	320,802	619,260	52%
Moroto	9,005	49,411	18%	3,850	63,087	6%	12,855	112,498	11%
Moyo	35,131	56,545	62%	18,696	62,205	30%	53,827	118,750	45%
Mpigi	224,597	298,070	75%	213,993	299,897	71%	438,590	597,967	73%
Mubende	104,207	166,577	63%	86,048	159,982	54%	190,255	326,559	58%
Mukuno	178,832	272,182	66%	152,977	268,945	57%	331,809	541,127	61%
Nebbi	66,426	99,683	67%	32,436	111,620	29%	98,862	211,303	47%
Pallisa	66,226	113,117	59%	43,825	122,755	36%	110,051	235,872	47%
Rakai	73,865	124,277	59%	63,634	128,895	49%	137,499	253,172	54%
Rukungiri	77,068	119,837	64%	65,829	132,500	50%	142,897	252,337	57%
Soroti	87,810	142,324	62%	51,706	154,210	34%	139,516	296,534	47%
Tororo	116,979	182,606	64%	79,527	190,661	42%	196,506	373,267	53%
Total:	3,408,038	5,369,766	63%	2,530,772	5,634,094	45%	5,938,810	11,003,860	54%

Source: The 1991 Population and Housing Census, Statistics Department, MFEP.

GDP BY SECTOR AT CURRENT FACTOR COST
In millions of U Sh

	1985	1986	1987	1988	1989	1990	1991
Agriculture	15028	36615	131417	353304	677044	812459	1082044
Cash Crops	680	1896	5558	12463	20798	31082	80064
Food Crops	10715	26447	96398	247346	505111	578546	725470
Livestock	2906	6410	20725	67767	107162	140272	191693
Forestry & Fishing	727	1862	8736	25728	43973	62559	84817
Industry	1629	4520	16588	52451	95969	155784	247499
Mining & Quarrying	47	122	302	847	1576	4532	8491
Manufacturing	773	2254	7683	25567	43044	60769	89541
Coffee, Cotton, Sugar	64	171	520	1644	3789	6830	21045
Food Products	89	173	737	2835	5191	6852	9632
Miscelleneous	620	1910	6426	21088	34064	47087	58864
Public Utilities	103	259	885	2993	5301	9160	15002
Construction	706	1885	7718	23044	46048	81323	134465
Services	8086	17990	63380	187373	339400	527017	774349
Trade	3089	7793	28620	85448	154079	197907	258817
Transport & Communication	866	2117	8165	21988	51360	96928	163008
Road	757	1807	5821	16361	38243	79514	139703
Rail	57	58	576	1206	2665	2360	3856
Air	41	85	286	745	1800	5232	7146
Communication	11	167	1482	3676	8652	9822	12303
General Government	1390	1633	6383	16114	22893	35585	67264
Education	937	1611	4935	15529	27544	46814	68524
Health	238	522	1515	4548	7913	15819	25608
Rents	470	1349	4482	15020	27142	54048	79858
Owner-occupied Dwellings	602	1617	4977	15140	25100	46760	66029
Miscelleneous	494	1348	4303	13586	23369	33156	45241
GDP – Factor Cost	24743	59125	211385	593128	1112413	1495260	2103892
o/w Non-Monetary	9274	23000	81407	215954	418971	507546	659094
Indirect Taxes	2065	3449	11085	26779	56374	95718	132179
GDP – Market Prices	26808	62574	222470	619907	1168787	1590978	2236071

Source: Statistics Department, MFEP.

GDP BY SECTOR AT CONSTANT 1987 PRICES
In millions of U Sh

	1985	1986	1987	1988	1989	1990	1991
Agriculture	124616	124897	131417	139549	148537	152877	156766
Cash Crops	5599	5342	5558	5316	5706	5469	6837
Food Crops	90211	91376	96398	102831	110622	113343	114517
Livestock	20567	19870	20725	22318	23104	24021	24976
Forestry & Fishing	8239	8309	8736	9084	9105	10044	10436
Industry	13401	13485	16588	19084	21499	23102	25484
Mining & Quarrying	371	365	302	286	330	622	755
Manufacturing	6993	6576	7683	9424	11223	12062	13762
Coffee, Cotton, Sugar	510	483	520	707	1023	1240	1794
Food Products	638	548	737	942	960	1063	1216
Miscelleneous	5845	5545	6426	7775	9240	9759	10752
Public Utilities	772	833	885	911	972	1049	1134
Construction	5265	5711	7718	8463	8974	9369	9833
Services	58791	59690	63380	68775	74014	77934	82168
Trade	26768	26199	28620	32078	35348	37262	39318
Transport & Communication	7137	7698	8165	8704	9136	9474	9869
Road	5184	5512	5821	6327	6753	6955	7303
Rail	468	543	576	592	648	738	710
Air	192	212	286	271	286	296	315
Communication	1293	1431	1482	1514	1449	1485	1541
General Government	6236	6299	6383	6489	6618	6765	6932
Education	4937	5090	4935	5180	5501	5964	6583
Health	1437	1476	1515	1556	1598	1641	1686
Rents	3688	4044	4482	5071	5677	6231	6696
Owner-occupied Dwellings	4719	4846	4977	5111	5250	5391	5536
Miscelleneous	3869	4038	4303	4586	4886	5206	5548
GDP - Factor Cost	196808	198072	211385	227408	244050	253913	264418
o/w Non-Monetary	76670	77626	81407	86150	91336	93652	95369
Memorandum Item:							
GDP Deflator (1987=100)	12.6	29.9	100.0	260.8	455.8	588.9	795.7

Source: Statistics Department, MFEP.

GDP BY EXPENDITURE IN CONSTANT PRICES
In millions of U Sh

	1985	1986	1987	1988	1989	1990	1991
Consumption	206170	203572	214265	229895	244467	251144	258486
Private	189458	189557	199865	216817	229324	235307	237337
Public	16713	14015	14400	13077	15143	15837	21149
Gross domestic investment	18005	18276	20535	21174	25247	30279	31574
Fixed investment	18005	18276	20535	21174	25247	30279	31574
Private	6610	6708	7342	8556	10000	12698	16019
Public	11395	11568	13194	12617	15247	17581	15555
Gross domestic expenditure	224175	221848	234801	251068	269714	281423	290060
Exports (g+nfs)	15959	13439	16303	15629	15800	15214	13949
Terms of trade adjustment	7095	6064	0	-2556	-4275	-6362	-6260
Import capacity	23054	19503	16303	13073	11525	8852	7690
Imports (g+nfs)	26901	25661	28633	29022	29096	26470	22979
Resource balance	-10942	-12222	-12331	-13393	-13296	-11256	-9030
Net factor service income	-2806	-2232	-2323	-2582	-3019	-2837	-4035
Net current transfers	4079	4936	4918	4872	4025	3135	4033
Current account balance	-9669	-9518	-9735	-11103	-12290	-10958	-9032
GDP at market prices	213233	209626	222470	237675	256418	270167	281030
GNP	210427	207394	220147	235094	253399	267330	276995
Gross domestic savings	14158	12119	8205	5224	7676	12661	16285
Gross national savings	15431	14822	10800	7515	8682	12959	16283
Gross domestic income	220328	215691	222470	235119	252143	263805	274771
Gross national income	217522	213458	220147	232538	249124	260968	270735

Source: Statistics Department, IMF and staff estimates.

BALANCE OF PAYMENTS
In millions of US$

	1986/87	1987/88	1988/89	1989/90	1990/91	Est 1991/92
Exports (g+nfs)	406	324	304	246	200	195
Merchandise (fob)	384	298	282	210	177	172
o/w Coffee	365	286	276	159	126	117
Non-factor services	22	26	22	36	23	23
Imports (g+nfs)	600	682	712	676	658	523
Merchandise (cif)	514	545	562	584	550	425
o/w Petrol	63	69	76	78	87	57
Non-factor services	86	137	150	92	108	98
Resource balance	-194	-358	-408	-430	-458	-328
Net factor income	-47	-57	-67	-77	-66	-142
o/w Net interest	-47	-57	-66	-77	-62	-87
Current private transfers	100	120	114	78	80	127
C/A balance (excl grants)	-141	-295	-361	-429	-444	-343
C/A balance (incl grants)	-101	-203	-230	-276	-239	-126
Official transfers	40	92	131	153	205	217
o/w Import support	0	33	49	29	87	77
Net M&LT loans	45	101	125	215	131	21
Disbursements	135	186	211	292	217	146
Project loans	135	141	143	125	118	77
Import support loans	0	45	68	167	99	69
Repayments	90	85	86	77	86	125
Foreign investment/Kenya comp.	28	10	13	6	1	2
Short-term, net	-31	37	-17	12	2	-4
Errors/value adjustment	-20	-10	7	0	0	-12
Overall balance	-79	-65	-103	-44	-105	-119
Financing:	79	65	103	44	105	119
Monetary authorities	22	-14	18	10	41	-2
Gross reserve changes	33	-4	12	11	-11	-23
IMF, net	-3	-17	7	-1	52	21
SAF/ESAF and purchases	57	34	94	42	89	55
Other, net	-8	7	0	0	0	0
Short term/commercial	10	-10	6	12	-2	-4
External arrears	-45	47	18	-19	65	124
Exceptional financing	92	41	61	41	1	1
Rescheduling	92	40	57	40	0	0
Debt cancellation	0	0	3	2	1	0
Residual finance gap	0	0	0	0	0	1
Memoradum item:						
Gross reserves (EOP) 1/	37	41	29.5	18.5	29.5	52.5
in months of imports	0.9	0.9	0.6	0.4	0.6	1.5

Source: Bank of Uganda, IMF, and staff estimates.

1/ Includes reserves of the Bank of Uganda held as tied import support.

COMPOSITION OF EXPORTS (FOB)

		1980	1981	1982	1983	1984	1985	1986	1987	1988	1989	1990	1991
Volume:	*'000 Tons*												
Coffee		110.1	128.3	174.7	144.3	133.2	151.5	140.8	148.2	144.2	176.5	141.1	127.2
Cotton		2.3	1.2	1.8	7.0	6.7	9.6	4.9	3.4	2.1	2.3	3.8	7.2
Tea		0.5	0.5	1.2	1.3	2.5	1.2	2.8	2.1	3.1	3.1	4.8	6.5
Tobacco		0.3	–	–	0.7	0.7	0.3	–	–	0.5	1.1	2.3	1.8
Maize		–	–	1.6	30.3	29.7	9.8	2.2	–	–	–	26.7	19.2
Unit Value:	*US$/kg*												
Coffee		3.10	1.90	2.00	2.40	2.70	2.30	2.82	2.10	1.83	1.45	0.99	0.95
Cotton		1.80	1.90	1.80	1.60	1.80	1.40	1.04	1.21	1.48	1.72	1.53	1.53
Tea		0.60	0.60	0.70	0.90	1.30	0.80	1.14	0.90	0.39	0.99	0.77	0.77
Tobacco		1.00	–	–	1.30	2.10	1.30	–	–	1.20	1.36	1.26	2.50
Maize & beans		–	–	0.40	0.40	0.30	0.30	–	–	–	–	–	–
Value (FOB):	*US$ millions*												
Coffee		338.7	241.6	340.0	339.7	359.0	355.0	397.3	311.2	264.3	256.7	140.0	121.0
Cotton		4.3	2.2	3.3	11.6	12.4	15.4	5.1	4.1	3.1	4.0	5.8	11.0
Tea		0.3	0.3	0.8	1.2	3.2	1.0	3.2	1.9	1.2	3.1	3.7	5.0
Tobacco		0.3	–	–	0.9	1.5	0.5	–	0.0	0.6	1.5	2.9	4.4
Maize & beans		–	–	0.6	11.3	10.1	3.1	1.1	0.0	0.3	–	7.5	5.0
Other exports		2.2	2.5	0.7	2.1	6.6	4.3	4.7	3.1	2.9	2.1	17.5	34.1
Total value		345.8	246.6	346.4	366.8	392.8	379.3	411.4	320.3	272.4	267.4	177.3	180.5

Source: Research Department, Bank of Uganda.

COMPOSITION OF RECORDED IMPORTS (CIF)
In millions of US$

	1986	1987	1988	1989	1990	First Semester 1991	1991
Imports not requiring foreign exchange							
Food and beverages	–	–	6.1	7.7	4.2	3.5	–
Other consumer goods	–	–	39.6	34.5	16.2	7.3	–
Intermediate goods	–	–	12.3	14.5	12.4	12.7	–
Petroleum and petroleum by-products	–	–	0.7	0.0	0.0	0.0	–
Capital goods	–	–	39.0	34.4	34.2	16.2	–
Total	125.9	97.7	97.7	91.2	67.0	39.8	–
Imports requiring foreign exchange							
Food and beverages	3.5	8.6	1.4	3.4	3.0	2.2	4.0
Other consumer goods	5.5	41.0	20.2	75.0	41.3	12.5	22.0
Intermediate goods	7.1	29.9	24.8	34.4	30.2	14.2	31.4
Petroleum and petroleum by-products 1/	77.7	43.3	61.7	66.2	75.6	36.2	65.9
Capital goods	19.1	24.1	6.6	66.9	56.8	15.8	26.4
Total	113.0	146.8	114.6	245.9	206.8	81.0	149.8
Total of recorded imports	238.9	244.5	212.3	337.1	273.8	120.8	–
Project-related imports 2/	129.5	165.0	181.0	192.5	202.4	108.9	193.4
Total imports	368.4	409.5	393.3	529.6	476.2	229.7	–

Source: Research Department, Bank of Uganda

1/ For 1986, this category also includes chemicals.
2/ Source is IMF for years prior to 1990.

Note: Details of project imports are not recorded. This table
in reported on a calendar year basis and does not include
barter imports. Consequently, it does not correspond to the
Balance of Payments (Table III.1).

SERVICE IMPORTS
In millions of US$

	1987	1988	1989	1990	1991
Overdue bills	8.1	22.8	4.4	0.5	0.1
Medical treatment	0.8	0.7	0.4	0.8	1.0
Education	1.9	2.1	1.6	0.9	0.5
Public	0.6	0.8	0.5	0.5	0.5
Private	1.4	1.3	1.2	0.4	0.0
Travel	9.6	11.4	11.8	10.1	10.4
Public	5.3	5.1	5.7	7.7	9.9
Private	4.3	6.2	6.2	2.5	0.5
Diplomatic missions	11.3	8.5	10.3	11.4	11.7
Savings and maintenance	1.1	1.2	1.0	1.1	1.5
Dividends and reinsurance	1.8	1.3	1.7	2.1	0.1
Others 1/	43.5	52.0	44.9	29.0	27.3
PTA clearing house settlements	--	--	--	14.4	8.0
External debt payments	--	70.3	38.8	58.5	35.6
Total services	78.1	170.3	114.9	128.8	96.1

Source:　　Research Department, Bank of Uganda.

1/　　Includes clearing/freight charges, fees, commissions
and services related to imports and exports.

EXTERNAL DEBT
In millions of US$

	1986	1987	1988	1989	1990	1991
Total external debt	1401	1916	1946	2231	2638	2832
Debt outstanding & disbursed	1085	1577	1611	1898	2213	2325
Long-term debt						
Public and publicly guaranteed debt	1085	1577	1611	1898	2213	2325
Official creditors	893	1289	1332	1619	1941	2093
Multilaterals	626	833	897	1007	1297	1446
IDA	370	534	585	673	935	1078
IBRD	43	50	44	37	34	29
Bilaterals	267	455	436	612	644	646
Private creditors	192	288	279	279	272	232
Commercial banks	55	65	82	102	93	77
Bonds	0	0	0	0	0	0
Other private	137	223	197	177	179	154
Private nonguaranteed	0	0	0	0	0	0
Use of IMF credit	249	273	252	225	282	330
Short-term debt	67	66	83	108	143	177
o/w Interest arrears on LDOD	32	34	43	57	86	115
Undisbursed debt	441	569	683	717	901	1166
Long-term debt	441	569	683	717	901	1166
Public and publicly guaranteed debt	441	569	683	717	901	1166
Official creditors	426	514	636	660	857	1123
Multilaterals	358	430	552	517	706	732
IDA	235	284	330	320	490	351
IBRD	0	0	0	0	0	0
Bilaterals	68	85	84	143	152	392
Private creditors	15	55	48	57	43	42
Commitments	108	471	321	368	469	435
Long-term debt	108	471	321	368	469	435
Public and publicly guaranteed debt	108	471	321	368	469	435
Official creditors	75	297	290	312	425	431
Multilaterals	23	155	258	124	378	180
IDA	0	126	132	95	354	0
IBRD	0	0	0	0	0	0
Bilaterals	52	142	32	188	47	251
Private creditors	33	174	31	56	45	4

Continued

EXTERNAL DEBT – *Continued*

	1986	1987	1988	1989	1990	1991
Disbursements	180	460	257	363	389	253
Long-term debt	180	400	185	312	305	175
Public and publicly guaranteed debt	180	400	185	312	305	175
Official creditors	148	269	148	266	268	171
Multilaterals	92	138	117	146	233	152
IDA	64	115	73	97	213	130
IBRD	0	0	0	0	0	0
Bilaterals	57	131	31	120	36	18
Private creditors	32	131	37	47	37	4
Commercial banks	0	6	22	41	1	0
Bonds	0	0	0	0	0	0
Other private	32	125	15	6	36	4
Private nonguaranteed	0	0	0	0	0	0
IMF purchases	0	60	72	51	84	78
Principal repayments	118	117	153	127	95	101
Long-term debt	31	42	74	58	49	68
Public and publicly guaranteed debt	31	42	74	58	49	68
Official creditors	14	22	41	28	23	29
Multilaterals	11	14	19	22	18	19
IDA	0	1	1	1	2	2
IBRD	2	3	3	5	4	5
Bilaterals	3	9	22	7	6	9
Private creditors	17	20	33	29	26	39
Commercial banks	2	1	1	13	13	14
Bonds	0	0	0	0	0	0
Other private	14	19	32	16	13	25
Private nonguaranteed	0	0	0	0	0	0
IMF repurchases	87	75	79	69	46	33
Interest payments	49	43	41	43	33	37
Long-term debt	22	23	22	23	15	24
Public and publicly guaranteed debt	22	23	22	23	15	24
Official creditors	18	21	19	19	14	20
Multilaterals	15	18	17	17	13	19
IDA	3	5	5	4	5	8
IBRD	3	3	3	3	2	2
Bilaterals	3	3	2	1	2	1
Private creditors	4	2	3	4	1	5
Commercial banks	2	1	0	1	0	3
Bonds	0	0	0	0	0	0
Other private	2	1	3	3	1	1
Private nonguaranteed	0	0	0	0	0	0
IMF charges	25	18	16	16	13	8
Short-term debt	2	2	3	4	5	5

Continued

EXTERNAL DEBT – *Continued*

	1986	1987	1988	1989	1990	1991
Total debt service	167	160	194	170	128	138
Long-term debt	53	65	96	81	64	92
Public and publicly guaranteed debt	53	65	96	81	64	92
Official creditors	32	43	60	47	37	49
Multilaterals	26	32	36	39	31	38
IDA	3	6	6	5	7	10
IBRD	5	6	6	8	6	7
Bilaterals	6	12	24	8	8	10
Private creditors	21	22	36	33	27	44
Commercial banks	4	2	1	14	13	17
Bonds	0	0	0	0	0	0
Other private	16	20	35	19	14	26
Private nonguaranteed	0	0	0	0	0	0
IMF repurchases and charges	112	93	95	85	59	41
Short-term debt (interest only)	2	2	3	4	5	5
Net flows	75	340	112	246	300	157
Long-term debt	149	358	111	254	256	107
Public and publicly guaranteed debt	149	358	111	254	256	107
Official creditors	134	247	107	238	245	142
Multilaterals	81	124	98	124	215	133
IDA	64	114	72	96	211	128
IBRD	-2	-3	-3	-5	-4	-5
Bilaterals	54	122	9	113	30	9
Private creditors	15	111	4	18	11	-35
Commercial banks	-2	5	21	28	-12	-14
Bonds	0	0	0	0	0	0
Other private	18	106	-17	-10	23	-21
Private nonguaranteed	0	0	0	0	0	0
IMF credit	-87	-15	-7	-18	38	45
Short-term debt	13	-3	8	10	6	5
Net transfers	138	390	166	288	326	161
Long-term debt	127	335	89	231	241	83
Public and publicly guaranteed debt	127	335	89	231	241	83
Official creditors	116	226	88	219	231	122
Multilaterals	66	106	81	107	202	114
IDA	61	109	67	92	206	120
IBRD	-5	-6	-6	-8	-6	-7
Bilaterals	51	119	7	112	28	8
Private creditors	11	109	1	14	10	-40
Commercial banks	-4	4	21	27	-12	-17
Bonds	0	0	0	0	0	0
Other private	16	105	-20	-13	22	-22
Private nonguaranteed	0	0	0	0	0	0
IMF credit	-112	-33	-23	-34	25	37
Short-term debt (interest only)	-2	-2	-3	-4	-5	-5

CENTRAL GOVERNMENT OPERATIONS
In millions of U Sh

	1986/87	1987/88	1988/89	1989/90	1990/91	Est. 1991/92	Budget 1992/93
Total revenue	5811	22548	47854	94526	136808	185995	290692
Tax revenue, fees & licenses	4946	20115	41692	90775	133366	179864	282100
o/w Coffee	1996	6299	5370	14931	12730	2005	0
Non-tax revenue	865	2433	6162	3751	3442	6131	8592
Total expenditures	11042	44300	91596	174928	269168	581496	774268
Current expenditure	6900	24700	60870	98296	130583	323017	369300
Wages & salaries	1200	3700	9778	12973	24132	47846	65000
Interest payments	500	2300	5800	8557	18656	90093	111502
Other	5200	18700	45292	76766	87795	185078	192798
Net lending/investment	0	0	1926	0	4500	8500	7500
Capital expenditure	4142	19600	28800	76632	134085	249978	397468
External	2307	11800	18037	42804	82015	213272	357363
Domestic counterpart	1835	2500	4105	5816	9855	13981	33105
Local capital	..	5300	6658	28012	42215	22725	7000
Current cccount balance	-1089	-2152	-13016	-3771	6225	-137022	-78608
Overall deficit (commitment)	-5231	-21752	-43742	-80403	-132360	-395501	-483576
Change in arrears, net	-30	-1248	-3222	-9441	-12385	2491	-62496
Overall deficit (cash)	-5261	-23000	-46964	-89844	-144745	-393010	-546072
Financing:	5261	23000	46964	89844	144746	393010	546071
Budgetary grants	562	6500	14160	20296	70185	194644	301793
External, net	400	8700	19404	91815	65152	142339	246278
Borrowing	1700	11200	22204	75641	96623	131605	246212
Repayment	1300	4900	13600	28355	58361	123839	86361
Other 1/	0	2400	10800	44529	26890	134573	86427
Domestic	4299	7800	13400	-22268	9409	56027	-2000
Bank	4699	7800	12300	-19326	3700	51391	-14000
Non-bank	-400	0	1100	-2942	5709	4636	12000
Memorandum item:							
Revenue and grants	6373	29048	62014	114822	206993	380639	592485
Overall deficit plus grants	-4699	-16500	-32804	-69548	-74560	-198366	-244279

Source: Ministry of Finance and Economic Planning and IMF.

1/   Includes debt rescheduling, moratorium interest, etc.

TABLE V.2

CENTRAL GOVERNMENT REVENUE

In millions of U Sh

	1986/87	1987/88	1988/89	1989/90	1990/91	Est 1991/92	Budget 1992/93
Taxes on income and profits	570	1792	4770	9461	13870	23639	34530
PAYE (Pay-as-you-earn)	34	76	495	705	1011	3207	2722
Company/individual profits	536	1716	4275	8756	12859	20431	31808
Taxes on goods and services	1674	8208	22436	38010	52030	63762	113192
Sales tax	1266	6273	16600	28890	36558	43318	84341
Local	634	2836	5304	9897	16455	22706	37738
Imports	632	3437	11296	18993	20104	20612	46603
Excise duty	340	1647	4905	6970	12416	15027	19251
Commercial transaction levy	68	288	931	2150	3055	5417	9600
Taxes on international trade	2591	9697	13217	39085	62312	78593	122992
Import duties	595	3381	7792	24150	49582	76588	122992
Petroleum	0	1100	3113	15858	36138	54785	83830
Other	595	2281	4679	8292	13444	21804	39162
Export duties	1996	6316	5425	14934	12730	2005	0
Coffee	1996	6299	5370	14931	12730	2005	0
Other	0	17	55	3	0	0	0
Other tax revenue	..	..	..	..	..	7660	2741
Fees and licenses	111	418	1269	4219	5155	6209	8646
Total tax revenue, fees & licenses	4946	20115	41692	90775	133366	179864	282100
Non-tax revenue	865	2433	6162	3751	3442	6131	8592
Total revenue	5811	22548	47854	94526	136808	185995	290692
Grants	562	6500	14160	20296	70185	194644	301793
Total revenue & grants	6373	29048	62014	114822	206993	380639	592485

Source: Ministry of Finance and Economic Planning and IMF.

CENTRAL GOVERNMENT EXPENDITURE

In millions of U Sh

	1986/87	1987/88	1988/89	1989/90	1990/91	Est. 1991/92	Budget 1992/93
Total current expenditure	6900	24700	60870	98296	130583	323017	369300
Economic classification	6900	24700	60870	98296	130583	323017	369300
Wages and salaries	1200	3700	9778	12973	24132	47846	65000
Interest payments 1/	500	2300	5800	8557	18656	90093	111502
Other	5200	18700	45292	76766	87795	185078	192798
Functional classification	6900	24700	60870	98296	130583	323017	369300
General public services	1272	3548	11241	16531	22493	..	80112
Defense and security	2917	8927	23965	48468	54502	..	77184
Education	838	5515	10386	11656	18687	..	49115
Health	210	986	2450	4431	6006	..	24334
Other social services	399	1121	2085	2398	2079	..	5881
Economic services	764	2303	4943	6255	8160	..	21171
Interest payments	500	2300	5800	8557	18656	90093	111502
Total capital expenditure	4142	19600	28800	76632	134085	249978	397468
Economic classification	4142	19600	28800	76632	134085	249978	397468
Domestic	1835	2500	4105	5816	9855	13981	33105
External	2307	11800	18037	42804	82015	213272	357363
Local capital	..	5300	6658	28012	42215	22725	7000
Functional classification	4142	19600	28800	76632	134085	249978	397468
General public services	726	6191	9914	34663	57362	..	131676
Defense and security	155	5296	1482	2588	3328	..	1298
Education	437	17	430	2359	9435	..	78189
Health	76	691	1672	2343	3683	..	34587
Other social services	232	333	1753	3987	2266	..	4822
Economic services	2516	7073	13548	30691	58011	..	146897
Net Lending/Investment	0	0	1926	0	4500	8500	7500
Total Expenditure	11042	44300	91596	174928	269168	581495	774268

Source: IMF.

Note: Because of different sources and classifications, this table
          may not necessarily be consistent with Text Tables 7.1 and 7.2.

MONETARY SURVEY
In billions of U Sh

	1986/87	1987/88	1988/89	1989/90	1990/91	1991/92
Foreign assets, net	-13.6	-18.7	-63.9	-89.1	-151.6	-277.6
Bank of Uganda	-14.0	-19.7	-66.0	-93.4	-165.8	-312.0
o/w Use of Fund Credit	-15.1	-14.0	-48.3	-97.7	-197.5	-399.4
Commercial banks	0.4	1.0	2.1	4.3	14.3	34.4
Domestic credit	8.2	24.2	68.5	79.7	120.7	200.8
Claims on Government, net	4.1	11.9	26.4	9.2	12.9	64.0
o/w Bank of Uganda	4.0	12.2	11.5	10.9	14.3	65.3
Claims on private sector	4.1	12.3	42.1	70.5	107.8	136.7
o/w Crop financing	1.5	4.5	19.5	24.4	40.5	41.4
Other	2.6	7.8	22.6	46.1	67.3	95.3
Total assets	-5.4	5.5	4.6	-9.4	-30.8	-76.9
Total liabilities	-5.4	5.5	4.6	-9.4	-30.8	-76.9
					42.6	
Broad money, M2	8.6	26.8	60.2	94.4	138.6	222.3
Money supply, M1	7.6	24.2	54.3	81.4	116.1	176.0
Currency in circulation	4.0	14.4	29.2	38.6	56.2	84.3
Demand deposits	3.6	9.8	25.1	42.8	59.9	91.7
Quasi-money	1.0	2.6	5.9	13.0	22.5	46.3
Other items, net	-14.0	-21.3	-55.6	-103.9	-169.4	-299.2
o/w Currency revaluation	-14.1	-14.1	-43.2	..	..	..

Memorandum items:

M2/GDP	6.2	6.4	6.8	6.8	7.2	7.9
Velocity	16.2	15.7	14.8	14.6	13.8	12.7

Source: Bank of Uganda and IMF.

INTEREST RATE STRUCTURE
In percent

	1984 Dec.	1985 Dec.	1986 Dec.	1987 Dec.	1988 Dec.	1989 Dec.	1990 Dec.	1991 Dec.	1992 June
Bank of Uganda									
Ways and means	2	2	5	5	15	15	14	14	--
Re-discount rate	23	23	35	32	38	48	43	40	43
Bank rate to commercial banks	24	24	36	31	45	55	50	46	49
Treasury bills									
35 days	20	20	30	23	33	38	34	35	--
63 days	21	21	32	25	35	40	36	36	--
91 days	22	22	35	28	38	43	39	37	--
Government stocks									
1 year	24	24	35	--	--	--	--	--	--
5 years	25	25	40	30	40	45	40	40	--
10 years	26	26	45	32	42	47	42	42	--
15 years	27	27	--	35	45	50	45	45	--
Commercial banks									
Deposit rates 1/									
Demand deposits	5	5	10	7	15	20	18	13	8
Savings deposits	18	18	28	18	28	33	30	32	35
Time deposits 1/									
3-6 months	20	20	25	15	28	33	30	34	36
7-12 months	20	20	30	20	30	35	32	35	38
Minimum 1 year	22	22	35	22	32	37	33	36	39
Lending rates 2/									
Developmental	24	24	38	22-25	32-35	25-40	36	37	40
Commerce	25	25	40	30	40	50	45	41	44

Source: Bank of Uganda.

1/   Minimum rates.
2/   Maximum rates.

EXCHANGE RATE MOVEMENTS

U Sh per US$

	Bureau Market Mid-Rate	Bureau Average FY & CY (Note 1)	Official Mid-Rate	Official Average FY & CY (Note 1)	Official/ Bureau	Official/ Bureau Period Average FY & CY (Note 1)	Real Effective Rate Sept. 1989=100
1989 January	396		165		41.7		70.2
February	406		165		40.6		77.9
March	460		192		41.8		80.8
April	520		200		38.5		80.6
May	566		200		35.3		85.2
June	612	438	200	304	32.7	53.9	90.6
July	613		200		32.6		94.9
August	592		200		33.8		95.5
September	611		200		32.7		100.0
October	620		232		37.4		86.5
November	714		342		47.9		60.3
December	720	569	370	222	51.4	38.9	55.6
1990 January	763		374		49.0		55.8
February	716		378		52.8		56.0
March	642		379		59.0		55.4
April	644		379		58.9		54.3
May	650		383		58.9		54.0
June	657	662	397	319	60.4	47.9	51.3
July	637		440		69.0		45.2
August	697		450		64.5		45.6
September	731		480		65.7		46.0
October	725		480		66.2		46.4
November	751		510		68.0		43.8
December	769	698	540	433	70.3	61.9	42.9
1991 January	778		570		73.2		42.0
February	787		600		76.2		40.1
March	815		620		76.1		40.9
April	847		640		75.5		41.6
May	888		670		75.4		40.0
June	939	780	700	558	74.5	71.2	41.2
July	957		800		83.6		39.5
August	973		800		82.2		36.3
September	981		850		86.7		34.3
October	1002		915		91.4		34.3
November	1070		915		85.5		32.7
December	1184	935	915	750	77.3	79.8	33.6
1992 January	1241		970		78.2		32.9
February	1260		985		78.2		35.0
March	1250		1160		92.8		36.0
April	1208		1159		96.0		34.6
May	1216		1165		95.8		35.4
June	1225	1130	1166	983	95.2	86.9	34.8
July	1248		1178		94.4		34.4
August	1256		1185		94.4		33.6
September	1233		1185		96.1		33.5
October	1222		1181		96.6		34.9
November	1241		1199		96.6		36.4
December	1248	1237	1214	1146	97.3	92.6	35.5

Source: Bank of Uganda and IMF.

Note: An increase in the real effective exchange rate implies that
Uganda becomes less competitive.

1/ FY refers to fiscal year, July to June, and is read from the June line;
CY refers to calendar year, January to December, and is read from the December entry.

FOREIGN EXCHANGE AUCTIONS

U Sh per US$

Auction No.	Date	Clearing Rate	Highest Rate	Bureau Rate Auction Day (Note 1)	Spread: Bureau/ Clearing (Note 2)	Total Sold US$ m	Declared Amount US$ m
1	31-Jan-92	970	1100	1199	20.7%	2.3	5.0
2	07-Feb-92	980	1100	1194	19.0%	1.4	2.5
3	14-Feb-92	990	1050	1188	17.1%	2.5	2.5
4	21-Feb-92	995	1050	1187	16.5%	3.3	3.5
5	28-Feb-92	1000	1050	1186	15.8%	1.9	4.0
6	06-Mar-92	1000	1050	1179	15.1%	3.2	3.5
7	13-Mar-92	1000	1050	1169	14.2%	1.3	2.5
8	20-Mar-92	1000	1050	1152	12.5%	3.4	4.0
9	27-Mar-92	1000	1175	1131	10.9%	2.2	4.0
10	06-Apr-92	1000	1050	1077	5.6%	2.0	3.5
11	10-Apr-92	1000	1020	1116	9.4%	2.1	3.0
12	21-Apr-92	1000	1010	1119	9.7%	1.7	3.5
13	24-Apr-92	1001	1030	1123	10.0%	0.9	1.0
14	04-May-92	1002	1050	1127	10.3%	1.0	1.2
15	08-May-92	1006	1050	1128	9.9%	0.3	0.6
16	15-May-92	1010	1015	1132	9.9%	3.5	3.5
17	22-May-92	1012	1030	1132	9.7%	2.3	1.5
18	29-May-92	1014	1020	1136	9.8%	1.2	2.5
19	05-Jun-92	1015	1030	1137	9.8%	1.1	3.5
20	12-Jun-92	1016	1025	1139	9.9%	1.6	2.0
21	19-Jun-92	1018	1022	1139	9.7%	2.0	2.0
22	26-Jun-92	1020	1025	1140	9.6%	1.7	2.0
23	03-Jul-92	1020	1026	1142	9.7%	2.5	2.5
24	10-Jul-92	1021	1027	1145	10.0%	1.8	3.0
25	17-Jul-92	1022	1026	1147	10.0%	1.5	1.5
26	24-Jul-92	1022	1026	1153	10.6%	1.0	2.5
27	31-Jul-92	1023	1025	1154	10.6%	0.4	1.5
28	07-Aug-92	1024	1200	1156	10.7%	3.1	3.1
29	14-Aug-92	1024	1026	1157	10.8%	0.3	1.5
30	21-Aug-92	1025	1026	1157	10.7%	1.3	1.5
31	28-Aug-92	1027	1028	1156	10.4%	0.9	1.0
32	04-Sep-92	1028	1031	1157	10.3%	2.7	3.5
33	11-Sep-92	1029	1031	1159	10.4%	0.6	1.5
34	18-Sep-92	1029	1035	1157	10.3%	1.4	1.5
35	25-Sep-92	1030	1033	1158	10.2%	1.5	1.5
36	02-Oct-92	1030	1033	1157	10.1%	1.4	2.5
37	12-Oct-92	1030	1034	1156	10.1%	1.4	1.5
38	16-Oct-92	1032	1036	1157	9.9%	1.4	1.5
39	23-Oct-92	1032	1044	1159	10.1%	2.8	3.0
40	30-Oct-92	1034	1035	1161	10.0%	2.0	2.0
41	06-Nov-92	1034	1036	1163	10.3%	1.5	2.5
42	13-Nov-92	1034	1038	1167	10.6%	1.6	2.0
43	20-Nov-92	1034	1038	1171	11.1%	1.6	2.0
44	27-Nov-92	1035	1037	1179	11.7%	1.6	3.0
45	04-Dec-92	1035	1038	1181	11.8%	2.5	2.5
46	11-Dec-92	1035	1040	1184	12.2%	1.2	2.0
47	18-Dec-92	1036	1039	1187	12.3%	0.8	1.5
48	28-Dec-92	1037	1039	1185	12.0%	1.0	1.0

Source: Bank of Uganda.

Notes:
1/ TC = Bureau travellers' check rate.
2/ For this calculation, the clearing rate includes BOU charges of 2.4% until auction no. 8 inclusive; thereafter, 2%.

PRODUCTION OF PRINCIPAL MANUFACTURED COMMODITIES

	Sugar	Beer	Soft Drinks	Cigarettes	Textiles	Cement	Electricity	Laundry Soap
Unit	Tons	'000 Ltr	'000 Ltr	Million	'000 Sq M	Tons	'000 Kwh	Tons
Annual								
1982	3,289	9,787	1,795	745.0	18,557	18,471	559,800	n.a.
1983	3,133	14,206	3,953	645.0	16,607	30,780	515,500	n.a.
1984	2,943	14,817	5,784	965.8	11,475	24,921	614,400	n.a.
1985	808	8,184	5,002	1,416.4	10,418	11,749	626,500	n.a.
1986	0	6,603	5,049	1,420.1	9,733	16,376	637,200	2,902
1987	0	16,484	5,875	1,434.8	10,465	15,904	618,087	15,508
1988	7,535	21,139	13,431	1,637.7	11,067	14,960	565,909	17,929
1989	15,859	19,516	16,178	1,585.9	11,589	17,378	659,971	26,872
1990	28,915	19,420	24,275	1,289.7	8,172	26,920	736,500	30,816
1991	42,456	19,529	25,982	1,688.2	8,901	27,138	782,518	33,283
Monthly								
1989 Jan	1,603	2,428	876	110.8	375	477	41,512	2,469
Feb	1,264	1,592	1,215	132.4	988	325	45,549	2,264
Mar	775	2,382	1,385	149.3	1,066	2,109	56,429	2,382
Apr	1,204	1,746	1,159	141.9	1,203	1,358	53,952	2,003
May	430	997	1,510	136.8	1,222	71	52,595	1,897
Jun	1,273	2,442	1,546	173.1	963	1,008	55,655	2,671
Jul	1,482	1,179	1,586	142.5	1,032	1,185	57,864	2,047
Aug	1,906	1,472	1,368	132.7	1,115	1,490	57,261	1,704
Sep	1,641	1,342	1,822	125.1	1,039	1,793	56,916	1,928
Oct	1,655	1,237	1,294	120.5	1,079	2,071	58,521	2,606
Nov	707	1,288	1,167	140.6	1,085	2,785	60,840	2,285
Dec	1,919	1,411	1,250	80.2	422	2,706	62,877	2,616
1990 Jan	2,701	1,667	1,617	102.7	572	3,412	62,089	2,601
Feb	3,093	1,275	1,409	125.9	997	1,210	52,675	2,283
Mar	2,095	1,531	1,655	105.1	1,186	3,705	54,587	3,033
Apr	2,275	1,576	1,943	57.0	777	503	65,978	2,484
May	2,911	1,804	2,336	101.5	901	2,405	64,174	3,200
Jun	2,949	1,811	2,217	103.1	655	5,104	63,794	1,966
Jul	3,797	1,857	2,014	96.2	677	1,054	62,666	2,420
Aug	2,595	1,897	2,008	125.3	824	783	62,641	2,343
Sep	1,453	1,147	2,066	133.1	597	2,661	66,154	3,508
Oct	1,388	1,843	2,441	109.1	503	2,142	67,119	2,050
Nov	1,484	1,497	2,161	120.9	343	3,011	57,442	2,439
Dec	2,174	1,515	2,408	109.8	140	930	57,181	2,489
1991 Jan	3,146	1,464	2,229	139.0	8	2,659	56,266	2,280
Feb	3,604	1,222	1,976	136.1	170	2,944	50,592	2,916
Mar	3,387	1,572	2,523	112.6	743	4,315	55,672	3,024
Apr	2,059	1,501	1,869	127.7	774	899	51,683	3,137
May	2,418	1,529	1,909	139.4	875	2,022	53,314	2,325
Jun	2,850	1,206	1,877	154.1	860	2,620	66,264	2,163
Jul	2,674	1,581	1,767	143.6	1,164	686	73,172	1,587
Aug	5,142	1,638	2,159	146.1	1,111	2,679	74,677	2,561
Sep	4,273	1,678	2,188	137.1	1,036	401	66,180	3,392
Oct	4,679	1,822	2,353	135.7	1,153	739	77,662	3,123
Nov	4,190	2,038	2,080	160.6	824	5,346	76,139	3,202
Dec	4,034	2,278	3,052	156.2	183	1,828	80,897	3,573
1992 Jan	4,295	1,846	2,132	121.2	324	3,142	82,575	3,814
Feb	2,716	1,380	1,376	142.6	855	3,125	75,923	3,165
Mar	4,745	1,890	2,316	138.2	1,120	2,453	82,761	3,680
Apr	4,371	1,752	2,063	129.0	991	3,391	85,448	2,531
May	5,105	1,569	1,561	155.7	1091	4,482	77,100	3,486
Jun	4,599	1,592	1,529	140.3	800	46	72,486	2,430
Jul	4,498	968	1,482	191.3	1,005	4,038	87,485	2,304
Aug	5,022	1,153	1,458	126.3	1,074	2,251	87,111	3,008
Sep	4,595	1,253	1,540	140.0	1,079	1,260	77,957	3,156

Source: Statistics Department, MFEP.

INDEX OF INDUSTRIAL PRODUCTION

Annual Summary, 1987 = 100

	No. of Estabs	Weight	1985	1986	1987	1988	1989	1990	1991	1992**
Food processing	51	20.70	93.9	85.3	100.0	128.0	153.7	174.9	227.4	242.9
Meat, fish and dairy	10	1.70	106.4	72.5	100.0	149.4	109.4	127.2	166.8	207.3
Grain milling	13	4.30	83.5	77.3	100.0	139.5	139.1	134.7	114.9	90.6
Bakeries	9	1.40	83.8	70.6	100.0	131.7	153.4	206.6	284.1	319.8
Sugar and jaggery	4	1.80	125.9	72.2	100.0	277.5	514.7	789.3	1220.5	1504.1
Coffee roasting	3	0.20	101	102.0	100.0	73.1	48.2	74.2	74.3	120.3
Coffee processing *	–	8.62	90.1	98.9	100.0	95.6	106.0	81.0	92.8	73.2
Tea processing *	1	1.39	153.2	97.4	100.0	98.6	130.9	184.1	238.1	219.0
Other food processing	4	0.30	56.3	69.3	100.0	115.4	104.9	100.9	91.1	68.4
Animal feeds	7	0.99	32.8	52.1	100.0	101.9	121.0	116.7	161.2	151.3
Tobacco and beverages	12	26.10	84.8	82.2	100.0	139.6	143.7	155.2	176.1	150.0
Beer and spirits	5	6.61	55.4	43.4	100.0	127.1	124.2	125.0	129.3	111.6
Soft drinks	6	5.40	84.5	85.8	100.0	221.3	253.8	362.4	385.5	289.5
Cigarettes	1	14.09	98.7	99.0	100.0	114.1	110.5	89.9	117.7	114.5
Textiles and clothing	13	16.30	98.9	92.9	100.0	121.8	132.7	116.3	110.9	121.4
Textiles	4	12.00	102.6	93.8	100.0	106.4	110.4	79.8	88.2	100.0
Textile products	4	3.09	55.9	65.9	100.0	84.3	107.7	116.5	48.7	49.9
Garments	5	1.21	173.2	153.8	100.0	370.9	419.1	477.8	556.0	518.3
Leather and footwear	7	2.30	86.9	90.0	100.0	62.0	62.9	75.3	60.1	78.9
Timber, paper and printing	22	9.00	76.8	72.0	100.0	135.1	169.4	183.6	198.2	212.7
Sawmilling and timber	4	3.20	53.3	60.8	100.0	96.0	61.5	58.0	58.1	62.9
Furniture & foam products	7	2.90	65.5	86.9	100.0	140.0	221.9	190.9	162.3	167.6
Paper and printing	11	2.90	114.0	69.6	100.0	173.7	236.1	315.2	389.0	423.4
Chemicals, paint and soap	19	12.30	58.6	58.8	100.0	111.2	162.9	183.5	192.9	238.0
Chemicals	1	0.31	87.4	68.4	100.0	88.1	88.1	79.9	110.9	140.7
Paint	4	0.51	176.2	88.2	100.0	98.3	167.5	62.0	168.2	443.8
Medicine	4	0.50	106.6	104.2	100.0	70.1	166.8	284.3	103.6	318.8
Soap	10	10.98	50.2	55.1	100.0	114.3	164.6	187.4	200.4	227.6
Bricks and cement	14	4.30	122.7	120.6	100.0	94.5	109.0	154.2	162.6	194.1
Bricks, tiles, etc.	12	2.23	171.2	137.3	100.0	98.8	105.2	149.0	167.8	208.3
Cement	2	2.07	70.6	102.8	100.0	89.7	113.2	159.8	157.1	178.3
Steel and steel products	19	5.30	133.1	105.9	100.0	87.2	98.9	107.7	149.3	191.4
Iron and steel	6	1.51	249.4	95.3	100.0	125.1	74.1	57.5	130.8	253.5
Structural steel	4	2.28	73.8	71.6	100.0	66.4	134.6	131.0	166.9	152.4
Steel products	9	1.51	107.1	167.7	100.0	80.9	69.9	122.6	141.2	188.4
Miscellaneous	17	3.70	139.1	141.0	100.0	134.0	204.2	181.3	251.2	262.4
Vehicle accessories	5	0.91	164.4	146.7	100.0	104.5	164.0	224.8	299.9	350.7
Plastic products	4	0.63	84.2	90.4	100.0	58.2	105.0	107.2	187.1	264.4
Electrical products	2	1.15	83.5	76.1	100.0	100.9	142.9	110.5	82.1	108.5
Miscellaneous products	6	1.01	214.1	241.2	100.0	245.4	372.0	269.0	440.1	356.8
Index – all items *	174	100.00	91.3	86.1	100.0	123.7	145.2	155.5	178.2	187.7
Annual percentage change				-9.6	-5.7	16.1	23.7	17.4	7.1	14.6	5.3

* Data include production data as provided by the coffee and tea marketing boards.

** Average based on the first nine months of 1992.

Source: Statistics Department, MFEP.

INDEX OF INDUSTRIAL PRODUCTION
Monthly Summary, 1987 = 100

	Food Process	Drinks and Tobac.	Text. and Cloth.	Leather and Footwear	Timber Paper ect.	Chem. Paint Soap	Bricks and Cement	Steel Prod.	Misc.	All Items
No. of Estabs	51	12	13	7	22	19	14	19	17	174
Weight	20.7	26.1	16.3	2.3	9.0	12.3	4.3	5.3	3.7	100.0
Annual										
1982	106.7	48.6	196.7	77.9	68.2	64.6	163.7	81.6	87.6	97.3
1983	103.7	59.8	177.6	152.8	79.6	68.8	177.4	118.5	124.3	103.7
1984	99.8	79.4	136.9	175.5	88.7	61.2	156.5	110.7	139.5	101.0
1985	93.9	84.8	98.9	86.9	76.8	58.6	122.7	133.1	139.1	91.3
1986	85.3	82.2	92.9	90.0	72.0	58.8	120.6	105.9	141.0	86.1
1987	100.0	100.0	100.0	100.0	100.0	100.0	100.0	100.0	100.0	100.0
1988	128.0	139.6	121.8	62.0	135.1	111.2	94.5	87.2	134.0	123.7
1989	153.7	143.7	132.7	62.9	169.4	162.9	109.0	98.9	204.2	145.2
1990	174.9	155.2	116.3	75.3	183.6	183.5	154.2	107.7	181.3	155.5
1991	227.4	176.1	110.9	60.1	198.2	192.9	162.6	149.3	251.3	178.2
1992 **	242.9	150.0	121.4	78.9	212.7	238.0	194.1	191.4	262.4	187.7
Monthly										
1989 Jan	187.5	132.0	62.5	40.4	138.7	172.9	71.1	76.7	151.0	130.8
Feb	154.8	141.6	131.2	42.6	162.4	163.5	59.6	96.4	156.2	139.3
Mar	139.9	168.8	135.4	69.2	169.1	167.3	121.3	104.0	121.9	147.7
Apr	157.4	141.5	149.3	61.6	162.0	141.2	109.9	96.9	228.7	145.5
May	143.4	147.1	162.5	39.3	220.2	146.3	51.4	107.7	227.4	149.6
Jun	136.2	182.7	150.9	52.7	194.5	194.0	100.0	116.3	299.3	164.6
Jul	168.3	150.2	141.6	73.7	126.9	148.1	99.0	100.7	263.9	147.8
Aug	185.1	138.3	149.3	81.9	124.8	136.8	116.5	99.7	216.3	147.0
Sep	157.0	149.1	146.1	64.1	205.1	149.3	138.5	106.6	274.3	155.3
Oct	151.2	127.9	145.0	93.2	195.1	181.9	134.4	103.0	174.8	148.1
Nov	115.2	130.9	147.6	71.1	186.6	167.2	157.3	129.7	196.6	142.0
Dec	148.6	113.7	71.3	64.7	147.1	186.5	149.4	48.9	139.6	123.9
1990 Jan	177.9	137.7	74.8	78.4	181.9	194.7	183.2	66.1	131.2	143.3
Feb	181.9	133.4	124.5	74.0	154.2	175.6	109.4	86.1	146.0	144.6
Mar	173.0	141.8	159.2	85.2	174.0	228.4	199.7	117.6	199.7	166.7
Apr	162.6	129.2	116.7	71.9	145.9	181.7	74.1	95.2	234.6	140.4
May	167.4	171.9	131.7	84.8	188.3	226.5	166.5	101.6	235.7	169.0
Jun	165.5	165.1	130.7	68.9	198.6	144.9	244.4	113.5	206.4	160.1
Jul	211.6	152.9	126.7	67.9	202.2	171.3	105.6	117.6	173.9	162.4
Aug	196.5	166.5	149.7	75.3	160.1	163.3	112.1	139.8	181.2	163.7
Sep	145.7	156.5	126.6	106.0	194.3	237.6	186.6	100.5	132.8	159.1
Oct	160.8	174.6	113.9	104.3	208.0	146.4	182.7	98.0	163.9	155.7
Nov	161.2	163.5	96.7	51.7	224.5	165.7	181.2	160.0	181.5	156.6
Dec	195.1	168.9	43.8	34.6	171.3	166.4	104.7	96.6	189.1	144.9
1991 Jan	219.7	170.8	37.7	41.8	179.7	150.6	166.1	117.1	168.5	151.4
Feb	217.2	156.6	62.1	42.8	173.2	189.7	166.7	124.0	248.8	158.8
Mar	196.6	173.5	112.9	34.1	161.3	197.2	221.8	156.5	264.9	171.6
Apr	151.7	157.1	111.2	60.0	177.3	203.0	103.5	107.1	283.5	153.5
May	169.5	165.0	124.6	78.2	219.7	165.7	146.8	125.2	306.2	164.7
Jun	189.3	161.8	125.6	71.8	193.9	155.8	178.9	171.6	315.0	168.6
Jul	221.4	166.5	158.1	69.6	213.6	118.7	130.4	167.3	308.4	176.4
Aug	304.9	177.5	144.5	42.0	214.0	184.9	178.6	172.3	265.5	202.6
Sep	258.0	178.1	132.3	53.7	220.5	248.1	102.5	192.1	166.5	193.8
Oct	274.5	186.0	145.5	80.0	214.0	231.0	143.9	151.1	228.4	201.2
Nov	264.0	188.4	114.9	69.5	215.3	226.8	273.6	175.1	252.5	201.8
Dec	261.5	231.4	61.2	77.1	195.8	242.7	138.9	132.1	206.8	194.4
1992 Jan	261.1	165.2	69.5	94.3	180.9	264.4	180.0	193.1	282.1	187.9
Feb	197.1	154.1	121.0	78.1	211.0	234.4	191.3	152.3	295.1	177.6
Mar	255.4	185.0	145.2	48.0	201.0	278.3	170.7	154.2	324.0	205.7
Apr	232.9	165.5	132.7	110.5	184.8	230.4	190.3	188.4	301.2	189.9
May	256.4	157.2	138.8	74.1	234.1	292.3	226.5	171.5	349.7	207.2
Jun	231.6	148.9	109.1	81.8	254.2	205.7	108.2	203.0	290.3	180.8
Jul	243.7	138.2	134.1	112.4	227.1	188.6	265.9	208.0	241.6	186.0
Aug	258.7	131.1	118.9	72.4	233.2	237.7	191.2	200.1	194.8	185.1
Sep	238.0	142.6	147.4	45.1	182.9	248.9	174.0	241.4	216.6	186.9

**   Average based on the first nine months of 1992.

Source: Statistics Department, MFEP.

PRODUCTION AND EXPORTS OF PRINCIPAL AGRICULTURAL PRODUCTS

	COFFEE			TEA			COTTON		TOBACCO		
	Deliveries	Exports		Prod	Exports		Exports		Prod	Exports	
			US$			US$		US$			US$
	Tons	Tons	'000	Tons	Tons	'000	Tons	'000	Tons	Tons	'000
Annual											
1982	161,866	174,700	349,400	2,580	1,200	800	1,800	3,200	647	0	0
1983	148,224	144,300	346,300	3,054	1,300	1,200	7,000	11,200	1,650	700	900
1984	145,971	133,200	359,600	5,214	2,500	3,300	6,700	12,100	1,969	700	1,500
1985	143,995	151,500	348,500	5,758	1,200	1,000	9,553	13,979	1,613	300	400
1986	159,881	140,800	394,200	3,335	2,800	3,100	4,875	5,086	949	0	0
1987	167,067	148,153	307,535	3,511	2,100	1,900	3,443	4,097	1,214	0	0
1988	151,157	144,254	265,279	3,512	3,079	3,079	2,088	2,968	2,639	39	58
1989	169,042	176,453	262,811	4,658	3,195	3,195	2,321	4,020	3,456	490	569
1990	128,747	141,489	140,384	6,704	4,760	3,566	3,808	5,795	3,322	2,269	2,821
1991	147,368	124,819	117,641	8,877	7,018	6,780	7,819	11,731	5,140	2,467	4,540
1992	111,524	119,795	95,699	..	7,816	7,711	7,740	8,488	6,305	2,544	4,800
Monthly											
1990 Jan	13,537	12,492	11,736	556	444	348	0	0	373	0	0
Feb	11,933	17,731	16,111	526	278	167	64	113	0	80	122
Mar	11,188	10,688	10,601	595	331	273	314	497	0	90	133
Apr	8,252	12,503	13,048	602	327	269	426	672	45	270	377
May	5,633	14,462	15,008	689	287	208	500	784	91	136	192
Jun	4,388	10,510	10,761	638	412	309	648	1,005	35	346	370
Jul	11,793	8,196	8,157	402	484	364	537	834	96	127	155
Aug	15,308	10,616	9,810	296	386	311	685	1,075	147	0	0
Sep	12,280	14,899	14,667	373	470	352	192	296	398	219	210
Oct	10,348	12,057	12,481	623	460	329	150	238	652	166	92
Nov	8,645	9,350	9,576	649	420	338	181	207	885	309	309
Dec	15,442	7,985	8,428	755	461	298	111	74	600	526	861
1991 Jan	16,456	9,849	11,227	773	455	455	149	165	854	248	481
Feb	12,408	11,108	11,376	667	515	592	352	545	5	169	331
Mar	6,657	11,599	11,873	674	923	932	682	968	152	205	410
Apr	3,268	12,248	12,825	793	573	596	446	728	49	917	1,670
May	3,569	5,922	5,923	853	814	806	439	722	0	136	102
Jun	5,980	3,366	3,399	822	585	572	1,134	1,874	0	0	0
Jul	18,197	6,066	5,361	733	616	567	1,196	1,935	63	0	0
Aug	22,013	14,027	11,822	590	488	430	1,457	2,237	276	0	0
Sep	17,282	20,337	17,050	684	495	416	339	411	953	0	0
Oct	13,346	9,206	7,079	674	459	369	947	1,239	711	163	337
Nov	13,422	9,705	8,740	720	662	626	345	501	888	267	463
Dec	14,770	11,386	10,966	894	433	419	333	406	1,189	362	746
1992 Jan	14,807	14,606	13,649	637	761	740	360	470	90	359	764
Feb	12,500	11,118	10,429	488	675	543	472	518	193	270	537
Mar	8,596	14,783	12,148	318	380	370	720	770	122	87	180
Apr	4,520	9,579	7,596	586	462	448	1,122	1,147	118	127	206
May	4,271	9,241	6,998	1,139	659	657	1,006	1,071	0	0	0
Jun	4,225	6,142	4,527	668	583	634	694	772	0	0	0
Jul	12,164	6,463	4,872	789	758	700	1,167	1,356	6	113	232
Aug	12,374	5,740	3,979	757	845	735	285	304	856	59	74
Sep	9,206	14,121	9,659	702	657	738	574	583	1,652	247	287
Oct	7,799	10,988	8,140	1,274	741	748	553	641	1,585	326	587
Nov	8,042	7,534	5,702	768	815	868	233	212	1,153	417	775
Dec	13,020	9,480	8,000	na	480	530	555	644	530	539	1,158

Source: Statistics Department.

Note: Owing to different sources, this table might not be comparable to Tables III.1 and III.2.

NEW CONSUMER PRICE INDEX: KAMPALA

September 1989 = 100, All Households

		Food	Drink & Tobacco	Clothing & Footwear	Rent, Fuel & Util.	HH & Pers. Goods	Trans. & Comm.	Other Goods/ Serv.	Weighted Average CPI	Annual Percent Change	Monthly Percent Change
Weights (%)		*48.6*	*10.2*	*6.1*	*12.5*	*10.4*	*4.6*	*7.6*	*100.0*		
1988	December	64.6	62.3	92.4	69.0	84.5	84.5	66.5	69.7	143.7	-0.9
1989	January	66.7	62.7	92.0	67.1	83.4	84.5	84.2	71.8	82.4	2.9
	February	70.8	62.9	95.2	68.3	81.5	84.6	84.9	74.0	91.0	3.1
	March	74.4	80.8	101.5	72.0	85.2	88.6	85.7	79.0	93.5	6.8
	April	83.4	82.2	98.1	72.8	86.1	88.8	86.8	83.6	91.5	5.8
	May	87.8	85.2	98.6	87.2	89.9	89.3	88.2	88.4	82.0	5.7
	June	88.4	88.6	99.1	98.3	94.8	91.4	92.0	91.4	76.8	3.3
	July	93.6	97.3	100.0	96.3	98.0	99.8	94.0	95.5	41.5	4.5
	August	97.1	98.5	100.0	97.8	98.7	99.5	95.6	97.7	37.5	2.3
	September	100.0	100.0	100.0	100.0	100.0	100.0	100.0	100.0	40.6	2.4
	October	107.5	104.4	102.6	97.2	101.6	110.6	100.2	104.6	48.8	4.6
	November	108.3	114.6	102.7	101.1	102.4	113.7	102.5	106.9	52.0	2.2
	December	109.9	116.7	103.1	104.7	108.1	120.4	103.2	109.3	56.7	2.3
1990	January	111.4	123.5	126.0	127.8	117.4	124.8	136.9	118.8	65.5	8.6
	February	108.3	125.8	129.5	132.3	119.4	126.3	137.1	118.5	60.2	-0.2
	March	106.6	126.6	129.2	138.7	120.1	126.3	140.4	118.9	50.4	0.3
	April	106.9	118.5	129.9	134.1	118.9	127.6	140.4	117.6	40.6	-1.1
	May	103.7	118.5	129.9	146.0	115.4	127.4	140.1	117.2	32.5	-0.4
	June	100.0	113.5	131.6	154.1	114.0	131.4	139.6	116.0	26.9	-1.0
	July	94.2	128.4	141.7	155.6	117.4	132.6	140.9	116.0	21.5	0.0
	August	101.4	123.9	139.3	154.7	119.5	143.7	150.4	120.2	23.1	3.6
	September	109.9	122.0	139.8	158.2	122.0	146.8	154.0	125.3	25.3	4.2
	October	118.9	126.0	140.9	165.5	125.9	161.4	156.4	132.3	26.5	5.6
	November	119.3	130.5	146.1	160.6	129.6	161.5	158.3	133.2	24.6	0.7
	December	116.8	139.0	144.8	168.2	130.6	161.5	158.0	133.8	22.4	0.5
1991	January	122.0	153.1	147.0	199.0	134.0	162.7	159.1	142.3	19.8	6.3
	February	120.7	151.1	160.3	185.4	136.6	162.8	180.2	142.4	20.1	0.1
	March	126.8	151.7	163.6	184.3	137.5	163.6	181.6	145.7	22.6	2.3
	April	136.5	155.8	163.5	180.0	142.0	163.8	178.8	150.6	28.0	3.3
	May	134.4	153.8	171.8	182.3	143.1	163.7	184.3	150.7	28.6	0.1
	June	131.4	148.9	177.6	207.5	145.4	163.7	192.8	153.1	32.0	1.6
	July	131.2	158.3	183.5	216.6	147.2	188.0	196.1	157.0	35.4	2.6
	August	132.3	162.9	184.1	232.8	150.3	188.8	202.5	160.9	33.9	2.5
	September	131.1	162.2	180.9	244.4	156.8	190.2	213.9	163.2	30.2	1.4
	October	134.6	167.4	176.0	238.7	162.7	192.8	215.1	165.2	24.8	1.3
	November	143.7	171.3	181.2	233.6	176.0	195.8	221.6	171.7	28.9	3.9
	December	149.9	169.7	185.1	238.3	183.6	198.9	228.6	176.9	32.2	3.0
1992	January	155.0	192.7	207.8	250.5	197.4	213.8	241.9	187.7	32.0	6.1
	February	166.4	196.6	212.9	261.7	210.2	244.2	268.7	200.1	40.5	6.6
	March	190.4	219.0	221.7	261.3	222.2	245.1	274.6	216.3	48.4	8.1
	April	227.6	234.7	224.4	264.2	228.7	250.9	296.2	239.1	58.8	10.5
	May	240.9	237.8	225.2	288.9	229.9	252.4	313.2	250.5	66.2	4.8
	June	239.4	229.2	222.9	295.9	225.1	253.9	316.9	249.5	62.9	-0.4
	July	234.1	266.1	232.0	314.4	224.3	288.9	323.4	255.6	62.7	2.4
	August	227.7	273.8	230.9	306.0	227.2	290.5	327.4	252.8	57.1	-1.1
	September	220.4	278.3	237.2	298.1	227.4	289.6	352.4	251.0	53.8	-0.7
	October	227.1	285.2	233.0	307.4	229.8	290.6	362.5	256.9	55.5	2.4
	November	226.2	278.7	229.1	309.8	226.4	289.3	360.3	255.3	48.7	-0.6
	December	218.5	251.4	240.1	316.8	225.0	289.1	362.8	250.4	41.6	-1.9

Source: Statistics Department, MFEP.

Note: This series is based on the 1989–90 Household Budget Survey.

NEW CONSUMER PRICE INDEX, KAMPALA

September 1989 = 100, All Households

	All Items Index	Annual Percent Change
Calendar Year (January – December)		
1982	0.6	..
1983	0.7	18.3
1984	1.0	37.5
1985	2.5	158.0
1986	6.4	161.0
1987	19.2	199.8
1988	56.9	196.3
1989	91.9	61.4
1990	122.3	33.2
1991	156.6	28.1
1992	238.8	52.4
Fiscal Year (July – June)		
1982/83	0.6	..
1983/84	0.8	19.8
1984/85	1.6	104.1
1985/86	3.9	148.0
1986/87	12.3	216.5
1987/88	32.8	167.9
1988/89	75.7	130.5
1989/90	110.1	45.4
1990/91	137.1	24.6
1991/92	194.8	42.1

Source: Statistics Department, MFEP.

ORPHAN CENSUS DERIVED FROM THE 1991 NATIONAL CENSUS
Provisional Results

District	Children	Orphans	Orphans as % of Children	Total Population in Final Census Count
Kumi	104,134	17,447	17%	236,694
Rakai	187,483	30,766	16%	383,501
Soroti	189,825	30,969	16%	430,390
Gulu	151,260	21,819	14%	338,427
Kitgum	163,895	23,256	14%	357,184
Moyo	81,542	11,222	14%	175,645
Luwero	217,201	29,330	14%	449,691
Masaka	419,116	56,582	14%	838,736
Kalangala	5,306	712	13%	16,371
Kiboga	68,131	8,431	12%	141,607
Moroto	84,076	9,879	12%	174,417
Mpigi	443,311	48,371	11%	913,867
Rukungiri	194,756	21,162	11%	390,780
Kabarole	337,901	36,654	11%	746,800
Kotido	96,095	10,282	11%	196,006
Mubende	244,973	25,650	10%	500,976
Lira	230,973	24,027	10%	500,965
Mbarara	439,977	44,963	10%	930,772
Kampala	311,998	31,244	10%	774,241
Mukuno	392,524	36,441	9%	824,604
Masindi	120,356	10,706	9%	260,796
Kabale	208,445	18,350	9%	417,218
Nebbi	146,819	12,911	9%	316,866
Bushenyi	368,834	32,025	9%	736,361
Bundibugyo	54,842	4,728	9%	116,566
Arua	295,074	24,976	8%	637,941
Apac	214,102	17,501	8%	454,504
Kibale	110,594	8,836	8%	220,261
Hoima	93,330	7,447	8%	197,851
Tororo	250,225	19,897	8%	555,574
Kisoro	98,497	7,477	8%	186,681
Jinja	132,835	9,634	7%	289,476
Pallisa	164,188	11,500	7%	357,656
Iganga	446,753	29,443	7%	945,783
Kamuli	226,493	14,577	6%	485,214
Mbale	324,316	20,812	6%	710,980
Kapchorwa	56,719	3,597	6%	116,702
Kasese	173,546	10,562	6%	343,601
Total:	7,850,445	784,186	10%	16,671,705

Source: The 1991 Population and Housing Census, Statistics Department, MFEP.

Note: Children are under 15 years. Orphans are children under 15 years
              who have lost one or both parents.

PATTERN OF FOOD EXPENDITURE BY REGION

In percent

Urban	Kampala	Mbale	Masaka	Mbarara
Bread and cereals	14.4	10.6	14.8	18.8
Meat and poultry	10.0	14.8	9.7	8.7
Fish	6.5	3.3	8.5	3.1
Milk, cheese and eggs	9.8	5.5	4.3	10.9
Oils and fats	3.3	3.6	2.2	2.7
Fruit, nuts and vegetables	16.7	20.4	19.8	22.8
Matoke and tubers	25.0	21.5	27.5	25.6
Sugar	10.0	9.3	10.2	5.3
Salt	0.6	0.7	0.7	1.0
Other food	3.8	10.3	2.3	1.3
Total food expenditure	100.0	100.0	100.0	100.0

Rural	Central	Northern	Eastern	Western
Bread and cereals	11.0	32.0	15.5	14.6
Meat and poultry	8.5	9.5	12.0	8.3
Fish	7.5	8.1	6.4	3.6
Milk, cheese and eggs	4.3	1.5	4.0	5.0
Oils and fats	1.5	1.5	1.3	2.0
Fruit, nuts and vegetables	21.8	12.0	22.7	22.2
Matoke and tubers	38.1	28.4	28.2	39.4
Sugar	3.5	2.1	3.5	2.0
Salt	1.2	2.4	1.6	1.6
Other food	2.7	2.6	4.4	1.3
Total food expenditure	100.0	100.0	100.0	100.0

Source: Household Budget Survey.

PERCENTAGE SHARES SPENT ON SELECTED EXPENDITURE CATEGORIES
In percent

	Urban	Rural	Total	Non-poor	Poor	Poorest	Total
	<--------		Percent accounted for by		-------->		
Health	13	87	100	72	20	8	100
Education	17	83	100	70	21	9	100
Clothing	23	77	100	71	20	9	100
Charcoal	66	34	100	77	19	4	100
Firewood	13	87	100	70	18	12	100
Market food	32	68	100	64	31	5	100
Bread and cereals	33	67	100	77	18	4	100
Meat and poultry	23	77	100	72	23	5	100
Fish	22	78	100	62	31	7	100
Milk, chees and eggs	42	58	100	81	17	2	100
Oils and fats	32	68	100	77	20	3	100
Fruit and vegetables	36	64	100	72	22	6	100
Matoke	51	49	100	79	19	2	100
Potatoes and tubers	35	65	100	64	27	9	100
Sugar	34	66	100	77	20	3	100
Salt	10	90	100	55	32	13	100
Other food	24	76	100	73	22	4	100
Non-marketed food	3	97	100	64	29	8	100
Bread and cereals	3	97	100	61	30	9	100
Meat and poultry	6	94	100	65	30	5	100
Fish	3	97	100	72	22	6	100
Milk, chees and eggs	4	96	100	79	20	2	100
Oils and fats	6	94	100	75	22	3	100
Fruit and vegetables	3	97	100	63	29	8	100
Matoke	3	97	100	71	25	4	100
Potatoes and tubers	3	97	100	53	35	13	100
Sugar	38	62	100	71	29	0	100
Salt	3	97	100	81	11	8	100
Other food	5	95	100	54	38	8	100

Source: Household Budget Survey

Annex II

Poverty: A Child's View

MAKONJE - RHODA

Rich people sleep on a bed (top left house) and have electricity (light bulb hanging from ceiling in top left house). They own many things, such as spoons (bottom row in top right house), cups (above spoons), plates and knives (above cups). Their houses have tiled roofs (bottom house) or iron sheets. They can afford shoes and handbags, and even have cars (they look like buses, but it is because they have to fit the whole family!).

Rich homes are tidy (see items arranged in boxes) and there are many things in them, including glasses, cups, dresses, chairs. They have electricity (bulb is hanging from the ceiling, between boxes of items) and ironsheet roofs. Here too, rich people are depicted as wearing nice clothes, with shoes and handbags, and having a car.

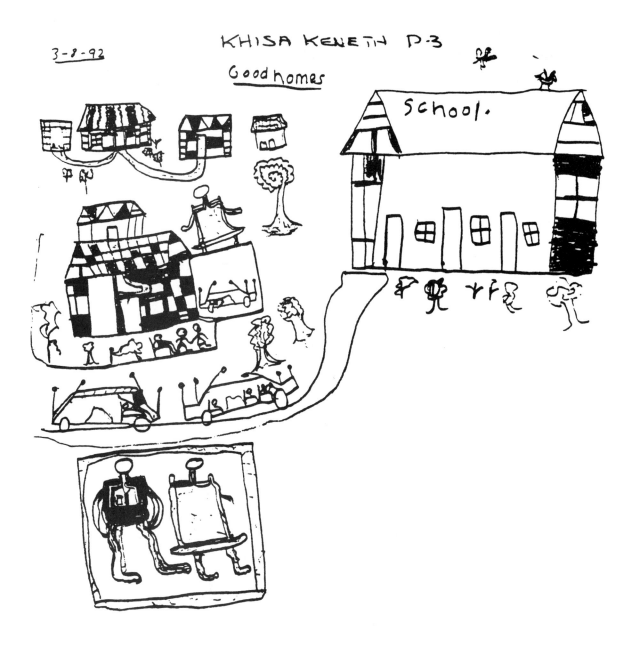

The symbols of wealth are cars (with radios!), enough money to go to a nice school (two-story building with trees around it), a television (square at the bottom). This is the only child who depicted a television, while many drew radios.

A poor household.

The poor use a hand hoe because they cannot afford ox ploughs. The family owns a bicycle, used by the father. Houses have a thatched roof, often leaking (that's why there is a person on the roof to repair it). Water is carried in old fashioned clay pots (home made) rather than in modern but expensive plastic jerry cans.

Poor people live in simple huts with thatched roofs. Their schools are in poor shape (note shaky lines) and pupils have to sit on benches rather than having proper desks. Poor households may own a few chickens, but certainly not cows. Farmers can only afford locally made hand hoes to cultivate their fields (see two people at the bottom), and grain has to be pounded by hand because more efficient technology is not available (see person with stick, on right). There are snakes near the schools and houses of the poor, because compounds are poorly kept (a reflection of high dependency rates and time-consuming work practices?).

Poor houses are untidy and have thatched and often leaking roofs. Poor people receive donations from the rich (here they receive 100 Sh) and have to eat cassava. They are barefoot. Women can't afford plastic jerry cans to carry water.

Poor people receive donations from the better off (the child and the person on the chair are both receiving a donation). They carry water in clay pots rather than in modern but expensive jerry cans. Even the pots used for cooking are homemade rather than metal ones (see them inside the house).

Annex III

Adjustments to the HBS Data

Annex III

Adjustments to the Household Budget Survey Data

1.   The fieldwork for the Household Budget Survey (HBS) took place over the course of the year from April 1989 to April 1990 and the enumerators visited a different set of parishes in each district on six different occasions during the year. Inflation in Kampala over this period was about 40 percent. Consequently, if we imagine two identical households, with identical purchases of goods, one sampled at the beginning of the fieldwork and the other sampled at the end of the fieldwork, then the second household will have expenditures which are approximately 40 percent higher because of inflation over the year. So if we had simply added up total expenditure for each household for comparison, we may have concluded that otherwise identical households had a 40 percent difference in welfare. Similarly price variations across the country would lead to biases in comparing households. Therefore, in order to correct for inflation and other regional price variations, we calculated a set of unit-values for each parish sampled, using the information in the HBS on the quantities of food consumed, from which we derived a food price index. For the adjustment of food expenditure, we simply used this food price index. For total expenditure, in the absence of any additional information on non-food prices, we assumed no non-food price variation in constructing an overall price index.

2.   In the HBS, when households were asked about the value of food from own-production, the values sought were equivalent to farmgate, or producer, prices. So the reported values of food consumed out-of-own-production are understatements of the consumption value of that food. So we have revalued the recorded values of consumption out-of-own production at market prices, so that the consumption value of all food is equally reflected in the valuations recorded in the HBS.

3.   It needs to be stressed that like all large survey data, the HBS data will carry statistical noise from unavoidable sampling and enumeration errors. The information from the HBS has proved to be robust in aggregate; but we are utilizing a level of detail, particularly in the calculation of the price adjustments, which could lead to some increases in the statistical noise, rather than unambiguous improvements in the estimates. Further refinements are presently being made to the data by the Central Statistical Office and, as mentioned in Chapter 1, there is also further analysis planned to estimate "equivalence scales" for Uganda. All of these efforts, together with the ongoing SDA survey, are expected to further develop the database and provide additional insights into the poverty situation in Uganda. The results presented in this report represent a first attempt to put together a poverty profile for the country, based on the HBS and other supplementary information, and should in no way be taken as final.

Distributors of World Bank Publications

ARGENTINA
Carlos Hirsch, SRL
Galeria Guemes
Florida 165, 4th Floor-Ofc. 453/465
1333 Buenos Aires

**AUSTRALIA, PAPUA NEW GUINEA,
FIJI, SOLOMON ISLANDS,
VANUATU, AND WESTERN SAMOA**
D.A. Books & Journals
648 Whitehorse Road
Mitcham 3132
Victoria

AUSTRIA
Gerold and Co.
Graben 31
A-1011 Wien

BANGLADESH
Micro Industries Development
   Assistance Society (MIDAS)
House 5, Road 16
Dhanmondi R/Area
Dhaka 1209

   Branch offices:
   Pine View, 1st Floor
   100 Agrabad Commercial Area
   Chittagong 4100

   76, K.D.A. Avenue
   Kulna 9100

BELGIUM
Jean De Lannoy
Av. du Roi 202
1060 Brussels

CANADA
Le Diffuseur
C.P. 85, 1501B rue Ampère
Boucherville, Québec
J4B 5E6

CHILE
Invertec IGT S.A.
Americo Vespucio Norte 1165
Santiago

CHINA
China Financial & Economic
   Publishing House
8, Da Fo Si Dong Jie
Beijing

COLOMBIA
Infoenlace Ltda.
Apartado Aereo 34270
Bogota D.E.

COTE D'IVOIRE
Centre d'Edition et de Diffusion
Africaines (CEDA)
04 B.P. 541
Abidjan 04 Plateau

CYPRUS
Center of Applied Research
Cyprus College
6, Diogenes Street, Engomi
P.O. Box 2006
Nicosia

DENMARK
SamfundsLitteratur
Rosenoerns Allé 11
DK-1970 Frederiksberg C

DOMINICAN REPUBLIC
Editora Taller, C. por A.
Restauración e Isabel la Católica 309
Apartado de Correos 2190 Z-1
Santo Domingo

EGYPT, ARAB REPUBLIC OF
Al Ahram
Al Galaa Street
Cairo

The Middle East Observer
41, Sherif Street
Cairo

FINLAND
Akateeminen Kirjakauppa
P.O. Box 128
SF-00101 Helsinki 10

FRANCE
World Bank Publications
66, avenue d'Iéna
75116 Paris

GERMANY
UNO-Verlag
Poppelsdorfer Allee 55
D-5300 Bonn 1

HONG KONG, MACAO
Asia 2000 Ltd.
46-48 Wyndham Street
Winning Centre
2nd Floor
Central Hong Kong

INDIA
Allied Publishers Private Ltd.
751 Mount Road
Madras - 600 002

   Branch offices:
   15 J.N. Heredia Marg
   Ballard Estate
   Bombay - 400 038

   13/14 Asaf Ali Road
   New Delhi - 110 002

   17 Chittaranjan Avenue
   Calcutta - 700 072

   Jayadeva Hostel Building
   5th Main Road, Gandhinagar
   Bangalore - 560 009

   3-5-1129 Kachiguda
      Cross Road
   Hyderabad - 500 027

   Prarthana Flats, 2nd Floor
   Near Thakore Baug, Navrangpura
   Ahmedabad - 380 009

   Patiala House
   16-A Ashok Marg
   Lucknow - 226 001

   Central Bazaar Road
   60 Bajaj Nagar
   Nagpur 440 010

INDONESIA
Pt. Indira Limited
Jalan Borobudur 20
P.O. Box 181
Jakarta 10320

IRELAND
Government Supplies Agency
4-5 Harcourt Road
Dublin 2

ISRAEL
Yozmot Literature Ltd.
P.O. Box 56055
Tel Aviv 61560

ITALY
Licosa Commissionaria Sansoni SPA
Via Duca Di Calabria, 1/1
Casella Postale 552
50125 Firenze

JAPAN
Eastern Book Service
Hongo 3-Chome, Bunkyo-ku 113
Tokyo

KENYA
Africa Book Service (E.A.) Ltd.
Quaran House, Mfangano Street
P.O. Box 45245
Nairobi

KOREA, REPUBLIC OF
Pan Korea Book Corporation
P.O. Box 101, Kwangwhamun
Seoul

MALAYSIA
University of Malaya Cooperative
   Bookshop, Limited
P.O. Box 1127, Jalan Pantai Baru
59700 Kuala Lumpur

MEXICO
INFOTEC
Apartado Postal 22-860
14060 Tlalpan, Mexico D.F.

NETHERLANDS
De Lindeboom/InOr-Publikaties
P.O. Box 202
7480 AE Haaksbergen

NEW ZEALAND
EBSCO NZ Ltd.
Private Mail Bag 99914
New Market
Auckland

NIGERIA
University Press Limited
Three Crowns Building Jericho
Private Mail Bag 5095
Ibadan

NORWAY
Narvesen Information Center
Book Department
P.O. Box 6125 Etterstad
N-0602 Oslo 6

PAKISTAN
Mirza Book Agency
65, Shahrah-e-Quaid-e-Azam
P.O. Box No. 729
Lahore 54000

PERU
Editorial Desarrollo SA
Apartado 3824
Lima 1

PHILIPPINES
International Book Center
Suite 1703, Cityland 10
Condominium Tower 1
Ayala Avenue, H.V. dela
   Costa Extension
Makati, Metro Manila

POLAND
International Publishing Service
Ul. Piekna 31/37
00-677 Warzawa

   For subscription orders:
   IPS Journals
   Ul. Okrezna 3
   02-916 Warszawa

PORTUGAL
Livraria Portugal
Rua Do Carmo 70-74
1200 Lisbon

SAUDI ARABIA, QATAR
Jarir Book Store
P.O. Box 3196
Riyadh 11471

**SINGAPORE, TAIWAN,
MYANMAR, BRUNEI**
Information Publications
   Private, Ltd.
Golden Wheel Building
41, Kallang Pudding, #04-03
Singapore 1334

SOUTH AFRICA, BOTSWANA
For single titles:
Oxford University Press
   Southern Africa
P.O. Box 1141
Cape Town 8000

For subscription orders:
International Subscription Service
P.O. Box 41095
Craighall
Johannesburg 2024

SPAIN
Mundi-Prensa Libros, S.A.
Castello 37
28001 Madrid

Librería Internacional AEDOS
Conseil de Cent, 391
08009 Barcelona

SRI LANKA AND THE MALDIVES
Lake House Bookshop
P.O. Box 244
100, Sir Chittampalam A.
   Gardiner Mawatha
Colombo 2

SWEDEN
For single titles:
Fritzes Fackboksforetaget
Regeringsgatan 12, Box 16356
S-103 27 Stockholm

For subscription orders:
Wennergren-Williams AB
P. O. Box 1305
S-171 25 Solna

SWITZERLAND
For single titles:
Librairie Payot
Case postale 3212
CH 1002 Lausanne

For subscription orders:
Librairie Payot
Service des Abonnements
Case postale 3312
CH 1002 Lausanne

TANZANIA
Oxford University Press
P.O. Box 5299
Maktaba Road
Dar es Salaam

THAILAND
Central Department Store
306 Silom Road
Bangkok

**TRINIDAD & TOBAGO, ANTIGUA
BARBUDA, BARBADOS,
DOMINICA, GRENADA, GUYANA,
JAMAICA, MONTSERRAT, ST.
KITTS & NEVIS, ST. LUCIA,
ST. VINCENT & GRENADINES**
Systematics Studies Unit
#9 Watts Street
Curepe
Trinidad, West Indies

TURKEY
Infotel
Narlabahçe Sok. No. 15
Cagaloglu
Istanbul

UNITED KINGDOM
Microinfo Ltd.
P.O. Box 3
Alton, Hampshire GU34 2PG
England

VENEZUELA
Libreria del Este
Aptdo. 60.337
Caracas 1060-A